EXPLORE WINE TOURISM
Management, Development & Destinations

Donald Getz, Ph.D.
Professor, Faculty of Mangement
University of Calgary
2500 University Dr. N.W.
Calgary, Alberta, Canada T2N 1N4

tourism dynamics

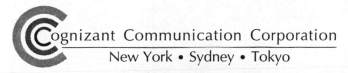
Cognizant Communication Corporation
New York • Sydney • Tokyo

EXPLORE WINE TOURISM
Management, Development
& Destinations

Cognizant Communication Offices:

USA   3 Hartsdale Road, Elmsford, New York 10523-3701
Australia P.O. Box 352 Cammeray, NWS, 2062
Japan   c/o OBS's Bldg. 3F, 1-38-11 Matsubara, Setagaya-ku, Tokyo

Library of Congress Cataloging-in-Publication Data
Getz, Donald, 1949-
    Explore wine tourism: management, development & destinations/donald Getz
      p.cm.
    Includes bibliographical references (p.).
    ISBN 1-882345-33-99 (soft bound)
      I. Wine and wine making. 2. Tourism. I. Title
TP548.5.T68 G48 2000
641.2'2--de21   00-023026

Printed in the United States of America

Printing: 1 2 3 4 5 6 7 8 9 10 Year: 1 2 3 4 5 6 7 8 9 10

Book design: Lynn Carano Graphics

Contents

List of Figures

List of Tables

Preface

This book looks at the business of developing and marketing wine tourism, complete with principles and concepts, research summaries, market intelligence, exemplary case studies, profiles and interviews with industry leaders. Numerous examples and detailed case studies are provided from the USA, Canada, Australia, New Zealand and Europe.

Explore Wine Tourism has been written for winery owners and wine industry managers, destination marketing organizations, and dedicated wine tourists who want to learn more about the world of wine tourism. Its focus is on wineries and destinations with potential to develop this increasingly valuable niche market. It is designed to give the reader insights into the industry and the potential for other businesses available to the industry and travelers. It will also serve as a text or reference work for those interested in the study of tourism and hospitality as it relates to the wine industry.

Sadly, the wine world lost one of its legends with the passing of Murray Tyrell in October of 2000. also, by the time of publication, Barbara Nixon had sold Victorian Winery Tours.

My interest in the subject is twofold. Previous research and writing on the subjects of destination planning and marketing, rural tourism, and family businesses, introduced me to this and other niche market opportunities. As well, I have a personal interest in wine and the allure of wine country. That comes from being a global traveler, wine lover (not connoisseur), and cultural tourist. I hope readers share in some of these passions.

My favorite anonymous quotation on the subject of wine sums it up: Wine improves with age - the older I get, the more I like it.

Acknowledgments

I am greatly indebted to numerous individuals and organizations for providing material, ideas, and hospitality during the research and writing stages of this book. Specific thanks are owed to the following:

- Augusta-Margaret River Tourist Bureau
- Australia, Department of Industry, Science and Tourism
- Anne Ruston, National Wine Centre, Australia
- Barbara Nixon, Victoria Winery Tours
- Barbara Storey, Barossa Vintage Festival
- Barry Salter, Barossa Wine and Tourism Association Inc.
- Bob McLean, St. Hallet Winery
- Bruce and Murray Tyrrell, Tyrrell Winery
- Cathy Parsons, Office of National Tourism, Australia
- Colin Michael Hall, University of Otago
- Conor Lagan, Chateau Xanadu Winery
- Chris and Hamish Laurie, Hillstowe Winery
- Chris King, Edith Cowan University, Bunbury
- Daniel Howard, Napa Convention and Visitor Bureau
- David Gilbert, University of Surrey
- Debra Eagles, Robert Mondavi Winery
- Denis and Tricia Horgan, Leeuwin Estate
- Deutsche Weinakademie
- Don Anderson, University of Calgary
- Edith Cowan University, School of Marketing and Tourism, Perth, Western Australia
- Firestone Vineyard, California
- Fetzer Winery, Redwood Valley, California
- Gail Sambidge-Mitchell, Wine Australia
- Gus Maher, Hunter Valley Wine Country
- Inniskillin Wineries, Canada
- Jack Rasterhoff, Victoria Wineries Tourism Council
- Jim Smith, Adelaide
- John King, Global Tourism and Leisure
- Johnathan Pedley, MW, London
- Larry Lockshin, University of Adelaide
- Marc Rheaume, Calgary
- NFO Research Inc. (permission granted to utilize data in Figures 3.1, 3.1, and 3.3)
- Office International de la Vigne et du Vin, Paris (permission granted to utilize data in Tables 2.1 and 2.2)

- Paul McCallum, Grapevine (Texas), Convention and Visitors Bureau
- Paula Crayford, Tasting Australia
- Peter Butcher, Southcorp Wines
- Peter and Louise Fergusson of Fergusson of Yarra Glen
- Peter Sesterka, Office of National Tourism, Australia
- Petra Giegevich, Deutscher Weinfolds
- Philip Gregan, Wine Institute of New Zealand
- Robyn Morris, Edith Cowan University, Bunbury, Western Australia
- Rod Hand, Fleurieu and McLaren Vale Visitor Centre
- Rosemary Fletcher, Toast Martinborough
- Scott Collet, Woodstock Winery, McClaren Vale
- Shane Crockett, Western Australian Tourism Commission
- Sonoma County, California Welcome Center
- South Australian Tourism Commission
- The Wine Institute (California)
- Tim Dodd, Texas Wine Marketing Research Institute, Texas Tech University
- Tri Cities Visitor and Convention Bureau
- Tony Spawton, University of South Australia
- Tourism New South Wales
- Tourism Victoria

Don Anderson and Marc Rheaume cooperated with the research on critical success factors. Both are dedicated wine tourists.

Explore Wine Tourism

THE AUTHOR RESTS ON
AN OLD WINE PRESS AT
DOMAINE CHANDON,
NAPA VALLEY.

Photo: Courtesy of Mark Rheaume

LINDEMANS, NSW AUSTRALIA:
ONE OF THE MORE FAMOUS
BRANDS OF SOUTHCORP WINES
AND A LANDMARK OF THE HUNTER
VALLEY

Photo: Donald Getz

THERE'S NO MISTAKING THE
WINE ROUTES OF CANADA'S
BRITISH COLUMBIA!

Photo: Courtesy of Don Anderson

Explore Wine Tourism

AN IMPRESSIVE ENTRY
STATEMENT FOR THE
WORLD FAMOUS NAPA
VALLEY
Photo: Donald Getz

THE NAPA VALLEY WINE
TRAIN: UNIQUE ATTRAC-
TIONS ADD TO THE
APPEAL OF WINE
COUNTRY
Photo: Donald Getz

SIGNAGE
FOR MOTORING WINE
TOURIST IN THE HUNTER
VALLEY: SOLAR PANELS AND
NIGHT-LIGHTS, MAXIMIZE
EFFECTIVENESS
Photo: Donald Getz

SPECTATOR SPORT AT THE FAMOUS BAROSSA
VINTAGE FESTIVAL, SOUTH AUSTRALIA
*Photo: Peter Fuller, courtesy of the Barossa
Wine and Tourism Association*

GRAPE STOMP AT
GRAPEFEST:
AUDIENCE PARTICIPATION
HELPS MAXIMIZE WINE
FESTIVAL APPEAL
*Photo: Courtesy of the Grapevine
Convention and Visitors Bureau*

TAKE YOUR TIME! TASTING
AND JUDGING AT
GRAPEFEST'S PEOPLE'S
CHOICE WINE TASTING
CLASSIC
*Photo: Courtesy of the Grapevine
Convention and Visitors Bureau*

HILLSTOWE WINERY IN
HAHNDORF, NEAR
ADELAIDE, SOUTH
AUSTRALIA: A NEW
WORLD WINE VILLAGE
IN THE MAKING
Photo: Donald Getz

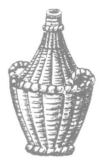

FOOD AND WINE,
PERFECT PARTNERS IN
SOUTH AUSTRALIA'S
BAROSSA VALLEY
*Photo: Peter Fuller, courtesy of the Barossa
Wine and Tourism Association*

AN INTIMATE WINERY
SETTING IN TOAST
MARTINBOROUGH, ONE
OF THE PREMIER WINE
AND FOOD FESTIVALS OF
NEW ZEALAND
Photo: Donald Getz

KROEV, ON THE MOSEL
RIVER: QUINTESSENTIAL
GERMAN WINE VILLAGE
Photo: Courtesy of Deutscher Weinfolds

Chapter 1

INTRODUCTION TO WINE TOURISM

THE APPEAL OF WINE TOURISM

"Wine tourism" is an evocative phrase. To those who love travel, a visit to the world's many wine regions offers considerable appeal: of authentic wine festivals, visits to wineries reflecting regional architectural styles, local cuisine, tasting new and rare wines, and delightful rural scenery. To wine lovers, travel allows for on-site education leading to more informed purchases of wine, or perhaps to the tasting and acquisition of otherwise unavailable wines. The *Wine Spectator* ("Ready, Set, Go," 1997) eloquently noted: "As anybody who loves wines knows, the regions where the finest wine is made are special places—even magical."

Gary Peters, author of *American Winescapes—The Cultural Landscapes of America's Wine Country* (1997), summarized the appeal of "wine country." "These are working landscapes, but to many they seem to offer much more. At their richest, they can be synonymous with civilized enjoyment; food, wine and conversation often come together here in harmonious ways." In the book *Appreciating Fine Wines* (1996), Jim Budd recognized the value to wine lovers of visiting wine regions, recommending both large and small wineries. Gary Johnson (1997) argued that wine tourism is different from most forms of tourism, in that it heavily involves the senses of smell and taste. In this way it fits perfectly with gastronomy. Wine tourism is also closely linked to the experience of a sense of place in which all the senses come into play. Brock Cambourne (1999), himself a wine tour operator, noted that "The very nature of the wine industry lends itself to a union with tourism, providing the tourist with the opportunity to experience history, food, culture, new smells, sounds and tastes . . . a combination of culture, lifestyle and territory."

The appeal of wine tourism therefore involves a complete sensory experience:

- **Taste:** of wines and regional cuisine; fresh grapes and other produce from the roadside market.
- **Smell:** of the land and the grape; fresh, country air; wineries during fermentation; barrel rooms and cellars; cooking in fine restaurants and country bed and breakfast places; the leaves and soil in vineyards; roses and herb gardens.
- **Touch:** hands-on interpretation of winemaking; the bottle and the glass; cooking with wine; picking grapes.

- **Sight:** vineyards and blue skies; unique and regional architecture; other people enjoying themselves; traditional festivals; the colors of wine.
- **Sound:** bottling; opening and pouring sparkling wine; festive music; winemaking equipment; the kitchen.

In addition to the senses, wine tourism should also be:

- culturally authentic (involving lifestyles associated with wine and food, festivals and events, wine villages, architectural heritage),
- romantic (based on the notion that wine, food and attractive surroundings foster romance),
- fun,
- educational (consumers want to learn about wine and culture).

DEFINING WINE TOURISM

Most existing definitions of wine tourism relate to the traveler's motivation and experiences. For example, Hall and Macionis (1998) defined it this way:

> visitation to vineyards, wineries, wine festivals and wine shows for which grape wine tasting and/or experiencing the attributes of a grape wine region are the prime motivating factors for visitors.

The South Australian Tourism Commission (1997) focused on activities:

> any experience related to wineries or wine production in which visitors participate when on a day trip or longer visit. . . .Wine tourism can range from a visit to a single cellar door outlet while en-route to a main holiday destination to intensive week long, live-in experiences focused on the wine process. (p. 4)

The Australian (draft) National Wine Tourism Strategy (1998) also concentrated on the experience, but deliberately broadened the definition:

> visitation to wineries and wine regions to experience the unique qualities of contemporary Australian lifestyle associated with the enjoyment of wine at its source—including wine and food, landscape and cultural activities.

These are consumer-focused definitions, which makes a lot of sense because ultimately it is the consumer who defines the wine tourism "product," but it should be remembered that there are at least three major perspectives on the subject: that of wine producers, tourism agencies (representing the destinations), and consumers. Thus, "wine tourism" is, simultaneously:

• a form of consumer behavior,

• a strategy by which destinations develop and market wine-related attractions and imagery,

• a marketing opportunity for wineries to educate, and to sell their products, directly to consumers.

As consumer behavior, wine tourism includes the travel of wine lovers to wineries, winemaking regions, or wine-themed attractions and events. Some wineries and wine-related attractions are located close to consumers, but these attractions are still part of the wine tourism product mix. It also includes visits to wineries made by those whose primary travel motives are not related to wine (this might even be the largest part of the market), lifestyle experiences that involve food and wine in wine regions, and even the passive enjoyment of the beauty of wine country.

This definition of wine tourism attempts to incorporate all three perspectives:

> Wine tourism is travel related to the appeal of wineries and wine country, a form of niche marketing and destination development, and an opportunity for direct sales and marketing on the part of the wine industry.

THE WINE TOURISM SYSTEM

Wine tourism is dependent on the successful integration of consumers, suppliers, and the destination, as illustrated in the model of the wine tourism system (Figure 1.1). Each major element is discussed in the following sections.

Consumer Experiences

Wine tourism is initiated by consumers who travel specifically for wine-related experiences, or by travelers who include wine experiences in their destination visits. Their interests might be based on sophisticated wine preferences, or on the image of wine regions as romantic and beautiful places to visit. Their activities in the destination might be very focused on visiting wineries for tastings, or more in depth to include learning about viticulture and wine production. They might very well incorporate gastronomic experiences, reinforcing the lifestyle (or "good life") image that wine creates or enhances.

Many wine-themed and other activities and attractions can be part of their experience. But wine regions also attract a wide variety of visitors, and many will have only a peripheral interest in viticulture or wine production. A whole range of essential services will be consumed, and non-wine-related leisure pursuits are likely to be desired. Shopping is a favorite pastime for tourists, with wine regions having the advantage of being able to sell local wines and other produce, plus wine-themed merchandise.

Suppliers

Suppliers provide both essential and augmented services to wine tourists. Essential services include accommodation, catering, and transport. Beyond the basics, entrepreneurs will tend to offer a variety of other leisure opportunities and tours, which might or might not include wine interpretation. Special events, such as community wine festivals or concerts at wineries, add considerably to the experience. Little if any research has been conducted on how the suppliers emerge and develop, and what is needed to facilitate growth and quality in this sector.

Figure 1.1. The wine tourism system.

Destination Marketing/Management Organizations (DMOs)

The third major component of the system is shaped by the destination. While wine tourism can exist with little or no coordination or planning, it is evident that some form of concerted marketing is at least needed to stimulate growth. Existing tourism organizations such as visitor and convention bureaus can easily fill this role if they recognize the potential of wine tourism and know how to exploit it. A minimal effort will include the provision of information to visitors, especially through effective sign posting and maps, while a more sophisticated organization will conduct research, evaluate trends, and engage in target marketing. A large question that must be addressed is that of whether or not a public or industry-based organization should attempt to stimulate development or invest directly in wine tourism enterprises.

Another key destination role is that of conserving the resource base—a vital function that requires collaboration of many parties and sound planning. Wine tourism can be threatened by overcommercialization, lack of land use controls, inadvertent destruction of attractive scenery, pollution and soil erosion, and a lack of public support. Individual wineries obviously must take the lead on environmental issues, but the entire community has a stake in ensuring that resources and support are sustained.

Destination organizations and suppliers must therefore become partners in ensuring that the essential ingredients of wine tourism are always in place:

• a suitable resource base, including climate, soils, moisture and drainage;
• viticulture (grape growing);
• winemaking;
• accessibility to the region and its wineries/wines;
• essential visitor services: transport, accommodation, dining, information.

In addition, there are several elements that attractively augment the basic product:

• interpretation of the region, winemaking, and the wines;
• tours to and within the region;
• festivals and special events with a wine theme;
• recreational and social activities to expand the visitor's choices;

• shopping, both at wineries and throughout the area;

• authentic regional architecture and heritage attractions;

• access to other aspects of the local culture/lifestyle.

A number of key questions flow from this discussion of the model, and I try to answer these in later chapters:

• Who are the best wine tourism consumers, and how are they motivated?

• What elements and combinations in the wine tourism system work best to attract and satisfy different target markets?

• What are the key roles to be played by tourism organizations and others in developing and marketing wine tourism?

• How can suppliers be stimulated, and what makes them effective?

• What can be learned from popular wine regions?

BENEFITS OF WINE TOURISM

Benefits to the Wine Industry

• increased wine sales,

• educate visitors and foster brand loyalty,

• attract new market segments,

• higher profits from winery sales,

• improved links with the wine trade,

• new partnerships (e.g., with other attractions),

• test new products.

Benefits to Destinations

• generate increased visitor numbers and spending,

• attract new and repeat visitors,

• develop a unique, positive destination image,

• overcome slow demand periods.

Benefits to Host Communities

• attract new investment,

• develop new facilities and amenities (e.g., restaurants and attractions),

• foster community pride,

• create successful events for residents and visitors.

Is it big business? Surprisingly little research has been directed at answering that question, and much of what does exist has been completed in Australia. The Winemaker's Federation of Australia (Australian Wine Foundation, 1996) estimated there were 5.3 million visits to wineries in Australia in 1995, with associated spending of A\$428 million. In October 1998 the draft national Wine Tourism Strategy argued that this reflected mainly cellar door sales, and that direct and indirect spending of wine tourists has to be included.

In the Australian state of Victoria, wine tourists were found to be "high yield." Visitation at wineries increased by 19% from 1.6 to 1.9 million visits between 1994/5 and 1995/6, rising to 2.3 million in 1996/7. The Victorian Winery Tourism Council estimated that total wine tourism expenditure in that state alone was A\$185 million, of which A\$70 million was cellar door sales and the balance related to food, accommodation, fuel, and other goods and services purchased by wine tourists.

Any number of problems can occur when attempting an estimate of economic value. Not all visits to wineries are made by legitimate tourists, as locals often buy their wine direct and attend winery events. Furthermore, many visitors to an area might visit a winery, but did not travel because of wine. As well, estimates should be based on visits to wine regions, not just wineries or wine events.

As with any form of special-interest tourism, the actual motivation of visitors must be known before economic impacts can be attributed. Following the logic of evaluating the impact of event tourists (Getz, 1997), the value of wine tourism to an area should be measured by the following steps:

1. determining who travels to the area because of the appeal of wine (preferably only including visitors who travel totally or at least "mainly" because of wine; if visitors travel both for wine and other reasons, assign a percentage of their expenditure to wine tourism);

2. measuring the total expenditure of wine tourists within the area;

3. it is also legitimate to include some of the expenditure made by any visitor who stays longer and/or spends more because of wine attractions and events;

4. secondary economic impacts can be estimated through application of an income or value-added "multiplier," but no research has been completed to determine what this secondary effect might be (to do so requires knowledge of what happens to tourist money spent at wineries or on other purchases in wine country—how much of it is retained locally as opposed to "leakage" for imports, profits and wages sent away).

Note that determining the economic impact of wine tourists (or any other types of traveler) is not the same as estimating the direct and indirect impacts of tourism in general. If one adds up all the nominal impacts of individual events and attractions within a destination, as calculated above, it will result in multiple counting of enormous proportions of the same expenditures. The truth is that there is no simple and accurate method for estimating the economic benefits of wine tourism. The best indicators of its impact are the numbers of visitors specifically attracted to a destination because of wine, followed by an estimation of their direct spending in the area.

The local economic benefits of wine tourism will be maximized when the following conditions apply:

• tourists are attracted specifically because of wine;

• wine tourist "yield" is maximized (i.e., increased length of stay and higher spending than normal tourists);

• seasonality of demand is reduced (some wine tourists will be interested in visiting wine country all year round);

• local ownership of wineries and other attractions and services is high;

• wine, food, and other products sold to wine tourists are produced locally, and include mostly local inputs;

• profits are reinvested in the community;

• local residents are mostly employed in the industry;

• services and amenities for residents are improved.

Model of the Wine Tourism Value Chain

It is useful to conceptualize wine tourism as a value chain in which each stage adds greater economic value (Figure 1.2). Viticulture adds value to the region's resource base, but the production and export of wine add much more. By adding tourism to the chain many new opportunities for adding value are presented, so that a wine region can diversify and grow its economy—as long as it conserves the resource base.

Wine tourism also reinforces wine exports, as consumers educated about and experienced in visiting a wine-producing region are more likely to become loyal customers and to spread a positive word about the wines. Travel to wine regions is in part motivated by consumption of wines, leading to a desire to visit the producing areas to learn more, and by the favorable image good wines create of the origin region. In this way wine production and tourism are synergistic, yielding more than the mere sum of their parts.

Figure 1.2. The wine tourism value chain.

The Seasonality of Wine Tourism

All forms of tourism are subject to seasonality, both related to supply (e.g., activities are not available all year round) or demand factors (mainly institutional and cultural patterns of holiday-taking, plus the influence of climate). Wine tourism is no exception, with peak demand normally occurring in summer when most people are traveling and the weather is best. However, wine tourism presents many opportunities for attracting visitors all year round. These stem in part from the inherent seasonality of the viniculture process, but also can be influenced by good marketing.

From the experiential perspective, there is something new and interesting for visitors to see and learn about in each of the four seasons:

• **Spring:** new plantings; first buds and leaves; vineyard spraying and/or organic methods of dealing with pests and fertilizing; maturing wines are racked from barrel to barrel.

- **Summer:** grape flowering and emergence of fruit; canopy management; grapes begin to ripen (the French call this period *veraison*); irrigation; last year's vintage is bottled.
- **Autumn:** grapes fully ripen; leaves may turn color; testing for sugar content and flavor; picking each varietal at its peak; transport of grapes to wineries; crushing, pressing and fermentation; settling and racking of new wines.
- **Winter:** vine pruning; icewine production; wines prepared for blending or bottling; barreling for maturation.

An additional consideration is that the Northern and Southern Hemispheres have opposite seasons, meaning that the wine tourist can potentially experience icewine production in January in Canada or Germany, then fly to Australia or New Zealand for summertime wine country tours. Southern Hemisphere destinations can use wine tourism to further capitalize on the propensity of "northerners" to escape winter.

From a marketing point of view, no season should be without its wine-related events and promotions. Chapter 8 discusses the numerous options available for winery and wine country events and functions, and Chapter 9 examines specific packages, such as the "short break" or "getaway" to wine country. There is no reason at all why winter should be a dead time, as people love winter breaks; the appeal of wine and food is sufficient in itself to motivate travel, but add winery events and the package is irresistible to many. In fact, in the Margaret River wine region of Western Australia, winter (not that they have snow or ice!) is the preferred season for short breaks in wine country and accommodation establishments are said to be booked solid on most weekends.

WINE TOURISM DEVELOPMENT ISSUES

Wine tourism in many areas has emerged unplanned and unregulated, based on whatever the wineries in an area do to provide facilities and market their attractions. But increasingly all forms of tourism (the special-interest or niche markets) are being actively developed and aggressively marketed by tourist organizations to gain competitive advantage. As well, the wine industry and wine tourism present a number of challenges to local authorities and environmental planning agencies that must be considered.

Cooperation

One of the main issues is fostering the cooperation necessary for effective planning and marketing. Macionis (1997) pointed out that tourism and wine industry operators are not necessarily easy to get together. Both tourism and wine industries contain numerous small operators, many of whom lack expertise in promoting tourism. She recommended that national, regional, and local plans be formulated to achieve wine and tourism integration, and argued that better research, information, and training are needed to foster wine tourism.

Wine and the Law

In many countries alcoholic beverages are subject to high taxation. A major issue in Australia is the imposition of federal taxes on wine given free to tasters at wineries. This makes it expensive to host visitors, leads to tasting fees or restricted tastings, and directly affects winery viability. A considerable amount of lobbying occurs by wine industry associations on these subjects.

Winery locations and facilities are regulated by zoning and environmental laws in most countries, with major impact on the development of wine tourism. Without some form of control, overcommercialization and environmental decay might easily follow, but all too often the authorities are not attuned to the specific needs of wine tourism and the wine industry.

The industry complains of many rules and regulations that impede its development. These vary from place to place, but include: drinking and driving laws; licensing of establishments and events to serve alcohol; hours of operation; mail-order restrictions (e.g., many US states prohibit wine shipments from wineries outside the state); and the legal drinking age.

Land Use Conflicts

The story of land use conflicts and planning in the Napa Valley (documented by Conaway, 1990; Sullivan, 1994) should be instructive for all other wine regions. In the Napa, so many wineries have been built explicitly for tourism, and to exploit the Napa brand name, that pressures for residential and other commercial development mounted and tourism congestion followed. Without effective regulation, "success" can breed a disaster.

Viticulture and winemaking also compete with other land uses, potentially pricing out other agricultural activities and the residents dependent on them. Animosity towards the industry can ensue, and if local politics are dominated by traditional forces, impediments to growth are likely to be encountered.

Investment

The funding of wine tourism infrastructure and marketing is a major issue. Who pays? Destination marketing/management organizations will certainly be expected to participate, but can the wine and tourism sectors work together to maximize their effectiveness? Will local and state governments contribute? What about economic development agencies, agricultural industry bodies, and roads departments? There are many essential partners to get involved.

Community Impacts

As observed by Hackett (1998), wine tourism can lead to a number of problems that, if not solved, can result in conflict with host communities. Many of these are typical of tourism development in general, although wine tourism can take large numbers of visitors (along with cars and buses) into previously quiet, remote rural areas. Some of the risks are:

• traffic congestion and related noise and air pollution;
• annoyances and complaints arising from viticultural and winemaking processes;
• overloaded community infrastructure and services;
• impingement on community amenities or sensitive ecological resources;
• commercialism: inappropriate types or scale of development;
• conflicts arising from new competition (e.g., wineries competing with local merchants).

Destination management agencies must consider and plan for the impacts of wine tourism on the host community, making every effort to involve residents and secure benefits for the community. Problems have to be anticipated and dealt with. The ultimate capacity of the area should be considered at the forefront.

Environmental Sustainability

Are viticulture and winemaking environmentally sustainable? Intensive agriculture of any kind can lead to devegetation, loss of wildlife habitat, soil erosion, and pollution of water, air, and land from pesticides and fertilizers. Winemaking adds special risks from chemical use (e.g., sulphates) and often a heavy reliance on fresh water for irrigation. The trend toward organic viticulture and winemaking will likely expand in response to perceived quality improvements, cost savings, and market forces, but the industry must realize that it requires an environmental code of conduct to ensure its long-term survival.

Marc Baum (1998) wrote an article entitled "Measuring and enhancing sustainability in California vineyards and wineries," which refers to the first ever sustainability survey of California wineries and vineyards. The goal is to maximize ecological and economic efficiency, including consideration of the following issues:

- integrated pest management, which emphasizes natural resources to replace polluting inputs;
- balanced nutrient cycles;
- preservation of a diversified environment (i.e., biodiversity) to avoid many of the problems related to monoculture;
- concern for the welfare of all animal species;
- preservation and improvement of soil fertility;
- use of renewable energy and energy reduction.

A holistic view of the entire operation is required in order to become sustainable. Practical examples of this approach include protected buffer zones, ground plantings, and watershed management for erosion control and water purity. Organic viniculture is a related movement that is discussed in Chapter 3. The motivation for following environmental codes of practice is to save money, ensure protection of the resource base, and satisfy growing demand for environmentally friendly products and services.

Chapter 2
GLOBAL OVERVIEW OF WINE TOURISM DEVELOPMENT

PATTERNS OF WINE PRODUCTION, EXPORTS AND IMPORTS

Wine tourism is related to both the world's wine-producing regions and its wine-consuming nations. While most wine tourism will occur within nations, international wine-oriented trips are bound to grow, and these trips will be heavily weighted towards movement between the major wine-producing and -consuming nations listed in Table 2.1. A related factor is that of wine exports, because countries with major export markets can be expected to perform better in wine tourism—as long as their reputation for quality remains high.

It is very apparent that Europe accounts for most of the world's wine production and consumption. According to 1997 data provided by the Office International De La Vigne et Du Vin (OIC) in Paris (1999, personal communication), the United States is a fairly small producer (9.5% of total volume in 1997) but is more important as a consumer nation (9.3%). The United Kingdom produces very little, but is a significant market for wine (3.6%). Australia produces 2.3% of the total, but its relatively small population ensures that it is out of the top 10 consumer nations. There is little chance of Russia or the former USSR nations becoming major players in wine tourism in the near future (for reasons of both low quality and lack of tourist attractiveness), but all the other countries in the top 10 list of producers can certainly develop this business sector. In addition, other countries like Canada and New Zealand, both small producer and consumer nations, already have a thriving and expandable wine tourism sector.

Top Producers		Top Consumers	
France	20.3%	France	15.6%
Italy	19.2%	Italy	15.1%
Spain	12.8%	United States	15.1%
United States	9.5%	Germany	8.3%
Argentina	5.1%	Spain	6.5%
South Africa	3.3%	United Kingdom	3.6%
Germany	3.2%	Russia	2.6%
Romania	2.5%	Romania	2.6%
Australia	2.3%	Portugal	2.5%
Portugal	2.2%		
Source: Office International De La Vigne et Du Vin (OIV).			

Table 2.1. World's Top 10 Wine-Producing and -Consuming Countries: 1997

As noted by Tony Spawton (1998), who teaches wine marketing at the University of South Australia, most wine is consumed in the nations that produce it, especially the leading European producers. Three of the top 10 producers, however, are also major importers of wine (see Table 2.2). The United States (and Canada) tends to import higher quality wines from all over the world. France tends to import bulk wines for blending, while Germany only produces about one half of its consumption and so imports a wide variety of wines. The United Kingdom is near the top of the list of importers, and that long-standing fact has contributed to its prominence in the wine world, including wine tourism. Japan is the only other non-European country in the top 10 importers and represents a potentially strong wine tourist source, as do other Asian countries that are just now becoming significant purchasers of wine.

What is the exact connection between wine trade and wine tourism? This has not been researched specifically, but it is clear from the Australian experience that United Kingdom tourists are the leading wine tourists Down Under. When wine consumers are exposed to quality foreign wines it naturally arouses a curiosity about the source. If that interest is combined with historical travel preferences (e.g., within Europe, and between British Commonwealth countries), wine tourism can flourish. The overall attrac-

Top Exporters		Top Importers	
France	24.0%	Germany	20.8%
Italy	23.9%	United Kingdom	14.3%
Spain	14.2%	France	10.2%
Portugal	3.8%	United States	8.1%
United States	3.5%	Russia	5.2%
Chile	3.4%	Netherlands	3.4%
Germany	3.3%	Switzerland	3.3%
Moldavia	3.1%	Canada	3.2%
Bulgaria	2.8%	Denmark	3.0%
Australia	2.7%	Japan	2.3%
Source: Office International De La Vigne et Du Vin (OIV).			

Table 2.2. World's Major Suppliers (Exporters) and Buyers (Importers) of Wine (by Volume): 1997

tiveness of a country or region (including its accessibility) will also figure prominently in the wine tourist's decision, so that several countries on the list of exporters, namely Chile, Bulgaria, and Hungary, might have a more difficult time developing this niche market.

On the other hand, it might be difficult to attract wine consumers from the big European producing countries to wine regions in other countries. Why? Because they consumer mostly domestic wines and possibly see little romance in visiting other wine regions. Three key geographic target markets therefore emerge:

• major wine-importing European countries (United Kingdom, Scandinavia, Netherlands, Belgium) without major wine production of their own and with high travel propensity;

• North America (major importing countries with high travel propensity);

• Japan and other emerging Asian wine markets (e.g., Singapore).

While the above analysis applies to the dedicated wine tourist, there remains the substantial potential to attract other tourists who are not traveling for any wine-related reason to visit wineries or attend wine and food festivals.

WINE TOURISM DEVELOPMENTS IN EUROPE

Europe possesses the world's most familiar and visited wine regions, its oldest wine routes, well-developed regional cuisine, and numerous, charming wine villages. Wine tourism has been a fact of life in Europe for generations, although until recently little was done systematically or by government policy to develop and promote it. Many commentators have remarked on the absence of good accommodations or restaurants in European wine regions, and on the difficulty of visiting many wineries because no facilities exist to service tourists.

Wine is an integral part of many European cultures, and has been since the time of the Roman Empire when grape growing became widely established on this continent. Until the fairly recent explosion of New World winemaking, good wine was assumed to be French, or perhaps Italian and German, and wine tourism anywhere else was nonsensical. Europe contains the most popular wine tourism destinations, partly because of the huge captive market (over 300 million residents live very close to many wine regions), and partly because of the general cultural allure of travel to Europe by residents of many other countries.

Wine tourism in Europe evolved differently from New World experiences, for many reasons, not the least of which is the enormous number of small grape growers and the dominance of a few large wine estates. The great wine chateaux of France were not in the tourism business, and did not need visitors, so potential visitors were traditionally ignored. Grape growers do not sell wine, so for the most part they are part of the scenery of wine country. Experiencing wine in Europe largely remains an exercise in individual cultural tourism—driving through wine country, soaking up the atmosphere of wine villages, and finding some wineries open to the public.

In parts of France, where wines of high reputation are certain to be sold every year, many wineries have *not* accommodated visitors at all. Robinson (1994) reported that Bordeaux was slow to develop wine tourism and Medoc did not have a hotel or more than one restaurant suitable for international visitors until the 1980s. The vast majority of wineries and vineyards in France are not open to the public, at least not without a prior appointment. This reflects the huge number of small and family operations, and the fact that the best *vignerons* have never had to worry about public relations in order to sell out. But increasingly the value of wine tourism is being recognized in France. Perhaps because the competition is finally worth noting?

Thevenin (1996) reported that in France two types of wine tourism development have appeared. The first involves a heavy investment in infrastructure, including museums, research centers, wine routes, restaurants, accommodations, and workshops, citing as a prime example the wine hamlet in Beaujolais. The second style has been through associations or clubs of winegrowers for marketing to tourists, such as the Great Wine Club of the chateaux of Languedoc. Alsace has 185 wine visitor sites and 12 wine museums, many of which are connected by a wine road. In Burgundy only 260 of 5000 winegrowers are involved in tourism. In Bordeaux there are 260 open wineries that attract some 70,000 visitors annually (Choisy, 1996).

Cognac uses tourism primarily as a means of communicating and marketing its famous product. The area has provided lots of infrastructure for visitors, including tasting rooms, bilingual staff, slide shows, exhibitions, and organized visits (Desplats, 1996).

Visitors can drive the Great White Wine Route of Burgundy while looking for the best Chardonnay. Start in Marsault and tour the *grand crus* and *premier crus* of Burgundy. Then drive the *Route des Grands Crus* between Vosne-Romanee and Gevrey-Chambertin for the highest density of *grand crus* estates. Most of these cherished vineyards are identified by special signs.

Georges Duboeuf put Beaujolais on the world wine map following World War II. Their Wine Experience is situated in the old railway station in Romaneche Thorins, and is part museum and part entertainment, designed to show large numbers of visitors the Duboeuf story.

Barge cruises on Burgundy's canals are popular, with some featuring local wines and gourmet meals, and private tours of chateaux. Optional cycling along the canal banks provides an athletic dimension to this romantic wine country experience. Add traditional wine villages and a visit to the Hospices de Beaune Hotel-Dieu (circa 1443), which has institutionalized Burgundy's most famous annual charity wine auction. Special wine appreciation cruises are packaged for the international market.

Dom Perignon has become the icon of Champagne, much to the benefit of Moet et Chandon. This venerable wine company in Epernay is a destination all onto its own, and has now constructed tourist-oriented wineries in Victoria Australia, Napa Valley, and Argentina.

Howley and van Westering (1999) described English wine tourism as being a new phenomenon and a prerogative of the higher socioeconomic groups. They described wine and gastronomic tours to Europe and further abroad, but said that most domestic winery visits are part of a day trip. With assistance from local tourist boards wine tourism has been promoted, but officially designated wine routes have had little success. The annual Festival of English Wines in Sussex attracts large crowds, so there is obviously a market. Denbies Wine Estate in Sussex was established specifically to be a tourist attraction and generates about 200,000 visitors a year to its winery visitor center that is complete with restaurant, educational theater, and indoor tour train. Other wineries have added restaurants to attract a broader customer base.

Gilbert (1990) looked at how Spain was developing new tourism concepts, especially cultural products including gastronomy and wine. The Rioja region was thought to possess the potential for wine and food tourism development, based on its good location and accessibility and well-maintained landscape and environment. To do so required better information and infrastructure for tourists, development controls, coordination in management and marketing, and quality products. Some of the elements of the wine and food tourism scheme were to be the renovation of buildings to hold wine courses, special tourist menus at restaurants, wine museums, and road signs.

In the south of Spain, the House of Sandeman has facilities open to the public at Jerez de la Frontera. Their visitor center is located in traditional cellars in the heart of this city. Here, Sherry and Brandy de Jerez are the products, and the tours include viewing of the traditional black aging caskets and tastings. Special services are offered for tour operators or other clients, including tastings for connoisseurs, events within the winery, and visits to sherry vineyards.

The Port Wine Route was initiated in 1996 by the wine industry of the Douro Valley Port Region in northern Portugal, and offers visitors 54 stops at estates, bottlers, and wine bars. For those so inclined, grape stomping is also on the menu! Tours start in Oporto, a World Heritage City and home to the great wine lodges, and take visitors up the narrow, vineyard-terraced river valley. The Wine Center of Cambres, built in the late 1960s, is a Sandeman's winery built for tourist visits. The Museum of Lagares offers a self-guided tour where visitors learn how grapes were once stomped in the open stone tanks called lagares. Nearby, Sandeman also operates a guesthouse for tired wine tourists. A notable wine tourism attraction in Oporto is the Sandeman Port Visitor Center (visit their Web site at: www.sandeman.com), which interprets the history and making of port, includes a tour of the cellars and a tasting. Also in the Sandeman lodges is the Sandeman Port Wine Museum (opened 1992 and remains the only one of its kind) and the Museum of the Douro (opened 1995).

The dedicated wine tourist should obtain *The Wines of Germany* (Deutcher Weinfonds 1993/4), a well-illustrated atlas and encyclopedia of this country's every wine region and site. It explains the German places of origin system and wine labeling, provides details on wine varieties and winemaking methods, and shows the location of each and every wine village and site in the country—it is the villages that give their names to the wines. Wines from all sites must meet high standards to receive the designation Quality Wine or

Quality Wine with Special Attributes. This system contrasts sharply with France, where individual vineyards are permanently quality designated.

The book covers "the sites and charms of the German wine regions. It includes tips on what to see and describes the wine routes recommended by the Regional Authorities, so that you can get to know the country and the people away from the main routes." For example, tourists can use the book to sample one of the most famous wine trips in the world, a trip down the Mosel and up the Rhine. The *Moselweinstrasse* (official wine route) runs from Koblenz to Perl, which is upstream of Trier, offering the car-based visitor access to quintessential European wine country scenery and history. There are medieval towns with half-timbered houses (e.g., oft-photographed Beilstein; Bernkastel-Kues), ancient churches, monasteries, and cathedrals (Bremm; Trier, Enkirch), steep, terraced vineyards, and many wineries with tasting rooms. The whole region is steeped in history, including Roman sites and relics like the wine boat on display in Trier's Landesmuseum, the excavations at St. Aldegund, and wine press at Piesport. Cochem is a tourist center with an old town and narrow, twisting streets. Bernkastel-Kues houses the Mosel wine museum.

The first German wine route—*Deutsche Weinstrasse*—was established over 55 years ago, through the Pfalz region. The Sachsen Wine Route, following the Elbe River, connects 13 towns and villages that welcome visitors, and 27 historic inns serving authentic regional food and wine.

NORTH AMERICA

In North America wine tourism is practically synonymous with California, and particularly Napa Valley. Nowhere else in the world has wine tourism developed to the extent it has here, even though the wine industry is relatively new. A combination of lifestyle elements, natural resources, quality wines, good marketing, and a large nearby population created the right mix for wine tourism to grow and flourish. Elsewhere in North America emerging wine regions are now competing to attract tourists, but not necessarily desiring the volumes experienced in Napa.

According to Richard Vine, author of *Wine Appreciation* (1997), wine popularity in North America surged in the 1990s with establishment of more than 1000 small, boutique wineries. "The typical estate was a few acres of prime Napa or Sonoma land planted to several select Vinifera varieties, centered by a state-of-the-art production facility housed in an architectural masterpiece" (p. 89). Wineries were created in almost every state, with the result that wine tourism followed—and in many cases is aggressively developed because it is essential to their survival.

In Napa Valley, the unofficial wine tourism "capital" of the world, "five million tourists a year swarm from town to town, blissing out on sun, vineyards and wine tastings" (Shapiro, 1998, p. 74). Legendary Robert Mondavi helped develop the culture of wine in America, and his Mondavi winery has become one of the major Napa attractions; indeed, it is almost like a pilgrimage to visit this shrine to the California lifestyle. Robert Mondavi Winery receives around 300,000 visitors a year, and Mondavi is also building a $70 million American Center for Wine, Food, and the Arts in the City of Napa. Scheduled to open in 2001, this facility will offer exhibits and programs, workshops and seminars, all available to the general public. It will certainly have a positive impact on the city, which, because of its 65,000 population, tends to be by-passed in favor of the rural areas and small towns of Napa. The Center will be run as a nonprofit educational organization with a prestigious board of directors (Eilender, 1998).

As with California, Texas can trace its wine origins back 300 years or more to the plantings of Spanish missionaries, but the modern industry was born in the 1970s when the state had only two commercial wineries. The number of wineries had grown to 27 in 1998 (Murphy, 1998, p. 45), producing close to 1 million gallons of wine annually from about 3000 acres of wine-grape vineyards (Texas Wine Marketing Research Institute, 1996). Many of these are small producers, but several have national and international markets.

The state has five appellations: High Plains, Hill Country, Bell Mountain, Fredericksburg in the Texas Hill Country, and Escondido Valley. Most of the grape growers are concentrated around Lubbock in the High Plains AVA, while a majority of the wineries are in the Hill Country. Like many of the 43 US states producing wine, most (96%) is consumed within the state of Texas. Research has found that 85% of winery visitors are from within Texas, and half live within a 30-mile radius (Murphy, 1998, p. 45). Smaller wineries have little choice but to pursue cellar door sales and stress the local and regional market areas. However, positioning wine within grocery stores has been credited with popularizing wine consumption in the state. For a more detailed and expert look at Texas wine tourism, read the interview with Dr. Tim Dodd.

Canada

Chidley (1998a) reported that Niagara region wineries attract 300,000 visitors annually (p. 40). A push to develop regional cuisine is gaining momentum. Vineland Estates winery was planning to open an international culinary institute with lodging for up to 70 students, visiting chefs, and agritourists. In Canada, "people are beginning to understand that our wines are some of the best in the world" (Chidley, 1998b, p. 42). And consumers are turning to finer quality wines. In 1989 Niagara had 15 wineries, and now it has 50! Between 1990 and 1997 British Columbia wineries nearly doubled, with 21 new ones. The cultural shift came in the 1980s. Impending free trade forced the industry to replace local with European varietal grapes. A new breed of winemakers like Donald Ziraldo of Inniskillin realized they could not compete at the bottom end of the market. Introduction of VQA (Vintners Quality Assurance system) was a Ziraldo project. Canadians still do not drink much wine by international standards, just 10 liters a year (Chidley, 1998, p. 43) compared with 83 liters of beer. (See the profile of Inniskillin's self-guided winery tour in Chapter 5.)

Will the Okanagan Valley someday rival Napa as a high-end center of year-round wine tourism? That was the question posed by Boddy (1998), perhaps wistfully in view of this wine region's newness and relative isolation. According to Boddy, "most Okanagan wineries operate out of tiny heritage houses or other unambitious facilities, inadequate for the bus tours and waves of automobiling boomers who now put chasing the grape at the top of their leisure agendas" (p. A17).

British Columbia is certainly making a concerted effort to develop wine tourism, and the Okanagan has the most potential. This is true despite the fact that the nearest city, Vancouver, is some 3-hours' drive away, and it relates to the valley's favorable climate, lakes, and scenery, which already attract large numbers of vacationers and retirees.

One direct tribute to the Napa Valley is the recent addition of a tour service between Kelowna and Vernon, called the Okanagan Wine Train. Original Super Continental Train cars from the 1950s and 1960s have been restored for the 90-minute one-way trip.

AUSTRALIA AND NEW ZEALAND

Patrick Iland and Peter Gago wrote the book *Australian Wine: From the Vine to the Glass* (1997). They note that every state in the country has at least one winery, but production is concentrated in the temperate south. South Australia has 55% of wine grapes, Victoria 24%, and New South Wales 18%. These vineyards cover a wide range of climate and terrain, with recent plantings occurring more in the cooler regions. "Typically, Australian wines are full of flavour. They are made from grapes that come from well managed vineyards in sunny, non-polluted environments; such conditions ensure clean, flavoursome grapes. . . ."(p. 15). There are approximately 60 varieties being cultivated, all *Vitis vinifera*.

Australians have given wine exports and wine tourism a very high priority at all levels. This country certainly leads the world in development of wine tourism strategies and planned destination initiatives. In October of 1998 a draft National Wine Tourism Strategy was released for consultation, and it is covered in detail in Chapter 7. Its authors (Global Tourism and Leisure) observed:

> During the latter half of the 1980's and through the 90's, Australia's wine and tourism industries have developed strong and positive images around the world. Of all the images and profile Australia enjoys worldwide, those established by wine and tourism are at the forefront. . . . At the same time, the image of wine was transformed from being an alcoholic beverage to one of a lifestyle product.

Similarly, the plan notes that tourism has changed from an emphasis on rest, recreation, or sightseeing to that of "lifestyle enhancement."

According to Delroy (1998), the wine industry in Australia is highly concentrated. There are approximately 1000 wineries, but 10 companies dominate the industry, with a combined market share of 84% of the annual crush (Rees & Grivas, 1998). Southcorp is by far the largest, followed by

Mildara Blass and BRL Hardy. A case study of the Southcorp wine tourism strategy is contained in Chapter 9.

Australia has achieved remarkable success in exporting wines (a 20-fold increase over the past 20 years), based on a number of competitive advantages (Delroy, 1998):

• favorable climate,
• few pests and diseases,
• innovative technology based on research,
• quality wines with intense, fruity flavors,
• value for money across all price points,
• a focus on markets.

Primary markets for Australian wine exports are the United Kingdom (almost half) and the United States, which leads directly to interest in visiting Australian wine regions from British and American consumers. Exports also help create wine region fame and identity, so that internationally the best known appellations are probably Coonawara, McLaren Vale, and Barossa Valley in South Australia, and Margaret River in Western Australia (Delroy, 1998). Within Australia, Hunter Valley also has considerable fame, and although less well known by appellation, the wines of Victoria are justly popular. The same factors have also led to establishment of many small wineries producing only premium wines, many of which are dependent on cellar door sales.

For a small country, New Zealand has the reputation of being a world-class tourist destination. While magnificent scenery and outdoor pursuits are dominant attractions, wine is gaining in popularity. Data from the New Zealand International Visitors Survey 1995/96 revealed that 13% of international arrivals had gone on a wine trail or visited a winery during their stay (New Zealand Tourism Board, 1996, pp. 17, 73). Lawson, Thyne, and Young (1997) reported on a survey conducted by the University of Otago in Dunedin, which found that almost 18% of New Zealanders visited a winery during their most recent holiday.

Campbell (1997), in his *New Zealand Wine Annual 1998*, recorded 30 new wineries over the previous year, and some 230 in all, and he predicted the high rate of growth would continue. About 93% of the country's wineries are small, or boutique wineries (Wine Institute of New Zealand, 1997). Four companies, Corbans, Montana, Nobilos, and the Villa Maria groups dominate production and sales (Campbell, 1997). For the bulk of small wineries, tourism is important because other means of distribution are prohibitively expensive (Johnson, 1997).

Analysis in 1995 revealed that 60% of New Zealand wineries had cellar door sales, compared to 80% in Australia (Deves, 1995, in Hall and Macionis, 1998). Very few operated tourist-oriented facilities other than eating establishments. Wine festivals have sprung up all over New Zealand, making it possible for event tourists to sample the best of food and wine in all its regions and cities. Two of the best known are the annual Marlborough Wine and Food Festival and Toast Martinborough (see Chapter 8 for a profile of this event). Martinborough has been promoting itself as a "wine village," and is close enough to Wellington to be included in any visit to the capital city.

Hall and Johnson (1999) reported that at least three wine regions in New Zealand use the term "wine country" in their promotions as a branding statement. Wine-related images are common in regional tourist organization materials. The majority of wine regions have published winery guides or wine trail maps for visitors. A number of domestic tour operators feature wine tours, but inbound wine tours are in their infancy.

INTERVIEW WITH DR. TIM DODD,
Director, Texas Wine Marketing Research Institute, and Assistant Professor, Restaurant/Hotel Management Program, Texas Tech University

Q: Tim, what is the current state of wine tourism in Texas and the United States?

A: Wine tourism has grown substantially in recent years throughout the United States, particularly in California. Texas and other wine-producing regions have also started to develop significant wine tourism industries. This has been a fairly recent phenomenon and has coincided with the increase in wineries within the state. Although the first wine in Texas was produced more than 300 years ago by Spanish missionaries, prohibition effectively eliminated the state's wine industry. It was not until the late 1970s and early 1980s that real interest once again developed in producing wine in Texas.

The majority of Texas wineries are only now beginning to recognize the potential of tourism to their business. Less than a decade ago, very few of the state's wineries fully embraced tourism. Fewer still considered tourists as their main focus. Most wineries put their efforts into distributing their wines through grocery, wine, and liquor store outlets, and restaurants. Tasting room sales were generally seen as a sideline. Increasingly, however, Texas wineries are recognizing the potential value of winery tourism, especially the smaller ones that have limited access to other means of distribution.

In the United States as a whole, the situation is similar. Although wine is produced in all but a few states, California produces close to 90% of the total wine made in the nation. In several regions of California, winery tourism is a huge business, one that has spawned new associated activities to meet the interests of winery tourists. Health spas, bed and breakfast accommodations, restaurants, and recreational activities such as balloon rides, horse rides, and bicycling have all arisen to target people who are interested in visiting the wineries.

In the smaller wine-producing states, winery tourism has also become a substantial industry. Wineries in these states often can't compete well in the retail environment because of the small volumes of wine they produce. However, a focus on tourism offers small wineries an excellent opportunity to start a new wine business without huge amounts of capital. The businesses can rely on tourists for sales without having to grow to the size needed to attract distributors and to keep shelf space in grocery and wine stores.

In Texas, many small wineries have made tourists their main focus. Larger wineries, while still putting most of their efforts into expanding their distribution both within Texas and to other states, have increased their attention to tourists. They are providing more festivals and other events at their wineries, publishing brochures and other materials for visitors, and are working more closely with convention and tourism bureaus to increase their exposure to visitors to their area.

Tourism has also helped with the general education of wine consumers within the state where per capita consumption is one of the lowest in the nation. This education of Texas consumers when they visit the wineries has been a major focus in the tasting rooms.

Q: Are there really good examples of wine tourism in Texas?

A: Texas has several distinct regions where grapes are grown and wine is produced and these regions have substantial differences in terms of supporting tourism. There are a number of good examples of wine tourism in Texas both in terms of individual wineries and in regions where groupings of several wineries have made them an attractive location for people to visit. Several small wineries have focused their marketing efforts entirely on the tourist. These wineries (mostly located in the Texas Hill Country region near Austin and San Antonio) do not plan to become involved in much distribution outside their tasting rooms. They focus on the traveler as their principal customer and were built with tourism traffic in mind. One winery, La Bodega, was even established at the Dallas/Fort Worth International Airport terminal. The winery sells its own wines, along with wines from many other Texas wineries, and especially caters to travelers between flights.

Some of the existing wineries have expanded by building tasting rooms close to large population centers. These wineries were originally built near vineyards or on land owned by the owner family and often in regions away from major population or tourism areas. During the past few years they have established these tasting rooms while still maintaining their original production facility. Most of these wineries have located their tasting rooms in the city of Grapevine, an historic township between Dallas and Fort Worth. Delaney Vineyards has a substantial facility in Grapevine that is open for tours and tastings while the main production facility is located near their vineyards in West Texas nearly 300 miles away. Two other wineries (CapRock and La Buena Vida) have also located a tasting room in Grapevine as well as maintaining a winery facility in another location. Homestead Vineyards has built their tasting room in the Dallas Fort/Worth region to be near tourists. Other wineries are also considering making the move and are being encouraged by a local community that wants to maintain an image as a tourism location.

Grapevine has also developed their own wine-related festivals that draw hundreds of thousands of people each year and link these events

with the historical and shopping aspects of the town. The city also provides music, art, and culinary events in conjunction with the Texas wine
theme that is the foundation for this tourism activity.

In the last few years a number of Texas wine stores have opened. These
stores specialize in selling a range of Texas wines and wine-related
merchandise. They are located in major tourist locations, such as near
the Alamo in San Antonio, and in tourist towns such as Fredricksburg
in the Texas Hill Country. Some of these stores produce their own
wines in limited quantities but the majority of their sales are of other
Texas winery products. Fredricksburg Winery is a classic example; they
originally produced very small quantities of their own wines and mostly sold other wineries products. However, they are now expanding production and are developing their own vineyards.

Local convention and visitors bureaus and state agencies such as the
Texas Department of Economic Development are beginning to see the
value of promoting wineries in their tourism literature. For example,
Lubbock is located in West Texas and heavily promotes the local wineries as items of interest for people visiting the city. One poster produced
by the Convention and Visitors Bureau depicts a worn cowboy boot
with a bottle of wine on ice inside. The three local wineries, CapRock,
Llano Estacado, and Pheasant Ridge, have been used substantially by
the Bureau when promoting the region. CapRock and Llano Estacado
wineries have in recent years started to capitalize more heavily on
tourists by offering a variety of festivals and other events.

Some of the advertising that the state does with respect to tourism
includes showing vineyards and wineries in their publications. One particular series of advertisements that was focused on tourists from
California highlighted the fact that Texas had an important wine industry.

In the Texas Hill Country, which is already a destination because of the
many items of interest already available to visitors, wineries have an
opportunity to capitalize on this substantial tourist traffic. Becker
Vineyards, Bell Mountain, Fall Creek, Hill Country Cellars, Sister
Creek, and Slaughter Leftwich Vineyards have all developed substantial tourist traffic in this area.

Perhaps the winery that has been most innovative in capturing the tourist market is Messina Hof Wine Cellars in Bryan. They have added a bed and breakfast facility, a restaurant, and other facilities designed to be of interest to both local visitors and out-of-town tourists. They have also become very prominent and well known in their local community, which helps to give the winery recognition with local hotels and restaurants.

Q: You have done pioneering work on winery visitors and the winery service environment. What would you say are critical success factors for wineries catering to visitors and specifically tourists?

A: There are many potential ways by which a winery can achieve success, and the first thing the owners should do is identify why they want tourists to come to the winery. For some smaller wineries, success may be the profitable sales of all the products they make along with a database of potential customers who will purchase wine by mail. Other wineries may aim at trying to ensure the highest degree of satisfaction for visitors. For larger wineries it may be to create a positive image that will translate into brand loyalty and subsequent sales in grocery stores and wine shops.

From my studies of visitors to Texas wineries and in working with wineries from other states, it is clear that a number of factors lead to a winery achieving their particular objectives, and the first thing it must do is clarify what these are. No one factor will prove to translate into success for wineries with respect to the tourist market. Most of the studies we have conducted at the Texas Wine Marketing Research Institute have investigated the factors that impact purchases of wine and wine accessory products so I will mainly discuss these.

In nearly all situations, multiple factors were found to influence wine sales. Characteristics of the individuals who visit wineries and visitor perceptions of various attributes associated with the winery are the two major factors that have been examined to date. However, there is still further work to be done to investigate how these issues are related and what other factors may be involved.

The four categories that seem to influence wine sales the most are as follows:

1. The service of winery personnel (especially the overall feeling of service provided, friendliness, and the degree of entertainment that people perceived). The overall service and the degree of entertainment received at the winery were the most significant service variables related to purchase of souvenir items.

2. Wine characteristics of particular importance to wine sales are the taste of the wine and overall perception of wine quality.

3. Aesthetics, especially the wine label, and the displays in the winery are the most strongly aesthetic characteristics related to how much wine people purchase. Displays are also the most significant influence upon souvenir purchases.

4. The price of wine is related to the total amount of money spent by tourists. The higher the perceived price of the wine, the smaller the amount that will be purchased.

With respect to personal factors, the most significant demographic variable associated with wine and souvenir purchases is the income of the visitor. In general, the higher the income the greater the amount spent at the winery. Product and purchase involvement, or the degree to which individuals consider the product of wine and the particular purchase situation as important, are also very significant variables related to wine purchases. Product involvement has been especially related to purchases of winery souvenirs. Thus, the greater the level of importance a person places on wine in their lives, they will tend to purchase more souvenir items to take with them, but the importance of the particular situation will only influence actual wine sales. These factors can determine how many people can be encouraged to visit the winery, how much wine and other merchandise they plan to purchase, the level of satisfaction attained, and the likelihood they will return One of the most significant implications from these studies is the need for winery personnel to excite people about their wine visit experience and make them feel like they are a special part of the success of the winery. Stories about how the winery was started, early struggles and amusing situations discussed by winery staff can make the visitor feel a special affinity with the winery. There is growing evidence that this translates into significantly higher sales of wine and winery souvenir products.

Chapter 3

THE WINE
CONSUMER AND
WINE TOURIST

MAJOR FORCES AND TRENDS IN WINE CONSUMPTION

Are all wine drinkers potential wine tourists? What about nondrinkers, will they visit a winery or tour wine country? In this chapter the wine consumer and wine consumption trends are examined, with implications drawn for wine tourism. That is followed by a detailed examination of available information about the wine tourist, organized around major market segmentation variables.

A number of basic facts should be considered first:

• although consumption of alcoholic beverages in general is declining in many countries, consumption of better quality wine has been increasing;

• global trade in wine is growing, carrying with it increasing exposure to new wine regions;

• wine has become identified with healthy, modern living, with fine dining and romance, and with attractive places to visit;

• developing Asian markets show good prospects for future wine consumption and wine tourism growth;

• wine consumers tend to be better educated, older, and with higher incomes—the same group that is mostly likely to engage in pleasure travel and particularly long-distance trips.

But there are concerns that wine consumption is overly concentrated in a narrow segment, that alcoholic consumption in general will shrink, and global overproduction of wine will affect future competitiveness. The industry will have to closely monitor trends and engage in continuous strategic planning. The following discussion should help wine tourism planners and marketers to find some competitive advantages.

Shifting Wine Consumption Priorities

The most important trend in global wine markets is that consumption levels in many countries are declining, as consumers are substituting quality for quantity (Fattorini, 1997; Spahni, 1995). In the European countries that traditionally consume the most wine, especially France, Italy, and Spain, dramatic decreases have been witnessed, resulting in a glut of wine and pressure to remove vineyards from production. Meanwhile, production and consumption of premium wines continues to expand.

The market research group Euromonitor (1998) reported that from 1992 through 1996 global wine sales declined, while the value of sales increased by 6.2% annually. North America has 15% of global wine sales by value, but less than 8% by volume, reflecting the trend to consume better wines. Euromonitor forecast continued growth in the value of wine sales, especially in Eastern Europe.

This trend can be beneficial for wine tourism, as it demonstrates increasing sophistication in tastes that can be converted into wine country visits. However, in all countries wine is one of the lesser beverages consumed, with beer generally being the number one alcoholic beverage by far. In the following paragraphs we look in detail at patterns and trends in several of the key wine-consuming countries.

United States

According to Edmondson (1998), writing in *American Demographics,* many more Americans drink beer than wine. Beer sales are driven by young males, and it is a "blue collar" beverage. Wine drinkers are highly concentrated in upper income groups. Edmondson noted that households in the $70,000 or more income range spend triple the national average on wine. Estimated spending on wine for home consumption was $88 per adult in the highest spending county, and the countrywide median was $47 annually.

Shapiro (1998, p. 74), writing in *Newsweek,* noted that Americans drink less than 2 gallons of wine each (in 1996), compared with over 54 gallons of soft drinks! The United States is the world's fourth largest producer of wine, after Italy, France, and Spain, but in terms of consumption it ranks fourth from bottom (just above Iceland). United States wine consumption (all types) peaked in 1986 at 2.43 gallons per capita (i.e., not just those of drinking age). Total "table wine" consumption dropped from 481 million gallons in 1986 to 381 in 1992, but has since rebounded to 462 million (Wine Institute and Gomberg, Fredrikson and Associates, personal communication, 1997).

In Figure 3.1 the United States wine consumer in 1997 is profiled by age (NFO Research Inc., personal communication, 1997). Thirty-three percent of wine (excluding coolers) was consumed by those aged sixty or more, but this older age category consumes only 15% of all alcoholic beverages.

Fully 68% is consumed by those aged 40 plus! It is the small amount consumed by 20-somethings (only 4%) that should worry everyone in the wine and wine tourism business, as this segment must be introduced to wine soon or the trend will take a nosedive towards zero. Wine coolers are the choice of 20-somethings, accounting for 29% of the total consumed.

In fact, many Americans do not drink alcohol at all; Kaplan, Smith, and Weiss (1996, p. 114) said about one third are abstainers. These authors also believed that 10% of wine drinkers consumed fully 90% of the wine. The market is therefore very narrow.

Cartiere (1997), writing in *Wine Business Monthly,* asked who is the next generation of wine drinkers after the baby boomers? The proportion of wine drinkers aged 35 plus had grown from 53% to nearly 70% since the mid-1980s, reflecting the population bulge of aging "boomers." Meanwhile, the percentage of wine drinkers under 35 dropped from 47% to 28%. The data also suggested that there had been no change in the gender of wine consumers, and that fewer low-income earners were consuming wine.

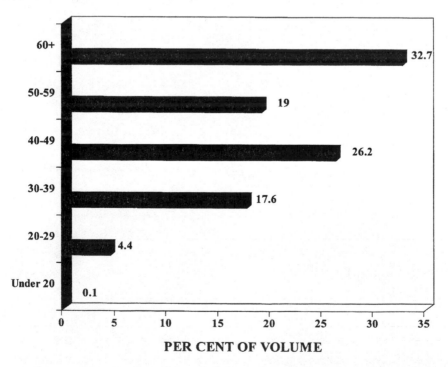

Figure 3.1. 1997 US wine consumption by age group (excludes coolers).

In Figure 3.2 the United States wine consumer of 1997 is profiled by household income, showing an obvious correlation between money and consumption. Almost half of wine (excluding coolers), and specifically of "table wine," is consumed by households with incomes of $60,000 or more. In contrast, this upper income group only consumes about 29% of all alcoholic beverages (NFO Research Inc., perconal communication, 1997).

Do the younger segments perceive wine to be too expensive? The above-mentioned data suggest they do, although cultural factors must also be considered. Ironically, as wine quality and prices continue to rise, placing higher profits in the hands of the industry, it might be simultaneously choking off future demand and sowing the seeds of decline in the domestic market. Wine consumption and hence wine tourism are now surging forward in direct response to the demands of the baby-boom generation, but it appears that in the absence of a concerted effort to reach younger generations that boom will eventually turn to a bust.

In Figure 3.3 the location of wine consumption is shown (excluding coolers). Most is consumed at home (71%) or at someone else's home. Restaurants only account for 13.4% of the total (NFO Research Inc., personal communication, 1997). Given the eating-out habits of North Americans, restaurants should be leaders in educating consumers about

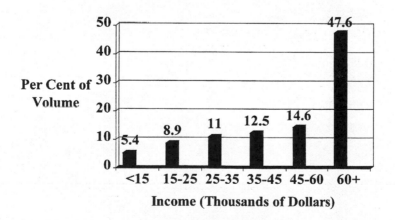

Figure 3.2. 1997 US wine consumption by household income.

wine, especially in light of the beneficial association of wine and food. Do servers know enough about wine? The younger ones presumably do not drink wine, and if they are of legal age they probably consume mostly beer and wine coolers. Are they effective ambassadors for the wine industry? This is an issue that should be addressed by the food service, tourism, and wine industries collectively.

Research conducted in 1996 by Simmons Market Research for *Wine Business Monthly* (1996) revealed other important characteristics of the United States market, especially that of the "typical" wine consumer. There were more females (55%) than males, they were highly educated (61.5% went to college), mostly married (63.5%), white (90.1%), and urban (87.55% in metropolitan areas); 75% owned their own residence and 64% had no children.

The Generational Factor

Fortunately, the huge baby-boom generation of Americans (and this holds true to varying degrees in Canada, Australia, New Zealand, and the United Kingdom) love both wine and travel. As they age, travel and fine-wine demand continue to increase, making the boomers our most important target segment. The downside, however, is what to do about the younger generations.

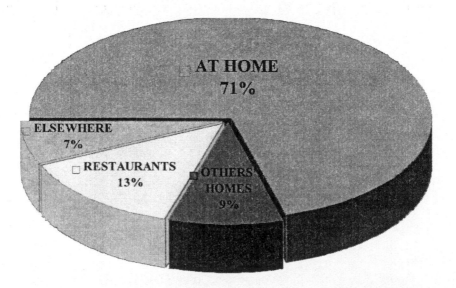

Figure 3.3. 1997 US wine consumption by location (excludes coolers).

The average age of Americans continues to rise as the baby-boom bulge progresses. Within a decade (by 2007) almost half of Americans will be aged 37 or older. The oldest boomers turned 50 in 1996, and each year 4 million more turn 50, right up to 2015! There are 78 million boomers in America (all born between 1946 and 1964), so it is a formidable generation (Canadian Tourism Commission, 1998). Many will have retired by 2010—the ranks of the retired will be swelling.

Boomers are the world's best educated and wealthiest generation ever, they are environmentally and health conscious, and travel like none before. They prefer independent travel; they search for less commercialism and more cultural authenticity. Lifelong learning is ingrained, and they like to take risks in traveling to new places. Fun and entertainment are part of their way of life. Computer and Internet use is high, and for making travel arrangements the Web has become a major factor.

Travel in general, and international travel in particular, will be fueled by the boomer generation for years to come. After 2007 the trend will start to reverse and young adults will again become a growth segment. While traveling, boomers will require healthy, comfortable, educational, and fun experiences. "Experience" is the key word, so wine tourism experiences must be customized to their needs.

America is not only aging, its cultural mix is rapidly changing. Because of differential birth rates and immigration patterns, the white majority is giving way to a population that will be dominated by today's "minority groups." Hispanics in particular will show the largest increase. In many other countries dramatic cultural change is also occurring. Because wine consumption is now dominated by white, middle-class boomers, these cultural changes present a major challenge.

So the next two decades are potentially the glory days of wine and wine tourism. The wine industry must meet the generational and cultural challenges, and wine tourism destinations must seize the opportunity now and secure a strong competitive position. Both sectors must recognize that the development of wine tourism can help capitalize on this great opportunity and use it to build future demand among the younger generation.

United Kingdom

The United Kingdom is one of the world's most important wine-consuming and wine tourist origin countries. British consumers are drinking about the same amount of alcohol as in the 1970s, but somewhat more wine and less beer (Fattorini, 1997). Wine use is concentrated in the middle classes and for many is seen as a luxury. The largest group of regular wine drinkers is aged 34–49, of which 34% were found to have consumed wine within the previous week, in 1994. Of 18–24 year olds, only 22% had done so. Males drink more than females, so heavy wine drinkers are mostly men. Women prefer white wine, and less of it.

Australia

In 1996 the Australian Wine Foundation's Strategy 2025 identified a number of trends or factors that made it desirable to attempt to increase domestic wine consumption:

• population growth in the prime wine-consuming age groups (over 25 years),
• forecast growth in discretionary income,
• increases in dining out,
• mounting evidence of health benefits,
• tourism growth,
• growth in demand for more individualized lifestyle experiences.

In 1997/98, per capita consumption of wine in Australia was at 19.3 liters and predicted to rise to 19.7 liters by 2002/03. Australian wine accounted for fully 94% of the domestic consumption, but threats were perceived to come from adverse social pressure regarding alcohol abuse, the popularity of other alcoholic beverages such as so-called "alcopops," import growth, and the need for developing the next generation of wine drinkers.

Canada

The unsettling demographic trends documented for the United States also apply in Canada. David Foot, the demographer who wrote *Boom, Bust and Echo: How to Profit from the Coming Demographic Shift* (1996), concluded that alcohol and tobacco "are losers in an aging population" (p. 92).

Consumption of both products declines with age, and the baby boom generation responsible for taking wine to new heights is definitely aging, and already past the prime consumption years.

Foot (1996), commenting on Canada's wine industry, noted: "The industry's timing was perfect, because these were the years (1980s) when the baby boom was switching from beer to wine and gradually learning to tell good wine from bad" (p. 93). He also observed that Australian wine sales did not surge until their boomers were in their late 20s and their 30s. Also to be affected by these trends are single malt whisky and specialty beers.

Wine consumption and wine tourism in Canada have largely followed American trends, so the issues are the same. The "echo boomers," children of "boomers," might or might not take up wine, and that is the big challenge.

CONSUMER-RELATED ISSUES AFFECTING WINE CONSUMPTION AND WINE TOURISM

This section covers several major issues affecting people's perceptions of, and attitudes towards, wine tourism, especially the health issue. Also, we examine wine tourism's relationship with other forms of special-interest travel, notably cultural and rural tourism.

Wine and Health

There are two countervailing health concerns affecting wine consumption. On the one hand, all alcoholic beverages are suspect in the minds of many people for contributing to alcoholism and drunk driving. Furthermore, some women are particularly concerned about the potential link between alcohol and cancer, and about Fetal Alcohol Syndrome. On the other hand, research has now shown that moderate daily consumption of alcohol does have beneficial health impacts. Wine drinking—especially with meals—has in many circles come to be accepted as being an integral part of a healthy lifestyle.

Kaplan et al. (1996) commented: "The ancients knew that drinking wine in moderation was an aid to health." These authors also observed: "As Americans travel more . . . there is a new interest in wine as part of the meal. Similarly, as Americans have become interested in healthy patterns of eating and drinking, they have looked to the Mediterranean diet as a model to follow" (p. 543). In particular, the *60 Minutes* television show in 1991, called The French Paradox, led to a jump in red wine sales as people latched onto the notion that wine will protect against heart disease. The French Paradox, applicable to other groups partaking of a similar diet, relates to the fact that they consume a lot of fat but have low rates of heart attacks. A correlation exists between higher wine consumption and lower rates of heart disease in many countries, but it is a sometimes overlooked fact that high alcohol consumption is also correlated with deaths by liver and other diseases. However, Shapiro (1998, p. 75) observed that relatively few new wine drinkers were generated by the French Paradox publicity; rather, existing drinkers consumed more wine.

A thorough discussion of the health issues related to wine consumption has been published by the German wine agency, Deutsche Weinakademie (1997). This brochure (write to PO Box 1660, 55006 Mainz, Germany) takes a balanced point of view, noting potential benefits and risks. Other books also cover this topic in detail (e.g., Vine, 1997). Evidence is readily available that shows the following potential benefits of moderate wine consumption:

• wine contains some useful vitamins and minerals;

• phenols (organic compounds that include color and tannins) are antioxidants and can act to reduce "bad cholesterol" (i.e., low density lipoprotein or LDL), thereby protecting against heart disease and cancer;

• calories from wine are different; wine drinkers tend to avoid becoming overweight, compared to drinkers of beer and spirits;

• wine helps digestion of the meal and contributes to a feeling of well-being by increasing levels of serotonin; it can also induce sleep.

A positive link between alcohol consumption and stroke prevention was announced in early 1999. Correspondent Dr. Steve Salvatore (for CNN) reported on a study published in the *Journal of the American Medical Association,* which indicated that one or two drinks a day can reduce the risk of ischemic strokes (which account for 80% of all strokes) by as much as 50%. It was also pointed out that heavy drinkers (seven or more drinks a day) have nearly a three times greater risk of stroke than nondrinkers, and that no study has recommended commencement of drinking by nondrinkers.

Researchers now associate moderate alcohol consumption, not just wine, with some major health benefits—although wine's contribution to digestion and association with dining (as opposed to drinking to get drunk) make it extra appealing. But how much is desirable and safe? Overconsumption of any alcohol can have the following negative impacts:

• reduction of blood clotting, leading to a higher risk of strokes,

• depression of the nervous system, impairing concentration and coordination (therefore, do not drink and drive),

• damage to the liver.

The famous U-shaped curve, derived from research, leads to the conclusion that one or two standard drinks a day ("moderate consumption") results in better health than no alcohol consumption or higher levels of drinking. In 1996 the US federal food guidelines for the first time suggested that moderate consumption of alcohol may have health benefits (Peters, 1997, p. 115).

Health issues often remain unresolved for years, and this is the case with the possible link between alcohol and cancer, miscarriages, and difficult conception—all factors that might influence the decisions of women, particularly those in their 30s (Shapiro, 1998, p. 75).

The Wine Institute maintains a database of thousands of scientific studies related to alcohol and wine consumption. For a synopsis, visit their Web site (www. wineinstitute.org).

Wine and Gastronomy

Wine and food, especially the appeals of unique, regional gastronomy, are inseparable. Indeed, most wine tourism destinations feature the two attractions together. This "packaging" reflects several underlying appeals of new cultural experiences, the healthy lifestyle of drinking wine with food, and the obvious fact that for most people wine usually tastes better with food, and vice versa.

Several of the case studies in this book feature restaurants at wineries and the promotion of wine and food experiences. In the packaging section is a profile of food and wine promotions from Victoria, Australia; as well, the *Great Southern Food and Wine Guide* is profiled in the section concerning wine routes. In the chapter on wine events, Tasting Australia is profiled. The concept of "food streets" is examined in the section on urban tourism later in this chapter.

The Victoria Wineries Tourism Council (1997) identified as an opportunity the "increased domestic demand for wine and food lifestyle experiences" and noted that increasingly Asian tourists, especially the younger ones, also wanted a Western lifestyle experience. But a major weakness was identified in the "poor integration between wineries and local food producers and restaurants," with "insufficient cooperation and networking between individuals and groups involved in food, wine and tourism" (p. 18).

While individual wineries having food services are clearly leading the way, as are regional restaurants featuring local wines, achieving an overall strategy for wine and food is more difficult. Victoria considers itself the "nation's food basket," but it has to work harder to consistently offer its produce and styles to the general-purpose visitor and thereby introduce them to more specialized wine and food tourism.

Victoria prepared a Food and Wine Tourism Development Plan 1998–2001, including an expansion of the mandate of the Victorian Wineries Tourism Council to develop and market food and wine tourism. The mission statement makes clear the state's goal and positioning:

> To position Victoria as the premier food and wine tourism destination in Australia. A destination where visitors can come and experience boutique accommodation, history and heritage, special events, art, culture, conferences and exhibitions, all backed by an array of fabulous food and wine. (p. 5)

What are the products of food and wine tourism? The Victorian plan identifies the following:

• dining out (especially regional cuisine and wines),

• food streets and precincts in cities (with wine bars and retailers),

• farmers' markets,

• wineries offering food services,

• combinations of wine and fresh produce,

• food and wine festivals and other events,

• food and wine touring packages (e.g., short breaks),

• food and wine trails, properly signposted.

Food (or gastronomic) tourism overlaps considerably with wine tourism, although it introduces new partnerships in the agricultural sector. Essentially, the Victorian planners recognize that the product is actually "lifestyle," in which food and wine are two of the most tangible and marketable products.

Wine and the Law

In most countries, anti-drunk-driving laws and related publicity campaigns are well established. Wine tourism must deal with this issue proactively, getting solidly behind programs like designated drivers and promoting responsible drinking. Other issues affecting consumers directly include: the legal drinking age; interstate shipment of wine; taxes; licensing of events and outdoor drinking; access to wine in stores and restaurants.

Wine and Cultural Tourism

"Cultural tourism" is a very broad concept, with most literature on the subject pertaining to heritage and architectural resources; the lifestyle dimension has been neglected. Richards (1996) concluded that learning is a "central distinguishing feature of cultural tourism" (p. 22), and the search for novelty is imbedded within the concept. Certainly wine tourism and other forms of cultural tourism occur with or without the provision of interpretation, but educational opportunities greatly enhance the experience.

A major research effort has been made to understand the cultural tourist in Europe (Richards, 1996), although global differences must be taken into account. The European researchers concluded that first-time visitors were much more likely to visit the well-known 'icons" of culture (i.e, famous sites), whereas repeat visitors would be more likely to seek "living culture" or lifestyle experiences.

Cultural tourism is more associated with those with higher incomes and age, but because of educational advances there are many more young cultural tourists than might be expected. The more educated specialty tourists are frequently seeking "symbolic consumption" of culture through visits and tours. One important lesson is that wine tourists are more likely to be drawn from the ranks of experienced travelers and repeat visitors to a country or region.

Cultural tourism products can take three basic forms (Munsters, 1996, p. 109). As applied to wine they are:

- the infrastructure of wineries and wine-themed events or facilities,
- packages featuring the wine destination,
- tours to wineries and within wine regions.

All three of these product types must be developed for a complete wine tourism destination. Cultural tourists might be interested in the interrelationships between wine production and the local people and their environment, including gastronomy and authentic traditions. Other cultural tourism themes tied into wine tourism include architecture, especially of wineries, and heritage conservation (see Dunstan, 1990). Wine festivals, especially those reflecting local customs and dress, also deserve attention (see Kenihan, 1991 and Ioannou, 1997 regarding the Barossa Vintage Festival).

Wine and the Arts

The fine arts are a particularly important aspect of culture that is often linked to wine tourism. This relationship in part reflects the cultural traditions of Europe where cultural tourists can easily feast on art, heritage, and gastronomic delights all at once, and to the notion held by many in the New World that wine *should* be part of a sophisticated lifestyle. But is also clearly dependent on the marketplace, in which wine consumers are also the best educated and wealthiest individuals.

Many wineries include art displays and retail galleries, as do some wine interpretive centers. Featuring local artists can add to the appeal of a visit, and increase sales. Wine tourists seek out antiques, wine-themed art and merchandise, and unique products they associate with wine country. Visual art is frequently an important element in winery branding, expressed in particular through the labels on bottles. Arts-related theming can also run through architectural design, background music, and special events—especially concerts. The case study of Leeuwin Estate (see Chapter 8) is a prime example.

Wine Culture

Is there a distinct wine culture? Marketers and wine country writers would have us believe it does, with the following as its (implied) differentiating qualities:

- sophistication (especially in terms of quality wines, fine dining, and the arts),

- elegance (wine goes with high fashion, interior decoration, and quality art),
- *joie de vivre* (revolving around wine, arts, and good food),
- luxury (visiting spas, foreign travel, living in the country, attending the best social events),
- romance and fun.

Many people, especially well-off, mature professionals living in cities, seem to aspire to belong to this vision of a wine culture, at least on weekends and vacations. It also exists as a lifestyle for the fortunate few who can afford to live in wine country (the real estate values alone are usually prohibitive). But if one examines the numerous lifestyle magazines that sing the praises of island living, coastal, mountain or country living, there is really little to distinguish them. Wine can be an important part of all these lifestyle choices, or not.

It seems more appropriate to talk about wine *and* culture, or the role of wine *in* certain lifestyles. In Europe wine is an integral part of culture but in many countries it has little or no impact. Overall in North America, as documented in this chapter, wine does not figure prominently in most people's lives, and probably will not in the future. It is one of many choices that consumers make based on their own interests and priorities. Furthermore, as long as the emphasis is placed on sophistication and elegance, it will be difficult to sell "wine culture" to the younger generation and to specific groups not currently interested in it.

Wine and Rural Tourism (Agritourism)

Wine regions are agricultural by definition, although wineries can be located in urban settings. As a particular form of agritourism (defined as tourism based on agricultural interests or situated within farming areas), wine tourism faces many of the challenges applying to rural economics and life in general, and rural tourism in particular.

"Rural tourism," like cultural tourism, is a broad and somewhat vague concept (see Page & Getz, 1997). Australia's National Rural Tourism Strategy (Commonwealth Department of Tourism, 1994) broadly defines rural tourism as the "country experience," which can encompass a wide range of attractions and activities that take place in agricultural or nonurban areas.

Its essential characteristics include wide-open spaces, low levels of tourism development, and opportunities for visitors to directly experience agricultural and/or natural environments. Lane (1994, p.14) argues that rural tourism enterprises should also be small scale, linked to local families, and reflect traditions of the region.

The cultural landscape, encompassing small settlements, indigenous architecture, and native peoples, is often an important component. In this context, wine regions offer a very unique and appealing rural experience, combining viticultural landscapes that generally make for attractive scenery, access to the means of wine production, the architecture associated with wineries and small villages, and a range of outdoor leisure pursuits.

Hackett (1998) pointed out that rural, and especially wine, landscapes are now commonly perceived to be recreation and tourism resources of the masses. Because of their unique resource base, wine regions are frequently popular with tourists, residential and resort developers, and other agricultural uses. This leads to a shift from a mind-set associated with agricultural production to one in which rural residents view themselves and their countryside as being "consumed" by visitors within a service economy. Conflicts can result from the changing economic conditions as well as changes in self-perception that accompany wine tourism development.

A number of trends were identified in the Australian Rural Tourism Strategy (Commonwealth Department of Tourism, 1994, p. 18) that relate well to the specific appeal of wine tourism, namely:

• higher levels of education result in more special-interest tourism;

• rising interest in "green" issues and ecotourism, with rural holidays being perceived as wholesome, especially if they provide education and adhere to sustainable practices;

• a growing interest in specialty food and beverages;

• the search for authenticity, including dealing with rural people;

• the need for peace and tranquillity;

• an aging population that often favors rural experiences for health reasons or nostalgia;

• health consciousness leading to more outdoor recreation (and, it should be added, an interest in the healthy properties of moderate wine consumption);

- growing REAL travel (i.e., rewarding, enriching, adventuresome, and a learning experience).

One of the main issues facing successful wine tourism regions will be the preservation of essential viticultural resources and the rural character in the face of developmental pressures. Tight control over land uses might be necessary. Another key issue will be that of environmental management to ensure that resources are not polluted or otherwise depleted, and that wine-related activities do not harm the ecosystem.

Who is the rural tourist? In a major review of rural tourism, Page and Getz (1997) concluded that identifying and segmenting the rural tourism market is probably the least researched and understood process in the rural tourism system. Just about any traveler is likely to somehow experience or pass through rural areas, so the real issue is how to determine which groups will consume or be interested in specific rural tourism products such as a winery visit. In general, Bramwell (1993, p. 21) believed the rural tourist to be more affluent and better educated, a seeker of quality, and a high spender. This seems to correspond well with what we know about cultural tourists.

Wine and Urban Tourism

The wine tourism experience is normally rural in character, but it is also somewhat tied to urban tourism. Most international travelers will use urban gateways to visit wine regions, so that an urban–rural experience can be packaged for them. Visitor information in gateway cities about nearby wine-related opportunities is important, as is the ability to enjoy local cuisine and wine in city restaurants, hotels, and conference centers. As well, visitors in cities can be lured into the countryside through organized wine tours.

There appears to be a trend towards wineries locating in or near cities in order to function more effectively as retail outlets. In this strategy, grapes (or juices) are brought to the winery, which is designed more as a store than a factory. A variation is for remote wineries to open stores in tourist towns or cities. The case of Spokane, WA is pertinent. This city boasts five wineries that engage in joint marketing to promote an urban winery tour, but almost all their grapes come from further south in the Columbia and Yakima Valleys.

Many wine tourism destinations are heavily dependent on the demand generated by nearby urban populations. Without doubt the success of wine regions such as Napa Valley in California (near San Francisco), Hunter Valley in Australia (near Sydney), and most of the famous European wine areas stems from large-scale domestic visits. More remote wine regions are challenged to work harder to attract day and overnight visitors.

There is a well-defined day-trip zone surrounding cities, and wine tourism planners must take this into account. A 2- or 3-hour drive is all that most excursionists will contemplate, so wineries within this belt can expect more frequent visits. If the wine country offers sufficient amenities, it can progress beyond day visits to attracting short-break visits—especially at weekends. Some are so attractive that they become resort areas, which introduces a whole new market.

Another connection between urban and wine tourism is the concept of "food streets." As highlighted by the Melbourne Food and Wine Festival (n.d.), a food street must include cafes and wine bars, specialty producers, delis, wine shops, and bookstores. "Diversity is good, so whatever your mood or budget there is something to suit." Australian and other warm-climate cities are favored when it comes to creating these streets, in order to accommodate *al fresco* dining and wine drinking. The challenge, of course, is to package this urban wine and food experience with wine country tours, or to use the urbanites' experience as a springboard to taking a wine country escape.

Other opportunities include the packaging of wine tours with urban-based meetings and conventions, and encouraging residents to take visiting friends and relatives into wine country. Wine routes almost certainly must start or finish in cities and towns, or connect them along a linear route, otherwise tourists will not find the choice of services they need, and urban residents will think winery tours are for foreigners.

Wine and Industrial Tourism

Industrial tourism focuses on visits to, and interpretation of, industrial activities, although a strong emphasis on heritage sites where industrial activities have ceased is an integral component. In one case, tourism is ancillary to manufacturing, while in the other it is likely to be the means to conserve a heritage site.

To the extent that wineries offer tours and interpretation of wine production, they can be considered to be one form of industrial tourism, and it might also appeal to those who are not primarily interested in wine itself. The manufacturer hopes to make direct sales, but usually it is more important to create product awareness and encourage brand loyalty. Many wineries, however, are more dependent on direct sales than are other manufacturers. Indeed, many wineries have been established with tourism as their primary source of revenue, so that production, sales, and marketing are virtually simultaneous. In the jargon of services marketing, the wine tourism "service" is produced and consumed simultaneously and cannot be inspected in advance. This, however, applies only to the winery or wine country visit, not the consumption of wine.

McBoyle (1996), speaking of Scotch whisky visitor centers and distillery tours, described the experience as industrial tourism that stems from the public's desire to not only understand how whisky is made, but also to observe other people's work. Many people are interested in understanding winemaking, but the notion that industrial tourism involves exposure to the nature of other people's work is perhaps new to the wine industry. To make this element work, wineries and vineyards will have to provide contact with owners and staff, interpret their work experiences and related skills, link these to regional lifestyles, and communicate the pride and satisfaction that comes from producing quality wines and other products.

Wine and Festivals/Events

It is little surprise that food and wine festivals have become very popular in many countries, given the general increase in cultural and rural tourism and global increases in wine consumption. Although they do not have to be located in a winery or viticultural area, most are closely tied to the wineries and vineyards or to the settlements dependent on wine-related activities. As such, they present the visitor with a potentially authentic lifestyle experience in very pleasant surroundings.

Event tourists, like other cultural tourists, fall into at least two general categories (Getz, 1997), including those motivated by the theme (wine or wine and food being very appealing), and those simply looking for a good social outing with family or friends.

Events are both products to attract visitors and a means for gaining publicity and shaping the image of a region. The Leeuwin Concerts are a world-class example of what can be done by an individual winery (with lots of community support), while the Barossa Vintage Festival (South Australia) and Toast Martinborough in New Zealand are excellent examples of district-wide wine events. These, and the wine festivals of Grapevine, TX, are profiled in a later chapter.

Dennis Schaefer (1997) observed that "the thought of visiting a tasting room intimidates many people" (p. ix). Events can overcome a degree of reluctance and thereby attract new segments. The intimidation factor is likely to be particularly strong in those "cathedral monuments to the art of wine" where "everyone whispers for fear of disturbing the wine muse."

Increasingly, wine trade events and consumer shows are gaining popularity. The industry, often combined with food and entertainment, seeks to educate, publicize, and sell product through these events, and to link producers with trade buyers—including tour companies.

Wine and Environmentalism

Major issues facing wine tourism development have been discussed, including the necessity of ensuring protection of natural resources, land use planning, and landscape aesthetics. Given that wine tourists are in large part pursuing an idyllic rural and cultural experience, environmental deterioration will have a great negative impact.

A related issue is the trend towards organic viticulture and winemaking. In part this is a reaction to perceived consumer preferences, which stem from health concerns and a desire for a cleaner environment; in part it is related to the constant need to improve techniques and reduce costs.

Organic Viticulture and Winemaking

Today's consumers, and especially the baby boom generation, have a strong environmental orientation. This has led to a movement called organic farming, and the wine industry has taken notice. Kaplan et al. (1996, p. 557) observed that organic practices were growing, especially in California where about 10% of the 600 wineries have had some or all of their vineyards certified organic by the California Certified Organic Farmers (CCOF).

Organic viticulture requires minimal or no use of chemical pesticides and fertilizers. Other practices include:

• composting to improve soil,

• use of cover crops like alfalfa or clover to enrich soils, cut down on weeding, and encourage beneficial insects like ladybugs,

• use of elemental sulfur instead of more dangerous chemicals to control fungi and plant diseases.

A leader has been Fetzer Vineyards (established 1968 in Hopland, Redwood Valley, Mendocino County). Fetzer has become the industry leader in farming grapes organically. Their approach is clear in these quotations from the Fetzer Web site (www.fetzer.com):

> Growing grapes organically is but one aspect of a company-wide philosophy of sustainability. We are an environmentally and socially-conscious grower, producer and marketer of wines of the highest quality and value. Working together in harmony and with respect for the human spirit, we are committed to sharing information about the enjoyment of food and wine in a lifestyle of moderation and responsibility.

Their goal is to be growing and purchasing 100% organically grown grapes by the year 2010.

Many practices help make Fetzer and industry leader, including:

• composting all organic material left over from crushing grapes and using it on the vineyards as natural fertilizer and mulch,

• minimizing energy consumption,

• minimizing packaging through bulk purchases (e.g., corks),

• protecting native oak trees,

• recycling, which results in lower dumping fees,

• restoration of used wine barrels to extend their life,

• established a blue heron sanctuary,

• contributions made to nature conservation programs,

• uses only recycled paper and other products,

• eliminated the use of Styrofoam,

• works in the community, including charitable donations.

Fetzer's recycling and safety programs are run by a team of managers and workers called the Fetzer Performance Team. The Fetzer Wine and Food Center is a major tourist attraction, encompassing a full-service deli, retailing of clothes and books, and a 5-acre organic garden with over 1000 varieties of vegetables, herbs, and flowers.

THE WINE TOURIST

Research on wine tourists or potential wine tourism segments has been very limited, making consumer research a high priority for the future. This section presents and assesses research findings from available sources (largely Australian in origin, because that is where the research has been most advanced) and attempts to use the information to create useful profiles for wine tourism marketing. The following discussion is organized under headings that relate to a comprehensive basis for segmenting the market, starting with geographical factors.

Geographic Segmentation: Origins of Winery Visitors

A general truth in wine tourism is that most visitors will be local and regional in origin. Research on visitors to six wineries in Texas (Dodd, 1995) determined that 85% were from within Texas (a total of 43% lived within 30 miles of the winery) and 15% were out of state. Some destinations, however, are likely to be favored with higher levels of international tourists.

According to Australia's international visitor surveys (cited by South Australian Tourism Commission [SATC], 1997), the number of international visitors who visited wineries in Australia increased at a rate of 19% per annum from 1993 through 1996, or approximately 10% in total. Among international visitors to Australia, Europeans (especially those from countries not known for their wines) and North Americans have been found to be the most interested in wineries (SATC, 1997). Data from New Zealand (New Zealand Tourist Board, 1996) showed that 13% of international visitors to that country had visited a winery or gone on a wine trail.

Research conducted by the Victoria, Australia Wineries Tourism Council (reported in Fuller, 1997a) found that 65% of winery visitors in the state were from the Melbourne area or the regions of the state, with 25% being interstate and 10% international visitors. In Margaret River, Western

Australia, fully two thirds of cellar door visitors were repeat visitors to the area, and were in small groups staying 2 or 3 days. Interstate visitors accounted for 29% of the sample, while international visitors constituted 9% (Morris & King, 1997).

Research in South Australia determined that 40% of all international visitors to the state included a visit to a winery. About 100,000 cellar door visits in total were reported (Fuller, 1997b). Around 20% of recent interstate visitors to South Australia visited a winery on their last holiday there (SATC, 1997) and fully 35% of international visitors to South Australia visited the Barossa Valley—its most famous wine region.

SATC (1997) concluded that wine tourism rates highly as a domestic and international tourist activity, with over half of domestic tourists in Australia considering winery visits to be appealing. An estimated 5–15% considered winery visits to be their most preferred holiday activity or as something they would organize a holiday around.

Implications

Winery visits definitely appeal to foreign and other long-distance tourists, but most demand will come from local and regional markets. Wineries near large cities have a distinct advantage, although more remote wine regions can potentially focus on attracting dedicated wine tourists without worrying about mass tourism. Internationally, it appears (from limited evidence) that wine tourists are most likely to come from major wine-consuming countries, other than those with their own major wine industries. In the future, it can be expected that Asian countries, now starting to enjoy wine, will become good sources.

As wine tourism promotion and packaging increases, it can be expected that more tourists will visit wineries and a higher percentage of visitors will be dedicated wine tourists. Research will have to concentrate on examining in detail the role of wine in luring visitors and shaping their activities.

Demographic and Socioeconomic Variables

Dodd (1995) concluded that winery visitors in Texas reflected the general population of American wine consumers, but were considerably different from the Texas population. Winery visitors were much more highly educated and had higher household incomes. They were mostly educated to some degree about wine. Income is one of the best predictors of wine consumption (Dodd & Bigotte, 1997) so it can be expected that high-yield wine tourists will not be tourists on cheap package deals.

In the Texas research Dodd and Bigotte (1997) found that age and income were the only demographic variables that explained major differences in spending among consumers at wineries. Older visitors had higher incomes and spent more money in total, but less per bottle. They rated wine attributes higher in importance, while younger respondents were more concerned about price. The older group also more highly rated environmental attributes, especially cleanliness, as factors influencing purchases.

In South Australia the SATC (1997) concluded that the most likely domestic tourists to visit wineries were those aged 40–60, couples with no children, and those with higher education and incomes in professional occupations. People in these categories with children face an impediment to winery visits, and are less likely to attend. For example, families with children were not well represented in the Margaret River sample (Morris & King, 1997) The majority of survey respondents in Margaret River were well-educated professionals aged 25–54 years.

Research in Victoria on winery visits determined that higher than average visitation (within the last 3 months) came from the following groups:

• people with advanced wine knowledge (59%),

• members of wine clubs (50%),

• those visiting small wineries (55%),

• nonurban residents (48%).

Higher than average first-time visitation came from:

• younger groups (18–24, 23%; 25–29, 20%),

• infrequent wine drinkers (25%),

• people with only basic knowledge of wine (18%),

• people on longer trips (26%),

• "blue collar workers" (19%).

This research also revealed that middle-aged segments were the most frequent winery visitors. Twenty-eight percent were in the 25–24 category,

26% were 35–44, and 22% were aged 45–54. Only 7% of winery visitors were in the younger category, aged 18–24; 12% were aged 55–64, and only 5% were 65 or older. Females accounted for 52% of the sample.

Implications

The correlation between wine drinking (and related knowledge) and wine tourism (particularly visits to and purchases at wineries) seems clear, but has not been tested in many areas. Certainly a primary target segment for wine tourism everywhere will be the middle-aged and older, higher income, knowledgeable wine consumer. However, wine tourism cannot thrive indefinitely on such a narrow market base. A number of special-interest groups, such as wine clubs and other affinity groups, have great potential.

Psychographic Segmentation of Winery Visitors

SATC (1997) reported findings of the Roy Morgan Holiday Tracking Study in Australia, in which holiday travelers are segmented on the basis of lifestyles and values. The 1996/97 data revealed that about 8% of those who had traveled on a holiday within the previous 12 months had visited a winery or vineyard, but this activity was much higher for those visiting Western Australia, South Australia, and Victoria. Segmentation revealed that all segments showed some degree of interest, but the highest levels of participation in winery/vineyard visits were among two groups called "visible achievers" (11%) and the "socially aware" (10%). These results also point to those with higher incomes and older married couples with no dependents as prime targets.

Implications

Much more research is needed on wine tourist personalities, attitudes, and lifestyles and how these impact on tastes and demand. Psychographic variables can be better predictors of behavior than demographics and socioeconomic factors.

Consumption Patterns and Spending

Wine tourists can be segmented on the basis of how they travel, make purchases, and their spending levels. Destinations and wineries want to find out who are the highest "yield" visitors, the ones who come back frequently and spend the most (from regional markets) and the origin countries that send the best yield tourists. However, little information is available on yield and other consumption patterns.

Dodd (1995) recorded pertinent data from visitors to six Texas wineries. They consumed an average of 3.55 bottles per month and spent $30 on wine purchases. Most of their wine (69%) was bought at grocery or liquor stores, 22% from restaurants, and about 8% from wineries. Mail-order sales accounted for only 1.3%. During the winery visit they spent $23.41 on average of which 78% was for wine and 22% for other merchandise. Most (61%) had not made previous purchases from the winery at which they were interviewed. Twenty percent of wine purchased was as a gift.

Another interesting conclusion from the Texas research was that older visitors (who are generally wealthier) spent more on wine at the winery, but spent less per bottle than younger visitors. Overall service and price were rated higher by younger visitors as factors influencing wine purchases at wineries (Dodd & Bigotte, 1997).

Respondents in Victoria said their preferred times for winery visits were "anytime" (56%), 12% at a festival, and 25% at "quiet times" (which were especially preferred by those aged 65 plus, the retired, and those on long trips). Only 1% preferred school holidays, showing this is not a family pastime. Six percent reported other times. In Victoria, interstate tourists visited more wineries than the average of 3.4 wineries per trip. Seven percent of respondents went to 10 or more, and 16% visited more than 6. Frequency of winery visits was found to be high. Fifty-two percent had made a previous visit within 6 months, although 13% had never been to one before.

SATC (1997) concluded that winery visits are strongly correlated with wine purchases, but almost one quarter of the Margaret River sample spent nothing at the winery, while 16% spent over $200 (this included some professional buyers). Factors influencing wine purchases were examined, revealing that taste was most important, followed by quality, price, knowledge of staff, and service. In addition to purchasing wines, 59% patronized winery restaurants, and others purchase local produce or arts and crafts and souvenirs.

An Italian survey (Pavan, 1994) found that 60% of winery visitors came to taste and buy, while 68% of them were habitual wine consumers.

Implications

One issue important to wineries is that of yield per visitor, as dedicated wine tourists will certainly spend more and potentially become more frequent buyers than larger tour groups full of general-interest sightseers (Morris and King, 1997).

Benefits Sought (Reasons for Visiting Wineries)

Winery visitors include both the dedicated wine lover, and the majority for whom it is an ancillary experience (SATC, 1997). Wineries attract small groups of family and friends, organized winery tours, and larger tour groups on general sightseeing trips. Those with restaurants and other facilities can tap into a variety of other market segments, including private functions and corporate meetings.

Evidence from South Australia (SATC, 1997) suggests that wineries make popular day-trip destinations, especially when residents are hosting visiting family or friends. Winery visitors tend to do so regularly, and visit more than one per trip. For most visitors, buying wine is a major motivator.

Research conducted in the Margaret River wine area of Western Australia (Morris & King, 1997) found that tasting and buying wine were the principal reasons for visits to wineries, although 20% did not make a purchase and 18% were found to be irregular purchasers of wine. A very high 88% said they were interested or highly interested in wine, but only 49% thought themselves to be knowledgeable of wine. Almost half made a visit on a random basis, either on impulse or deliberately to try a new winery, so advertising, visibility, and signage are important. Other reasons for a visit included: were on a tour; wanted a restaurant; the winery's reputation.

Macionis (1997) conducted a study of winery visitors in the Canberra, Australia region in 1994. She reported the following main motives:

- to taste wine,
- to buy wine,
- a day out,
- enjoy the rural setting,
- meet the winemaker,
- learn about wine.

Her respondents said that the most enjoyable aspects of their trip were: socializing with friends and relatives; relaxing; enjoying the service; having fun; doing something different; the scenery; food.

Research in Victoria, Australia, linked winery visits as a trip motivation with the number of wineries in each area—the more wineries there are, the higher the percentage who gave "visiting wineries" as their main trip motive. The conclusion was that a "critical mass" of wineries in an area is needed to generate a high level of special-purpose wine tourism. Overall, 53% of winery visitors in the state gave "visiting wineries" as their trip purpose.

Research in France found that fully 45% of visitors to Burgundy were motivated by food and wine, whereas in Bordeaux wine and food ranked only fourth highest in terms of visitor motivations (Choisy, 1996).

Implications

There will always be different motives for visiting wine regions and wineries, including functions and meetings. Although the search for dedicated wine tourists (those most highly motivated by the wine experience) is of paramount importance, wine tourism developers cannot neglect secondary markets, such as those more interested in culture, sightseeing, entertainment, or socializing. Wineries can lure passers-by and area residents with visiting friends or relatives to make spontaneous visits, and can seek to influence their purchasing behavior. The more wineries there are in an area, the greater the drawing power it will have for dedicated wine tourists.

Unfortunately, most research has concentrated on regional wine tourist demand, rather than the international visitor. More studies of potential target segments in origin countries, and comparisons between domestic and foreign visitor motives and activities are required.

Communications (How to Reach the Wine Tourist)

What information sources are used by winery visitors? Research in Australia (Victoria Wineries Tourism Council, 1997) found the following:

• family or friends: 32% (especially for those aged 18–29),

• wine regions of Victoria brochure: 30%,

• Tourism Victoria brochure: 22%,

- other brochures: 10%,

- previous experience: 10%,

- auto club guides: 7%,

- newspapers: 7%,

- magazines: 3%,

- other: 10%.

The same research found that 52% of surveyed winery visitors had planned to visit wineries in the region where they were interviewed, whereas 23% said their visit(s) was spontaneous. Another 24% had planned to visit the specific winery at which they were contacted. The Texas research (Dodd, 1995) found that most winery visits (88%) were planned, and only 12% were spontaneous visits while passing by.

Summary Profile of the Dedicated Wine Tourist

Although research on wine tourism has been inadequate, evidence suggests the following key points define the dedicated wine tourist (i.e., the people most likely to deliberately seek out wine country experiences):

- wine tourists are most likely to be middle-aged, higher income wine consumers living in cities,

- most are baby boomers (born 1947–1963),

- they are most likely to be local and regional in origin,

- key wine tourist origin countries are likely to be European (especially the United Kingdom) North Americans, and Australians; Asia presents major growth opportunities.

Challenges

Cartiere (1997), in *Wine Business Monthly*, emphasized three major challenges:

- demystification (most consumers do not want to invest much time learning about wine),

- social acceptance (especially among youth),

- increased fit with informal occasions.

The average wine consumer is getting older, and so is the average tourist. How can the younger generations be convinced to try the wine tourism experience? What specifically will appeal to them? Are wineries and destinations prepared for the older segments?

Wine consumption (especially in North America) is too closely linked with white, well-educated, middle and upper income baby boomers. What will appeal to other races and ethnic groups, to lower income persons, and to typical beer drinkers?

Chapter 4

THE WINERY AS TOURIST ATTRACTION

Wineries are the core attraction in wine tourism. Even though many are not built or managed as attractions, there is increasing recognition that wine tourism works to the benefit of most wineries and they are adapting to this market. Some, especially small, boutique wineries in emerging or nontraditional wine-producing regions, are heavily or entirely dependent on visitors for their existence (Cambourne, 1999). A few major wineries have been built as, or are becoming, hallmarks or centerpieces for wine tourism in their regions. Still others are being created or are evolving into integrated estates that function as self-contained destinations.

WHY SHOULD WINERIES GET INVOLVED WITH TOURISM?

Dodd (1995) summarized the various reasons for wineries to cater to visitors:
• allow people to try new products,
• build brand loyalty,
• increase profit margins,
• provide an additional sales outlet,
• generate marketing intelligence,
• educate your consumers.

In most of the world's wine regions, high competition and an abundance of small wineries has forced them to attract visitors and make on-site sales. For example, Saunders (1996) commented that Canadian grape growers have discovered they are in the tourism business. As noted by Dodd and Bigotte (1997), the majority of American wineries rely primarily on tourism for survival, reflecting both their inability to market widely and the fact that profit margins are highest at the source. Folwell and Grassel (1989) found that many wineries in the states of New York and Washington relied almost exclusively on direct sales, while Dodd reported from research in Texas that 19 wineries in his sample sold through tasting rooms and of these 7 realized over 60% of total sales that way.

Wineries in the Margaret River area of Western Australia reported that cellar door sales, on average, accounted for 34% of total revenue from wine sales (King & Morris, 1997). Fifteen percent of the sample reported that it exceeded 80% of sales. Reilly (1996) did a survey of wineries in South Australia and found that cellar door sales accounted for 20–30% of sales in the Clare Valley (with a high of 60%) and 30% in Barossa.

In the state of Victoria it has been estimated that cellar door sales account for 50% of total winery business at the 320 wineries in the state (Global Tourism and Leisure, 1998, p. 19). An earlier study by Spawton (1987) in Victoria revealed that for some wineries the cellar door in combination with mail order is the primary distribution channel, accounting for up to 100% of sales. Mail orders are largely based on visits to the winery and fol-low-up communications with customers.

In France, Choisy (1996) reported that direct sales accounted for 19% of the value of Burgundy's wine sales, and 11.8% of its volume. In Alsace, 23% of sales were made direct to consumers.

Boddy (1998) reported that in British Columbia, Canada, the winery gets about 18 cents gross revenue from a bottle for wine sold in the provincial liquor stores, as opposed to $5.98 for the same bottle sold at the cellar door. While the economics vary from place to place, they are similar because of heavy taxation on alcohol and/or huge transport, wholesale, and retail markups. This is a powerful incentive for wineries to develop wine tourism.

Even where direct sales are not of great importance, many wineries try to educate customers and develop brand loyalty, while a few, like Robert Mondavi, are primarily concerned with education. Another benefit can be market intelligence gained through tastings and direct customer feedback.

From a destination perspective, wine tourism is likely to be more important in newly emerging wine-producing regions where reputations have yet to be made and numerous boutique wineries lack the means or interest to develop alternative distribution channels.

Wine Tourism as a Sales and Distribution Option

Small wineries might have little choice—without visitors to the cellar door, nothing gets sold. As a winery develops, however, it has other sales and dis-tribution options available to it (Figure 4.1). The most likely expansions are into the areas of mail-order sales, as these can develop easily from visitors to the cellar door, and into local and regional retail outlets, as these can be secured without involving wholesalers. Tourists are not essential in any of these options, assuming there is a large, local population that buys wine. In remoter locations all visitors to the cellar door will be classified as tourists. Adding tourist segments to local markets makes a lot of sense, in all circumstances, because they are likely to bring distinct benefits, namely:

• higher spending per visit (on the part of dedicated wine tourists),

• wider word-of-mouth promotion,

• more evenly spread demand (where local demand is seasonal),

• higher volumes (especially when catering to tour groups).

On the other hand, wider distribution through retail and wholesale channels can create tourist demand as more-distant consumers discover the winery's products and build a desire to visit the area and the winery. With all these

Direct Sales at Cellar Door (Residents & Tourists)	Direct Sales to Wine Stores, Restaurants, & Hotels	Wholesale (Domestic & Export)	Mail Order
Costs: • Capital for facilities • Special staffing and training • Participation in events and other promotions to market the winery and the destination • Possible interference with vineyard and winery operations	Costs: • Sales visits (might require special sales staff) • Might require incentives to gain acceptance • Price discounting often required for volume sales	Costs: • Requires reliability in production volumes (potential penalties for non-delivery) • Must ensure consistent high quality in products • Might require domestic and foreign sales trips • More sophisticated business management (professional staff) • Risk of dependence on specific markets or wholesalers	Costs: • Maintain computer database • Regular mail-outs • Shipping costs • Discounts or reward programs to loyal customers
Benefits: • Higher profit margins • Can create brand loyalty • Allows database development for mail-order sales • Market intelligence • Enables consumer education • Save on advertising and sales visit costs	Benefits: • Higher volume sales • Wider distribution and awareness of products	Benefits: • Highest possible sales potential • Widest exposure to product leading to brand development and extensions	Benefits: • Can quickly expand from local to national and international sales • Higher volume sales • Larger purchases (usually by the case) • Fosters brand loyalty through relationship marketing

Figure 4.1. Costs and benefits of various sales and distribution channels for wineries.

points in mind, a strong case is made for utilization of all four sales and distribution channels as the winery grows.

As the reputation of many wine regions and specific wineries has grown, on-premise sales have frequently become the only way to get highly prized wines. Jeff Cox (1998) said: "There's a saying in California wine country: 'the best wine never leaves here'" (p. 38). Prerelease sales at wineries can attract numerous visitors looking for their only or best chance to get the wines. Such a case was the August 1, 1998 sale at Silver Oak Cellars (both Geyserville and Oakville facilities), in California, when an estimated 3500 showed up to acquire 1994 Alexander Valley Cabernet Sauvignon. Norm Roby (1998) reported that "the atmosphere was festive and the winery supplied live music and some light fare" but "people had come to purchase, not party" (p. 12). All prerelease vintages from 1985 through 1991 were sold out by noon, and the day's revenue was $1.3 million.

In another example, Clos du Val in Napa's Stags Leap District held a prerelease sale at which 2000 showed up, including winery club members who enjoyed a discount on purchases and members of the general public who had to pay $20 for the privilege. With this in mind, Roby asked if wine merchants were still needed, especially if they cannot secure popular wines for retail sales. Loyalty has shifted to wineries and away from knowledgeable retailers. And visitors can try the wines before making the purchase, which has a distinct advantage over mail-order acquisitions.

Why Some Wineries Are Not Involved in Tourism

Many winery owners are product oriented, concerned mostly or wholly with creating quality wines (Macionis, 1997). This is understandable, given the effort, skill, and capital required to run a winery. For these people tourism is either not recognized for its marketing potential or is actually shunned as an unwanted intrusion. For others, cellar door sales are not equated with tourism. They might be correct if all customers are local, but there might easily be a misperception as to who their drive-in customers are and why they are visiting. Either way, such winery operators are unlikely to become involved in tourism associations and related promotions. But a more fundamental problem occurs if the production-oriented winery owner is simply ignoring marketing, because that spells trouble.

Other reasons for not developing the tourism potential of wineries have been identified through interviews with numerous owners and wine industry representatives. Tourism-oriented developments and promotions can cost a lot of money and be unaffordable to small wineries. The costs can include: new access roads; signage; new or expanded visitor reception and cellar door facilities; increased staffing and training; parking areas; and advertising. And assuming there is a desire to capitalize on tourism, winemakers running their own business often lack the knowledge or time to devote to its development. In these cases, the help of tourism industry organizations is required.

A final reason for avoiding tourism is the perception, and it is often a misperception, that wine tourists are either not good customers (they are looking for free drinks), are likely to be rowdy drunks, or will not become loyal wine consumers. Although some wineries undoubtedly experience these negative elements, improved marketing and visitor services at the winery and destination levels can deal with the problem.

DEVELOPING THE SUCCESSFUL WINERY ATTRACTION

There are many choices available to wineries when it comes to attracting and serving visitors. Some are so small that visitors literally enter the winery itself and meet the owners or winemaker in a very minimal facility, and this has considerable appeal to many wine lovers. Others incorporate cafés, restaurants, museums, galleries, retail facilities, and overnight accommodations to create major tourist focal points.

John Doerper (1996), writing in his guidebook to *Wine Country: California's Napa and Sonoma Valleys,* provided insights to the rewarding winery visit. He values the attractive rural setting, good sign posting and ease of access, and relaxing tasting rooms. He suggested they should be designed to introduce novices to the pleasures of wines, as well as to provide a chance to expand one's knowledge.

Christian McIntosh (1997), in *Wine Business Monthly*, advised that it is no longer enough to simply greet customers and pour the wine. More sophisticated visitors are increasing and they often demand know-how from staff. More innovative wineries are using their vineyards as educational and selling features, while others add gardens to stress the food and wine connection. As an example, the Benzinger Family Winery (California) vineyard tram gives complimentary tours providing education on viticulture, wine, geography, and history.

The SATC (1997) concluded that popular winery features were the opportunity to buy wine not readily available elsewhere, and the chance to try the wine or meet the winemaker prior to making a purchase. Location is certainly another key factor. Research by Reilly (1996), involving Adelaide wine consumers, revealed that the highest frequency of winery visits within South Australia was to those regions closest to the city. This research determined the key factors affecting winery visits, namely (in descending order): shortness of the drive; restaurants; special features of the wineries; festivals; accommodation; other tourist activities; and other retail opportunities like crafts. Reilly also measured what was most highly valued about cellar doors at wineries, finding (in descending order): knowledgeable staff; tastings at no cost; lower prices than retail; the presence of winemakers; and unique surroundings.

The Historic Winery and Visitor Centers

Many wineries, both in Europe and the New World, are old enough or unique enough in their architecture or artifacts to have historic significance and may be identified as official heritage properties. This presents both challenges and marketing opportunities.

Dunstan (1990) examined the historic wineries of Victoria, Australia and documented a number of issues for wine tourism. He noted (p. 47) that "entrepreneurs have sought to make use of the wine industry's history and heritage of remnant material structures. . . . Regrettably, some of this is being undertaken with scant attention to appropriate heritage concerns" (p. 47). He did identify one very good example, that of Chateau Tahbilk, which had been over 60 years in the Purbick family. It conserved many aspects of its 19th century vineyard and winery complex, and even preserves its own historic grape, the marsanne.

It is not just buildings and artifacts that are of interest, although many cultural and industrial tourists will take a special interest in these things regardless of any major interest in wine. But vineyards, grape varieties, and viticultural practices are also important for conservation and interpretation. There might also be scientific value in these historic elements, such as the use of gravity in winemaking, or disease-fighting experiments.

The wine industry might learn much about heritage and marketing from Scotch Whisky distilleries. McBoyle (1996) discussed how the Scottish industry was conserving, adapting and marketing its history to promote whisky and specific brands. Distillery visitor centers in Scotland attracted over 1 million visitors a year, and many are in restored historic buildings. McBoyle suggested, "At the core of cultural tourism is the search for those characteristics about a place or a people that are outside the observer's normal experience" (p. 280), and whisky is a strong symbol of Scottish culture.

Of 85 malt whisky distilleries in Scotland, McBoyle observed that 26 had dedicated visitor centers and 15 others took visitors on appointment. As well, the industry had cooperated in establishing the Scotch Whisky Heritage Centre in Edinburgh to introduce visitors to that historic city to the romance and heritage of whisky. Also in Scotland, The Dallas Dhu distillery has been converted to a museum.

What are the elements in a successful whisky heritage center? McBoyle identified the following heritage elements:

• landscape,

• architecture,

• traditional materials,

• historical displays,

• production processes interpreted,

• features of the host culture (e.g., costumes, hospitality).

And in presenting and interpreting these heritage elements, the needs of cultural and industrial tourists must be met:

• authenticity (genuine culture; accurate restorations),

• quality,

• learning opportunities,

• participation (e.g., hands-on interpretation if possible),

• meeting locals (such as the staff),

• entertainment,

• personalized experiences.

Nontraditional Settings

Wineries are not always located in viticultural areas, so wine tourism is not necessarily locationally restricted either. There are some interesting examples, according to a report by Winters (1997) on the world's only airport winery, La Bodega, operated at Dallas–Fort Worth International. Wines from throughout Texas are sold, and the winery is producing its own brand. Another example cited by Winters is the Stone Hill Winery in Branson, MO, where over 6 million tourists a year come for country music. The approach has been to avoid pretentiousness and not go after elite market segments.

The basic strategy for these unconventional wineries is simple: you can either get tourists to come to you or you can take the product (and to a lesser extent, the wine experience) to the consumer. These innovators are tapping new markets and expanding the wine consumer base.

PRINCIPLES FOR DESIGNING A TOURIST-ORIENTED WINERY

Drawing on the case studies reported in this book, available literature, and the author's visits to numerous wineries, principles for designing a successful, tourist-oriented winery can be suggested. Obviously there is no single, winning strategy or formula. In fact, diversity is to be encouraged, as is adherence to regional architectural styles and traditions.

What Are Winery Visitors Looking For?

Earlier it was observed that winery visitors are not just looking to taste, but also to learn about, and buy, wine. Many wine tourists are on a social outing, looking for an interesting rural experience. Wineries, to be effective attractions, must provide for social experiences among groups of visitors and preferably cater to a range of activities such as picnicking, shopping, and more active recreation. Dining and accommodation can be specific attractions. Functions and events will motivate other visitors.

Once they get to a winery, a number of attributes become important. Research reported by Dodd and Bigotte (1997), using interviews with visitors to wineries in Texas, analyzed environmental and service perceptions as a factor influencing wine purchases. Older, wealthier visitors placed more importance on cleanliness as a factor in making a purchase. Younger visitors rated overall service to be more important. The tangible factors examined were: cleanliness; pleasant environment; winery smells; attractiveness of winery; and displays. Service elements covered were: friendliness; courteousness; overall service; knowledge of the staff; professionalism; believability of staff; and entertainment. More research on wineries as retailing, entertainment, and learning environments will have to be undertaken.

Access and Visibility

Some wineries have located on major roads, in urban areas, or tourist towns to maximize their visibility and accessibility to consumers. Those in rural areas have a greater challenge. Wineries, especially those in rural areas, are often at the mercy of road departments that do not appreciate the necessity of catering to visitors who (a) do not know their way around, (b) are uncomfortable on poor roads—especially dirt and gravel, and (c) can be lured to, or discouraged from, visiting a particular attraction by road and traffic conditions. Furthermore, tour coaches will not normally risk out-of-the-way itineraries over substandard roads.

The best solutions are at the regional level, involving the implementation of wine routes and themed signage. Wineries in the poorest access locations will have to go to extra lengths and expense to ensure that tourists can get to them comfortably and safely.

Signage

Directional signs are essential throughout the wine region and for each and every winery and attraction or service. Casual wine country tourists can be greatly influenced by signs and other information, including tour maps and brochures. Research has shown that many winery visits are spontaneous and therefore directly influenced by information at hand.

The entry sign is of particular importance, and will often be integrated with other elements designed to impress and invite the visitor (e.g., gates, arches, attractive landscaping, fencing, symbols of winemaking, like barrels or vines).

The Entry Statement

A combination of signage, physical layout, and other symbols can make an immediate impression about the attraction. The entry statement should be carefully designed to reflect and incorporate brands (names and symbols) and architectural/artistic themes used in the estate or winery facilities. It is at once a welcome, saying please enter (with signs giving details of open dates and hours) and a positioning statement, communicating to the visitor the tone of the establishment, quality of its products, and nature of the experience.

Small wineries have to rely on their own kind of statement, whether it be rusticity, down-home familiarity, unpretentious quality, or discovery through adventure! There are certainly wine tourists quite happy to poke around and try the unusual, but attention must still be given to their first impressions.

Parking and Special Access Provisions

Visitors want to be as close as possible to the attraction and service entrances, and provision must be made for the handicapped and coach tours. Parking is not just a necessary evil, it is an integral part of the entry statement and of the on-site experience. Bad parking facilities, with long walks over rough or wet surfaces, do not make for an enjoyable wine tourism experience. A gentle walk through gardens or along a path with views can be a very pleasant entry. Coaches require separate facilities with large bays and turning areas. Consideration should be given to separate access routes and facility entranceways if numerous coach parties are expected.

Internal Access (Including Handicapped)

The flow of visitors has to be planned, both to facilitate their desired activities (i.e., get to the tasting room, take a tour, use the washrooms, buy a meal) and to manage crowds. Visitor flows can be mapped and analyzed for problems like congestion points and activity conflicts, in combination with evaluation of service quality. The "service mapping" technique is described later.

Some visitors will have special needs, making it important (and in many areas legally mandated) to provide wheelchair access and separate washroom facilities. Also consider the unique perspectives of children, people with babies, the elderly, and large groups moving together.

Tours present a special challenge. Typically only larger, specially designed wineries offer scheduled tours. Wineries offering occasional tours, by reservation, must consider the extra risks associated with taking people into production and equipment areas, plus the comfort of guests that might be affected by moisture, temperature, noise, and odors. Furthermore, all aspects of the visitor experience must reinforce messages of quality and customer orientation.

Site Orientation (Views)

Wineries in attractive rural areas are often able to take advantage of views and landscaping to enhance the visitor experience, as well as to encourage longer stays, dining, and shopping. Making the site and facilities an attractive venue for picnics, recreation, walks, group functions, and special events will help realize these commercial objectives.

The Design Concept and Theming

Some wineries are indeed architectural masterpieces, attracting and rewarding visitors with a design concept that inspires aesthetic appreciation of the surroundings while simultaneously suggesting quality and sophistication of the wine. More traditional buildings also appeal to wine tourists, especially if their historical and cultural authenticity is evident. Even the modest, family-run, micro-winery has its rustic appeal, as long as it is clean and tidy.

As wineries became tourist attractions, particularly in the Napa Valley, there seemed to arise a competition for the most appealing or unique design. Some of the resulting facilities are not authentic in any way, nor are they going to have enduring visual appeal. Those that occupy unique sites have an advantage, but the most significant have incorporated traditional winery design elements to the fullest. These elements include original winery or farm buildings, native building materials, a functional arrangement suitable to the industrial process of winemaking, and attention to landscaping details. Add to this a care for visitor comfort and enjoyment, and a great winery attraction is born.

Reception and Direction

What impresses visitors most upon entering the winery or visitor center?

Some wineries feature the barrel room or barrel motif, others prefer to give patrons views of the fermentation rooms. There is no right or wrong approach, only the need to make a favorable impression and bring the visitor willingly to the tasting area, exhibitions, or sales areas. Probably more important than the design is the greeting people receive. Is there a staff person assigned to say hello and give directions? What happens when a crowd arrives and staff are overwhelmed? Many operators cater to groups only by appointment to avoid such problems, but the unexpected will occur!

A sequencing preferred by many winery operators places the tasting room first, preferably combined with exhibits and views of outside or of internal operations. In many wineries there is no other public room. If a tour is provided, returning the visitor to a tasting and/or sales area makes a lot of sense.

Tasting Rooms

Are they designed to maximize visitor enjoyment and education, or sales? A tasting room has a definite capacity and cannot handle too many people without problems arising. Some specifics to consider:

• physical orientation (views, exhibits, links to other areas),
• information on available wines, prices, procedures,
• facilitating the tastings (e.g., through staff–visitor interaction),
• roles of counter staff,
• separation of sales and tastings.

Ambiance

Music, lighting, décor, and staff can all contribute to the right atmosphere, whether for education, tasting, or sales. In a few wineries (such as Gundlach Bundschu in Sonoma Valley) a very youthful, upbeat (i.e., "cool") ambiance is communicated. This suits their positioning in the marketplace, with such irreverent but tasty products as the Bearitage label.

Internal Function Areas

Increasingly wineries are attractive function venues, and this market can generate substantial revenue. Examples include meetings, dinners, seminars, or cooking classes. Separate rooms can be constructed for private tastings and dinners, large banquets, or formal seminars and meetings complete with the latest in audio-visual equipment. Kitchens can be adapted to host small groups for demonstrations. Care must be taken to avoid conflicts between these types of groups and regular visitors.

Outdoor Event Spaces and Facilities

Numerous wineries host their own outdoor events or participate in regional festivals. Some have built special-purpose event areas, taking advantage of attractive landscape features like water, forests, and views to provide memorable experiences. The most common outdoor events seem to be concerts, picnics and other food events, and festivals.

Basic facilities or site improvements could include a covered stage, sloped seating areas, and lighting. Frequently tents are used for outdoor functions, requiring relatively flat, well-drained grassy areas. Hardened footpaths might be necessary for crowds, especially in wet climates.

Food Services and Catering

There is a big difference between providing snacks or a café and operating a full-service restaurant. Wineries in remote areas sometimes open their food services only on weekends and holidays, or for lunches, to cope with severe demand fluctuations or the difficulties of getting staff. Some clear choices are evident, ranging from least to most expensive to establish and operate:

• a refrigerator with prepared snacks and beverages,

• special snacks provided with tasting,

• small café or snack bar; lunch baskets or plates,

• limited-service restaurant (by hours and times of operation),

• permanent restaurant,

• catering service (in-house and by contract to outside clients).

The "destination" restaurant is in a different category altogether. This attraction will offer something truly unique (type of food, quality, wine selection, ambiance) that lures diners.

Other Retail Space

It is well known that travelers spend more money than locals, so wineries can go beyond wine retailing. Some develop their own specialty lines with a wine theme, while others adopt a country or ethnic theme. Distinct classes of products found at wineries include:

• souvenirs of the winery and the region,

• specialty items associated with wine (e.g., books, glasses, crystal),

• local produce (e.g., olives, fruit, vegetables),

• travel literature,

• clothing (usually displaying the winery name/logo),

• up-market goods unrelated to wine or the winery.

Departures

As discussed later, every visitor should be viewed as a potential loyal customer, so establishing a relationship (such as by getting them on a mailing list) is an important predeparture task. Normally it is wise to separate departures from entrances, but this is not always possible. Separation avoids potential congestion and allows the winery to structure visits so that departures are made under optimal circumstances. Usually this means having the exit beyond the retailing area, but it can also allow for personal contact from staff.

Essential Services

Every visitor facility must provide the essential services and amenities:

• washrooms,

• drinking water,

• comfort areas (seating, shade, line-up and waiting).

Picnic and Play Areas

To be family friendly, provision for visiting children is desirable. Picnic and play areas are inviting to casual travelers, and can lead to increased purchases from retail outlets.

THE WINERY TOUR

Winery visitors potentially have many interests, not the least of which is a desire to learn about and taste the product! But what else should be covered in a tour? Allegra and Gillette (1997), in their winery guide to the Napa Valley, provide a useful starting point by listing special interests catered to in various Napa winery tours. Other interests can easily be identified, and have been added:

• winemaking, varietals, viticulture;

• caves, cellars;

• barrels, barrel making, oak;

• food (to eat) and its links with wine;

• art, including sculptures, stained glass widows, wine labels;

• architecture (modern and traditional), interiors;

• landscaping, gardens, and views;

• personalities (meet the winemaker, owner, staff);

• history (of area, winemaking, the family);

• culture (of wine, the area);

• organic farming and wine production;

• bottling and bottles;

• marketing of wine (where to buy it, how to get the best, wine clubs);

• wine-themed and related merchandise (shopping);

• sensory stimulation (smell, taste, sound, feel);

• romance (of wine and wine regions, of drinking and dining in the winery);

• flora and fauna, microbiology, pest control.

A review of many winery guides and winery promotional materials, plus personal visits, suggests the following tour elements. This is a list of possibilities from which the winery managers must select the appropriate blend to suit their environment, markets, and goals:

• the tasting (before, during, and after the tour; from vats and barrels);

• providing views of actual operations;

• hands-on experiences (e.g., riddling, picking, crushing);

- meeting the owner, winemaker, and other staff;

- receiving instruction (winemaking, cellaring, buying wine, etc.);

- interpretation of history, processes, facilities, displays seen;

- providing technical and economic information about winemaking, the area, and industry;

- sales pitch;

- wine and food appreciation (with tasting);

- photo opportunities.

Technical Considerations Regarding Tours

Group size and composition:

- small tours (up to 10?) with guides are best for maximizing the learning experience and keeping control of guests;

- different approaches required in case of special group composition (e.g., children, seniors, foreign languages).

The guide:

- training in guiding and interpretation of wineries is required;

- must be friendly, helpful, neat, and verbally clear;

- a script is useful, but some degree of spontaneity is also desirable.

Frequency, flow, timing:

- constant tours appeal most to visitors but are troublesome to provide if staff are required;

- number of guides and length of tour are key factors;

- interference with operations must be avoided;

- determine how many guided tours can occur simultaneously, and if different routes or staged departures are needed.

Reservations:

- many small wineries provide tours only upon prior reservation and subject to maximum group size;

- likely to be needed at peak times to avoid overcrowding;

- employ tourist bureaus, toll-free numbers, and Internet to book ahead.

Staging:

• need a large space where groups can assemble;

• ensure the end-point of tours is suitable for safe dispersal (avoid congestion).

Audio-visual presentations:

• can be used to enhance learning/entertainment value;

• can replace guides under some circumstances;

• incorporate interpretation and marketing messages.

Music and entertainment:

• consider the desired ambiance for key target market segments (e.g., youthful or conservative?).

Personal comfort:

• dress codes might be required (e.g., no bare feet);

• temperature settings (cellars get cold and damp; outside/inside temperatures vary a lot).

Safety and risk management:

• support designated drivers;

• avoid operational hazards.

Security:

• video cameras might be required to prevent damage or theft;

• unescorted tours might pose a greater risk.

Many wineries opt for a self-guided tour, so it is worth discussing the pros and cons. At a minimum, this option requires the following:

• careful attention to the safety and comfort of guests;

• special signage, and interpretive stations or viewpoints;

• determination of the capacity of the tour in terms of numbers of visitors and group size;

• consideration of the length of time required

• attention paid to the entrance (from reception? or directly from parking?) and exit points (end at tasting room or retail area?).

See the case study of Inniskillin's self-guided tour presented in the next chapter.

SERVICE QUALITY

The winery visit, especially if motivated by more than making a simple wine purchase, is a social, leisure experience. High-quality and consistent service is required to ensure both visitor satisfaction and sales. "Service" is evaluated differently depending on the motives, characteristics (including culture), and actions of visitors, but two major service dimensions are involved: staff contacts and physical evidence. Poor service will be associated with rude, unhelpful, or uncaring staff (including owners!), with facilities and grounds that are dirty, unsightly, unsafe, or inconvenient, and with the ways in which important exchanges are conducted. The crucial exchanges consist of making purchases, taking a tour, eating a meal, tasting the wine, having a picnic, getting into and out of the attraction, and using essential services like toilets.

Owners and Staff Are the Experience

To the winery visitor, staff—and especially owners—constitute a large part of the experience. Staff and owners are actors, or cast members, and in small, family-run wineries the personality of the owners can make a big difference in sales. Winery staff are important elements in branding (the image they convey), wine appreciation and winery interpretation (the messages and clarity of presentations), sales (making the sales pitch in a friendly, helpful manner), and in solving visitor problems (for information, services, etc.).

Staff Training and Performance Evaluation

Training in "critical incidents" (CIs) will pay dividends. CIs occur wherever visitors require or look for service or a staff contact, and while many CIs experienced in wineries are similar to those found in other tourism and hospitality settings, some are unique:

• the tasting of wine in a controlled setting;

• a tour and interpretation of winery or vineyard operations, often while work is occurring;

• purchasing wine (often an anxious, emotional process);

• dining in a winery or picnicking outside (involving winery products);

• experiencing entertainment in a winery setting (a special atmosphere with undertones of romance and sophistication).

Regular hospitality training is useful for many of the incidents staff and owners can expect, but specialized training is required for the unique CIs listed above. Fortunately, more colleges are offering specific programs in wine appreciation, wine service, and winery operations.

Essential Components of a Service Quality Management System

Commitment must come from the owners and flow through all the operational divisions and staff positions. This comes from realization of the importance of quality products and service to the success and survival of the business. A focus on the customer is required. All too often owners and staff concentrate on winery operations, assigning marketing functions to a professional, or relegating marketing to a secondary position. But marketing subsumes all operations, including what products to make, their branding, theming of the winery, the presentation and actions of owners and staff, and all contacts with guests and potential customers.

Research into your customers is required, even if only by direct observation. Are they mostly casual and looking for a simple tasting experience, or are they sophisticated and demanding of high-touch services? Surveys will help, and these can be done collectively by area tourist or wine associations. The aim is to be able to meet and exceed all visitor expectations, or to shape their expectations to fit your style through target marketing.

The term "empowerment" is used to describe how owners or managers give staff (usually trained staff in key positions) the authority and means to determine and meet customer needs. Can the tasting room manager provide premium wines to discerning guests, waive the tasting fee for a regular customer, replace a spilled or broken glass, or otherwise set the standard of service provided? A lot of trust is required to truly empower staff.

Some kind of monitoring is required to ensure that visitors really are leaving the winery (and the destination) truly satisfied. Sales are certainly one measure of success, but other important measures are the number of repeat visits, positive word-of-mouth recommendations, and willingness to become a mail-order customer.

The Winery Audit

Figure 4.2 presents guidelines for conducting a winery audit. The audit can be self-performed, or experts can be brought in to do the work. Its purpose is to evaluate the winery and its operations from the perspective of visitors,

---

A) ELEMENTS TO BE EVALUATED

<u>Tangible Factors</u>
- Accessibility and visibility
- Signage
- Entry statement
- Parking and flow
- Special needs (disabilities compliance)
- Visitor comfort, safety, and health
- Themeing and Aesthetics
- Information and interpretation
- Tours
- Other facilities (e.g., dining, functions)
- Programming and events
- Retailing (sales)
- Relationship building

<u>Service Quality</u>
- Greeting and welcome
- Staff–customer interaction
- Critical incidents
- Interpretive efforts
- Sales efforts
- Management systems (e.g., training)

<u>Intangibles</u>
- Sensory stimulation
- Atmosphere

B) RESEARCH AND EVALUATION PROCESS

<u>Benchmarking</u>
- Comparison to industry leaders
- Determine HOW success is achieved

Determine Best Practices

<u>Visitor Surveys</u>
- Determine interests, motives, perceptions, satisfaction, etc.
- Get feedback on tangibles and intangibles
- Determine key target segments

Develop Market Intelligence

<u>Participant Observation</u>
- Use expert observers to simulate and evaluate the customer experience
- Create service maps

Improve Service Quality

<u>Risk Assessment</u>
- Use experts to assess risks (to customers, staff, owners)

Develop Risk Management Strategy

<u>Green Audit</u>
- Use experts to assess environmental friendliness and organic potential

Become a Green Winery

<u>Owner and Staff Input</u>
- Interviews and anonymous written input

Practice Internal Marketing

Figure 4.2. Guidelines for the winery audit.

leading to recommendations for improvements. It can be completed in isolation, but it should ideally incorporate an assessment of competitors, especially through the device of "benchmarking" against industry leaders.

Benchmarking can be done casually through visits to other wineries, or through a formal, reciprocal arrangement. Under the assumption that competitors can learn from each other, direct comparisons and sharing of information can be justified. As well, the winery can approach "competitors" in other regions that do not perceive a direct threat. Winery or wine tourism associations can undertake benchmarking more systematically, leading to larger scale improvements in the industry.

The essence of benchmarking is that it includes not only an assessment of what industry leaders do well, but—more importantly—how they achieve their success. The exercise must therefore identify quality *and* the management systems that enable it. For example, good service by winery staff must come from training and other management efforts; educational and fun winery tours stem from an underlying attention to customer preferences and behavior, as well as to relevant design criteria.

Employing Service Quality Audits and Service Mapping

One very useful audit tool is the service map, based on the work of Bitner (1993). Using the technique of "participant observation," in which observers go through the same experience as customers, the service encounter from beginning to end is documented and evaluated. Specific points of analysis include:

• the flow of movements from approach through arrival, on-site experiences, and departure;

• all contacts with owners or staff (or their absence when needed), assessing helpfulness, friendliness, knowledge, etc.;

• all physical evidence of service levels such as cleanliness, appearance, safety, comfort;

• critical incidents or "moments of truth" when the customer receives good, bad, or indifferent service.

With the help of managers, the mapping also shows unseen management practices and how they effect the customer. These systems can make or break service quality standards. For an illustration of service mapping see Figure 4.3.

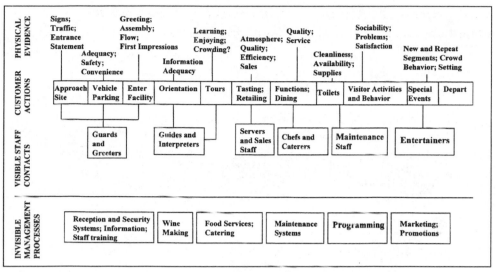

Figure 4.3. Service mapping for winery visits.

CREATING THE INTEGRATED WINE ESTATE DESTINATION

Larger wine estates can develop into complete destinations through integration of attractions (wine, food), accommodation (from simple bed and breakfast through luxury hotels or villas), programming (recreation and events), and other essential services. Capitalizing on brand name recognition, a reputation for quality wine and food, or unique settings, ambitious winery operators can capture more of the economic benefits of wine tourism for themselves. Most importantly, high-yield market segments can easily be attracted to a wine estate for a short break, longer holiday, or a business event.

A classic example of how the wine estate destination can evolve is provided in the draft Australian National Wine Tourism Strategy (Global Tourism and Leisure, 1998, p. 20). Warrenmang vineyard and winery is located in the Pyrenees wine region of Victoria, which is beyond a quick drive from central Melbourne. It commenced as a small, high-quality, low-volume operation, added a fine restaurant, then accommodation, and finally meeting and conference facilities. Weekends were in high demand for wine and food, but accommodation and other facilities were needed to even out demand. Active marketing, targeting corporate meetings, is an essential part of their success.

A number of serious obstacles can exist to this type of estate development, not the least of which is rural or agricultural zoning. In many

85

wine regions tight controls by municipal authorities have expressly prevented ancillary uses at wineries, and in the case of Napa Valley have now restricted the number of wineries. Certainly there is a potential resource-depletion problem that must be faced, as too much tourism development can both diminish the land available for viticulture and make it too expensive for expansion of grape growing. As well, the proliferation of tourism infrastructure would visually diminish the wine tourism experience. But many wine regions do not have the spatial concentration or large volume of tourism that Napa experiences, so some degree of controlled tourism development on wine estates should be permitted.

Accommodation

There are several good reasons for adding accommodation to the basic winery attractions:

• additional sources of revenue;

• year-round demand for wine, food, and merchandise on site;

• the enhanced cash flow can be an important counterbalance to the peaks and troughs of wine sales;

• internalizes visitor spending that is otherwise lost to competitors or the region;

• longer staying visitors can be offered a more in-depth experience, leading to brand loyalty and good word-of-mouth promotion;

• can generate an infusion of capital through real estate sales (e.g., strata title, condominiums, timeshare, or outright land sale).

There are, of course, major potential costs and risks associated with developing accommodation. Money and other resources devoted to accommodation might compromise the core business of wineries, and ongoing maintenance and staffing costs will be increased. It is possible that guests will get in the way of viticulture and winery operations, or even cause physical damage. And it is also possible that some overnight and day visitors will prove to be incompatible. To be compatible, on-site accommodation must be sited where visitor access and activities do not interfere with viticulture or winemaking processes, and where visitor enjoyment will not be reduced by other traffic, noise, smells, or unsightly structures and equipment.

Do wine estates have any unique advantages to offer as destinations? Can they really compete with resorts or other types of accommodation? Given the increasing number of successful accommodation establishments located on wine estates, the answer must be yes. To the consumer, the following benefits stand out, and should be promoted:

- pleasant, relaxing, rural ambiance with the added attraction of vineyards;
- unique architecture or heritage;
- the combination of good wine and regional cuisine;
- other cultural appeal (e.g., interpretation, master classes, events and entertainment).

Furthermore, given the close association of wine tourism with cultural and general rural tourism, broader packages can be created to combine the wine estate experience with regional culture and nature tours. Of course, it is possible to locate any kind of accommodation on a wine estate, and this makes sense in wine regions with few alternatives, but the best strategy is to develop in such a way as to capitalize upon, and enhance, the core wine tourism experience. This means that accommodation development on wine estates should adhere to several planning, design, and operational principles:

- small scale (do not encourage mass tourism);
- up-market and focused on niche market segments (avoid attracting visitors not interested in good wine and food);
- attractive and unique, fitting the overall winery image and architectural style;
- providing a quiet, relaxed atmosphere (e.g., avoid mechanized sports or large-group activities).

While up-market and therefore premium-priced accommodation makes a lot of sense, as it fosters an exclusive image and keeps the scale smaller, there is also the potential to attract corporate groups, functions, and incentive tours, especially if suitable restaurant/catering facilities are available.

RESEARCH ON CRITICAL SUCCESS FACTORS FOR DEVELOPING WINERIES AS TOURIST ATTRACTIONS

Discussion in this chapter can be supplemented by results of surveys in Australia and Washington State (United States) to shed light on what wine and tourism industry professionals think are the most important factors for destination and winery tourism development. The samples consisted of participants at the First Australian Wine Tourism Conference, held in Margaret River in early 1998, and participants in a wine tourism seminar (the first of its kind) held in the Tri-Cities of Washington State's Columbia Valley appellation in late 1998.

A very high level of agreement was achieved between the two samples on the point that it is the wine itself that attracts visitors to the winery, especially quality wine, special offers (not available elsewhere), and the ability to taste before purchasing. Australians seemed to think more of the appeal of ambiance and setting or (winery design), whereas Americans put more emphasis on education and staff.

Here are the critical success factors that have been identified, but it should be cautioned that consumer research is needed to confirm the importance of these factors in actually shaping travel and shopping patterns:

• quality of the wine and reputation of the winery;

• tasting before purchase;

• special offers of wine;

• knowledgeable and friendly winery staff leading to high customer service and a satisfying visitor experience;

• education: talking with (or meeting) owners or winemakers; tours; other interpretive opportunities;

• ambiance/mystique;

• setting and sign posting;

• attractive, visitor-oriented design.

Chapter 5

CASE STUDIES OF SUCCESSFUL TOURIST-ORIENTED WINERIES

FERGUSSON OF YARRA GLEN WINERY AND RESTAURANT, VICTORIA, AUSTRALIA (WINNER: VICTORIAN TOURISM AWARDS, BEST WINERY 1997)

The State of Victoria takes wine tourism very seriously, so winning their best winery award is truly an honor. What are the criteria, and how did Fergusson of Yarra Glen win the prestigious award? Are there lessons for other wineries? This case study provides a profile of the Fergusson family and their enterprises in building a successful, tourism-oriented winery, examines the key success factors, and draws some lessons for other wineries.

The Victorian Tourism Awards do not simply list criteria by which wineries are to be compared and judged. Rather, applicants are asked a series of questions and are required to respond in a detailed document. The questions do not stress the design of the winery, its size, or popularity, but focus on its success as a tourist attraction and its role in tourism development in the region. Each of the 11 questions forms the basis of the case study, starting with a profile of the region and the Fergusson winery.

Question 1. Provide a general overview of the nature and history of the winery and describe the unique and outstanding features of the attraction.

The Yarra Valley is certainly one of Australia's most convenient, beautiful and successful wine tourism destinations. Being within a 1-hour drive of central Melbourne ensures great access for residents and visitors, and its reputation for quality, cool-climate wines (especially sparkling wines, Chardonnay, Pinot Noir, and Cabernet Sauvignon) ensures widespread from wine lovers. Its attractions include 28 wineries with visitor services and facilities, and another 6 that are open for sales by appointment only (Yarra Valley Wine Growers Assoc. 1998 brochure). Several tour companies offer Yarra-specific tours and the area has a full calendar of events ranging from the large, valley-wide Grape Grazing Festival (March, annually) to individual winery programs.

Grape growing and winemaking date back to 1838 in the valley, but what today's visitor sees is the result of a major rebirth dating from the 1960s. Peter Fergusson planted his first vines in 1968, and was the first in the region to add a restaurant to an existing winery. Despite a disastrous fire in

1989, the business has gone on to become one of the region's popular wineries (Hardy & Roden, 1995). Within 7 months of losing the entire facility, husband and wife owners, Peter and Louise Fergusson, had opened their new complex, complete with restaurant and Australiana shop. It is now open every day of the year for wine tastings and sales, lunch and shopping, and caters to functions as well.

The soild-timbered restaurant in colonial style overlooks a picturesque vineyard and features a large open fireplace to warm the winter wayfarer and the roast beef. A rustic charm and friendly ambiance are thereby created. The luncheon menu is distinctive (it has been called "innovative country cuisine") and based on regional produce. Louise is an accomplished chef and has authored her own, colorful book called the *Beginning and the End of Cooking,* which features her creations for entrees and deserts. To enjoy the Yarra more, visitors can stay in Cabernet Cottage, which offers self-contained accommodation for up to four persons. To add excitement, daily balloon flights are offered in conjunction with Global Ballooning.

Fergusson of Yarra Glen is a family business (there are three children living on site) stressing friendly, personal hospitality, Continental attention to detail, fine Australian food and wine, and most importantly a high standard of customer service.

Question 2. List the goals and objectives of the winery for the qualifying period.

The first objective was to continue to promote and support the Yarra Valley and Dandenong Ranges as a destination. Peter has supported various organizations since 1968, believing that a strong region makes for successful business enterprises. His involvement has included a number of formal positions: president of the winegrowers association; vice-president of the tourism board; member of the Victorian Wine Industry Association.

Objective two was opening LouLou's fine dining facility. The idea was to have Louise develop a cooking Master Class, and this required expanding the kitchen and restaurant to accommodate classes of up to 30 students. Work was completed in 1996.

The third objective was to continue monitoring of customer service, which is done through formal means (the visitor book is full of flattering comments) and consulting with tour operators. To the Fergussons, the success of any service business is determined by pride in performance of all the workers, and a customer-first attitude.

Question 3. Detail the business success achieved by the winery and explain the effect on profitability.

Comparing 1996 with 1995, the business had achieved a 12% increase in restaurant sales, including a 66% increase in the winter month of June, which is attributed to the staging of three Christmas in June evenings. The Australia shop showed increased sales of 20%, cellar door sales grew by 32% (240% in the month of June, which featured a sale), and the overall growth in revenue was 15%. This was in spite of no significant increase in prices and is attributed to better operations, and to marketing by the winery and the region. Tour groups supply 30% of restaurant sales and a major part of shop sales. Working with accountants, the business has implemented a system to track cost movements and compare to industry standards, as well as providing accurate profit analysis for each department.

Question 4. Describe target markets and marketing activities, with results.

Evaluate and refine target markets was actually their fourth objective. Growing competition from larger wine companies and more wineries in the Yarra has meant that pursuit of niche markets is more important to the smaller operations. So, prior to departure for his annual international marketing trip, Peter identified specific targets: corporate meetings, conventions, and incentive groups; fully independent travelers, both international and domestic; regional day-trippers; special interest groups; and weddings and receptions.

Marketing activities often apply to various target segments and include the following:

a) Annual United Kingdom promotional tour, including tastings and seminars to promote the wine and Yarra in general.

b) Annual involvement in the Yarra Valley Grape Grazing Festival. Fergussons is one of the most popular venues for this March weekend event. On Saturday they feature musical entertainment, free balloon rides, pony rides, and face painting for kids. A three-course dinner with entertainment attracts 75 or more customers. On Sundays are an outdoor barbecue and sit-down dining with more entertainment. The Yarra Valley Grape Grazing Committee promotes the event, but Fergussons also use radio and print plus joint promotions with tour operators to promote their activities. Over 2000 visitors came to the winery in 1 day.

c) Participation in the Aussie Trading Post promotional tour in the United States (1996) to promote travel to Australia. Americans and Canadians constitute about 15% of visitors to Fergussons.

d) Participation in the annual Australian Tourism Exchange enables the winery to directly contact tour wholesalers and retailers from around the world. This is especially important in meeting operators from New Zealand, Europe, the United Kingdom, and Ireland, which collectively account for 56% of all international visitors to the winery. Peter emphasizes that it is imperative to attend such trade shows, especially for rural attractions. In 1996 Peter estimated he wrote A$50,000–60,000 of business at the Exchange.

e) Wine Australia is the biggest annual wine and food showcase in the Southern Hemisphere (see the profile in Chapter 8) and participation in this event allows Peter, in conjunction with other Yarra wineries, to promote regional wines, and for Louise to put on cooking demonstrations. As a direct result of the show, five special interest groups totaling 65 guests came to the winery within 6 months.

f) Running of the New Wine is another Yarra event, held in September, in which 13 wineries provide vertical tastings of new wines. Winemakers are present for questions and discussion, complemented by seasonal produce on the menu. This one focuses on food and wine enthusiasts, but also attracts free, independent travelers (FITs) to the region.

g) In 1996 Fergusson also participated in the Great Car Show in Melbourne where they had a Victorian Food and Wine Display. Following the event, 11 separate car clubs visited Fergussons for lunch.

h) The Australian Antique and Fine Art Dealer's Fair in Melbourne presented another opportunity to reach special interest groups. Fergussons was the only winery involved.

i) Hot air balloon flights are offered through a joint marketing effort with Global Ballooning. About 950 passengers took a balloon ride in 1996, including corporate incentive and special interest groups. After the morning flights, a champagne breakfast awaited plus a talk on the history of winemaking.

j) World Wide Web: The Fergusson winery first appeared on the Web courtesy of a coach driver in North America!

k) Twice in 1996 the Yarra was featured on national Australian television programs, with Fergusson of Yarra Glen featured in one of them.

Question 5. How has the winery contributed to the development of tourism in Victoria and Australia? Show how the attraction has cooperated with the regional and Victorian tourism authorities.

In addition to his membership in various organizations, described earlier, Peter helped initiate the Yarra Valley Wine Network to evaluate tourism business development in the region. Now working with the winemakers and tourism board, this group has a business plan to put in place strategies for development. Chief winemaker Chris Keyes serves on the Grape Grazing Committee.

Question 6. What training and staff development programs were conducted during 1996?

The winery was involved in two educational programs for hospitality students from area colleges, with over 120 students working and training at the winery during 1996. As it turns out, this relationship also benefits winery staff, who learn from the students. Staff take the AussieHost training program.

Question 7. Explain how the winery ensures a standard of quality in its customer service. Provide evidence of customer service and satisfaction.

Peter and Louise are hands-on owners and managers, as they believe in leading the staff by example towards a "customer first" ethos. An employee attitude survey was conducted in 1996 by a consulting firm, leading to "fine-tuning" of operations and instigation of multiskilling among staff. The winery guest book is full of complimentary comments, and the Fergussons receive letters from satisfied customers.

Question 8. How does the winery ensure it continually improves its attraction?

Continual improvement is reflected in expansion of the Asian Stroll Garden, planting of a palm tree for shade, marketing initiatives, and development of the Yarra Valley Business Network. One aim of the Network is to turn the Autumn Festival into a premier Victorian event.

Question 9. How does the winery promote itself to the tourist market?

Most of the communications methods have already been presented. Association with AAT Kings Tours and Australian Pacific Tours, as well as Victorian Winery Tours, are also very important. Fergussons, as a consequence, is featured alongside other area attractions like the Healesville (animal) Sanctuary and Puffing Billy steam train. Fergussons is also part of the Melbourne Country Gourmet Tour. These tour links mean that the winery caters to both small and large groups, which in turn generate positive word of mouth communications.

Quarterly visits are made by the winery's sales and marketing consultant to Melbourne and regional accommodation establishments to ensure the winery brochure is on display and that concierge staff are briefed. Recommendations from hotel staff have proven to be an important source of business. Joint marketing agreements with the Puffing Billy attractions and with the larger winery attraction of Domaine Chandon are very cost-effective. Promotional visits abroad have already been mentioned.

Question 10. What specific services are offered to tourists?

The owners realized early on that an all-year operation was necessary in the tourism business, thereby requiring a team of reliable, trained, full-time staff. The restaurant features lunch, but is open Saturdays for dinners and other nights by appointment or during special events. In addition to the already-described facilities and services, Fergussons also offers picnic facilities and gourmet hampers. The facilities cater to visitors with special needs, with easily accessible buildings, and they provide language assistance, and special dietary meals.

Question 11. Demonstrate the winery's contribution to the staging of festivals, special events, and other tourism-related opportunities to increase visitor numbers, length of stay, or expenditure.

Their involvement with events and recreational activities has already been partially covered. Other events include Jazz Amongst The Vines, and St. Andrew's Day Celtic Dinner Dance. Peter knows that many of the guests at their winery dinners, and for ballooning, stay overnight in the district.

As identified by the Fergussons, the following critical success factors explain why they won the best winery award and why they have become one of the most popular wine attractions:

- top-quality wines!
- innovative, gourmet cooking featuring regional cuisine;
- a strong visitor orientation: open all year, every day; high standards for customer service;
- attractive premises and cultivation of "country ambiance";
- niche marketing; knowing your target segments;
- joint marketing with other attractions and with tour companies;
- active development and promotion of the destination region;
- participation in regional festivals and development of their own functions and special events;
- promotions aimed at special-interest groups;
- attention to cost and revenue management;
- quality, trained staff; attention to employee concerns;
- continuous improvement philosophy;
- a range of facilities and services, including dining;
- accommodation, master classes, merchandise sales, picnics;
- ballooning, functions, and special events;
- excellent word-of-mouth promotion from satisfied customers.

Owners: Peter and Louise Fergusson
Staff complement: 11 full-time and 13 part-time
Address: Wills Road, Yarra Glen, Victoria 3775
Telephone: 059-65-2237; Fax: 059-65-2405

Established: 1968
Varieties: chardonnay, shiraz, cabernet sauvignon, cabernet franc, merlot, pinot noir, sauvignon blanc
Hectares under vine: 10
Average annual crush: 65 tonnes

ROBERT MONDAVI WINERY, NAPA VALLEY, CALIFORNIA

Established in 1966, the Robert Mondavi Winery quickly became an icon for not only the Napa Valley but for American wine in general. With its name brand recognition, distinctive Mediterranean design, and prominent position along route 29, it now attracts over 300,000 visitors annually and will soon expand to provide more wine tourists with a superb educational experience.

It is a family-owned and operated business, with all family members participating in the management of the company. R. Michael Mondavi is president and CEO, while brother Timothy acts as Managing Director and Winegrower; their sister, Marcia, is a director; the founder, Robert, is Chairman of the Board.

The Mondavi philosophy is to educate visitors, in contrast to the prevailing Napa Valley emphasis on sales. The facility (as of 1998) contained only a small sales area, almost insignificant by Napa standards. Deborah Eagles, marketing manager, believes that most visitors know little about wine and are very interested in taking a tour and hearing about the entire process, not merely having a taste.

During busy periods (May through October, weekends all year; Tuesday–Thursday is the quietest period of the week) it is best to arrange a tour time in advance—something that the Napa Visitor and Convention Bureau will do for tourists, or the visitor may have to stop by to make a reservation. The number of tours on a given day is fixed and the schedule is posted, so that crowding is avoided. Visitors may certainly drop by and get a tasting or make a purchase, but tours are restricted in size.

The facility was built specifically to facilitate tours, although growth in demand—particularly during the 1980s, has made expansion necessary (more about this later). Visitors register in the reception area (which doubles as the retail space) before meeting their tour guide. The trip through the winery is not about Mondavi, but covers winemaking, varietals, and viticulture.

Tours are free, but for a fee visitors may end their tour in one of several, specially designed, intimate tasting rooms for an additional experience of wine and food. A separate tasting area is also available for casual visitors, with tastings by fee.

At Mondavi, visitors are managed to create a more educational and enjoyable experience. Marketing focuses on the wine trade, with numerous industry familiarization tours occurring throughout the year.

Mondavi hosts numerous functions and events all year round, both on and off site. More detailed event programs became necessary as the number of repeat visitors increased dramatically. Most are priced to generate a profit for the company, although participation in community festivals and events is designed to generate money for charities and worthwhile local causes. The Mondavi Web site contains an event schedule, which can be searched on-line. Listings cover all wineries and off-site events throughout the year. Some examples:

- Robert Mondavi Winter Festival concert series: performances by internationally renowned artists, combined with either lunch or intermission wine and cheese tasting, proceeds donated to The American Center for Wine, Food and the Arts. The festival also incorporates dinner concerts.

- Annual Shareholder Meeting: over 600 shareholders attended the fifth meeting in 1998, at which expansion plans were unveiled; the meetings incorporate tours, dinners, seminars, and, for members of the Partners Circle (over 4000), result in major sales of exclusive and limited-release wines at special prices.

- Great Chefs at Robert Mondavi Winery: these weekend events cost $750 to $1650 per person in 1998; they include cooking demonstrations, lodging, transportation, lunches and dinners, private winery tours at Robert Mondavi and nearby Opus One (owned by a Mondavi-Rothschild partnership), and a variety of seminars. In addition, 1-day sessions with the great chefs are offered to professionals and serious amateurs, following the 2- and 3-day weekends.

- Annual Blessing of the Grapes: no charge; September 4, 1998.

The Mondavi Wine and Food Center is located in Costa Mesa, CA, and hosts many food and wine functions, including cooking classes and meals. It is a consumer-oriented, for-profit function center. Mondavi takes food and wine and other promotional events to its consumers in locations like New Jersey (dining at Doris and Ed's Seafood by the Seaside) and Virginia (Sunday Wine Nights at Sam and Harry's). Other examples: Wine Tasting with Riedel Crystal in Chicago; Wine Dinner at Disneyland Pacific Hotel; Robert Mondavi Wine Dinner at Rye Town Hilton Hotel, Rye Brook New York; New York International Wine Auction at Cooperstown.

In early 1998 Mondavi finalized development plans that include physical expansion of the winery and an innovative addition to Disneyland, CA. Expansion of the main Napa winery facility will in particular improve the company's ability to host trade groups and full dinners. They are not looking to expand the number of visitors.

In a press release dated April 30, 1998, Robert Mondavi announced plans to develop a "Wine Country Experience" with Disney's "California Adventure," scheduled to open in the year 2001. Disneyland resort is creating the California Adventure theme park on a 55-acre site adjacent to Disneyland in Anaheim. "The multi-faceted wine complex will offer an educational and entertaining introduction to premium California wines to millions of visitors," said the release. "The opportunity to showcase wine as part of the California experience on this level is the fulfillment of a life-long dream for my father and our family," says R. Michael Mondavi. "Introducing visitors to California's wine history and Robert Mondavi's role in it supports our global strategy."

Elements of the wine experience include: a real vineyard; film presentation; several wine-tasting counters; a special reserve tasting room for more in-depth food and wine experiences; gourmet food and retail area; restaurant modeled after the Vineyard Room—the private dining room at Mondavi's Napa winery. Naturally, it will feature Mondavi's various California wine brands.

"What distinguishes Disney theme parks is our ability to tell compelling and entertaining stories," said Mike Berry, Vice President of food operations and concept development at the Disneyland Resort. Celebrating the "fun and diversity" of California is the core of the concept.

In this development, wine tourism enters a new stage. Just as the Whisky Centre in Edinburgh brought the whisky trail and distillery experience to the visitors where they congregate in the greatest number, the Mondavi–Disney partnership will take wine tourism to the masses of tourists and residents who rely on the Disney name and tend to restrict their activities to the attractions of Los Angeles. If this gets them interested in wine country, so much the better. If not, it will certainly sell Mondavi brands. As well, the application of Disney's "edutainment" concepts to wine interpretation is bound to have a lasting and perhaps profound impact on the entire wine tourism sector. Wineries will be watching closely to see exactly how the wine story is told, and particularly if this new approach will generate interest among new market segments and especially younger audiences.

Critical Success Factors Learned From the Mondavi Experience

• Maintain the family vision and philosophy.

• Quality wines and brand name recognition attract visitors.

• A highly visible, easy to access site is a major asset.

• Unique and attractive winery design adds to the status of Mondavi as a must-visit attraction in Napa Valley.

• Commitment to education about wine in general and providing a quality visitor experience lead to customer satisfaction and loyalty.

• Functions and events generate profit and community relations; demand increases as repeat visitation grows.

• Innovation in developing partnerships and new wine tourism concepts (especially the Disney linkage) has been important.

• Expand to meet core objectives, not to encourage growth for growth's sake.

FIRESTONE, SANTA YNEZ VALLEY, CALIFORNIA

The quality associated with fine wine can be transferred to that other alcoholic beverage, the one that more people all around the world drink much more of than wine. Beer is especially more popular than wine among young adults, and because "craft" beers or "real ales" have become extremely popular in the same way that the quality of wine continues to improve, beer and wine *should* go together. It might be the best way to connect with the next generation of wine consumers.

Firestone winery in Santa Ynez Valley has a brand name associated with quality wines, and has created an excellent brand extension by establishing a partnership called Firestone Walker to produce a unique family of beers. Adam Firestone, president of the winery, and his brother-in-law David Walker, decided that some empty Chardonnay barrels might be used in starting a brewery. That experiment failed to produce good-quality beer, but new American oak barrels proved successful. Employing a traditional English method called the Burton Union process, the brewery in Los Olivos (just down the road from the winery) now produces Firestone Walker Double Barrel Ale and Windsor Pale Ale. Jeff Morgan (1996), writing in *Wine Spectator,* described the Double Barrel Ale as "rich and well balanced," and it has also been described as flavorful, mellow, and drinkable. The pale ale is lighter in flavor and body, but with the nuttiness and wood flavor derived from the Burton fermentation system.

Michael Lucas (1997), a staff writer for the *Los Angeles Times,* reported on the brewery and observed that "many winemakers see a common interest with their beermaking brethren in working with wholesome, natural foodstuffs. . . ." The brewmaster, Christian August, adds that "there is no compromise; ingredients are always the finest available, the equipment is state of the art. The final product is always consistent because it is filtered, cold stabilized and bottled on the premises."

But can beer and wine be marketed together? After all, beer is not generally perceived to be a sophisticated beverage—perhaps just the opposite. Clearly it is the emphasis on purity, quality, and taste that makes the fit between premium wines and beers, and many consumers certainly enjoy both. There is definitely a strange but welcome feeling involved in finding the beers available for tasting at the winery.

Just the way good restaurants are proud of their wine lists, having a quality beer list is also catching on. Servers will soon have to be trained in what beers and wines go together in the same meal!

Contacts: Firestone Vineyard: P.O Box 244, Los Olivos CA 93441-1244 Firestone Walker Brewing Company: P.O. Box 244, Los Olivos, CA 93441-0244 (www.firestonewalker.com)

SELF-GUIDED TOUR AT INNISKILLIN WINERY

In the book *Anatomy of a Winery: The Art of Wine at Inniskillin,* Donald Ziraldo (1995) described and illustrated the development of Inniskillin Winery in Niagara-on-the-Lake, Ontario, Canada, including their self-guided tour. Hugh Johnson, writing the book's Foreword, observed: "by the imaginative educational weapon of Inniskillin's self-guided winery tour he [Donald] is teaching the new generation of Canadians to understand and appreciate the wines their country can make."

The tour was developed in 1992 with the building of their new Barrel Aging Cellar, in recognition of growing visitation to the winery and in keeping with Ziraldo's leadership in the Canadian wine industry. Inspiration came from Sterling Vineyards in Napa Valley, which continues to offer one of the best self-guided tours anywhere. Apparently Inniskillin's approach has been quite successful, because the book follows from visitor demands for the same information they got on the tour.

What is different about the self-guided tour? Without an escort there are several important concerns related to the visitor, the winery's marketing, and to winery operations. After all, the tour guide has multiple roles, including that of interpreter, supervisor (enforcer of rules), entertainer, and sales representative:

• will visitors be safe, comfortable and satisfied with the experience?

• will visitor movements interfere with operations?

• can the winery communicate as effectively with visitors?

• will their be a negative impact on sales?

Inniskillin's tour involves 20 stations, all of which are described and illustrated in the book. Commentary, illustrations, and photography are set up at each viewing station, with specially designed windows giving views into the winery facilities. Let's look at each of them, in outline:

1. History of Inniskillin: includes the historic Brae Burn Barn, which now houses the winery boutique, visitor and tour center; stations 1 though 9 are located here.

2. The Climate: emphasizes cool climate viticulture, which produces wines higher in acid and aroma; the Lake Ontario micro-climatic influences are also highlighted.

3. Soil and geography.

4. Vintner's Quality Alliance (VQA): describes this appellation of origin system, now mandated by law in the Province of Ontario and also used in British Columbia.

5. Viticulture, including seasonal patterns.

6. Grape varieties.

7. Harvesting, covering the measure of sugar content.

8. Cooperage (barrel making).

9. History of the cork.

10. De-stemming and crushing: can be observed outside the winery.

11. Pressing (stations 11 through 16 are located in an open-air passageway from which winery activities can be observed through windows).

12. Fermentation: including primary and malo-lactic.

13. Red wines: the process from grapes through bottling.

14. White wines (and how different from red wine production).

15. Tank cellar: covering settling/clarification, fining, and filtration.

16. Barrel aging: and the influence of oak in wine.

17. Bottling line: including labeling and shipping (stations 18–20 are alongside the buildings, next to the vineyard).

18. Brae Burn Vineyard.

19. Icewine: how it is made and why it is special.

20. Frank Lloyd Wright: the design of Brae Burn Barn was inspired by the great American architect.

The main advantages of this self-guided approach can be summarized as follows:

• support for tour staff and related administration;

• no need for visitors to schedule or book tours;

• no direct interference with winery operations, and consequently no related safety or security problems.

Several potential disadvantages should also be considered:

• visitors might not get the full sensory experience of tours within the facility;

- the interpretive, entertainment, and sales roles of the guide are absent;
- it might therefore be harder to establish a relationship with visitors.

Inniskillin also offers VIP tours by appointment. Visit their Web site: http://www.inniskillin.com

Chapter 6

DEVELOPING THE SUCCESSFUL WINE TOURISM DESTINATION

Why did readers of *The Wine Spectator* (1997) select as their favorite wine regions Burgundy, Bordeaux, Tuscany, Napa, and Sonoma? These choices do reflect a particular readership's viewpoint, but no doubt these are all world-class in terms of appeal and visitation. Burgundy has famous gastronomy and history, Bordeaux its name-brand chateaux, Tuscany the superb climate and enchanting countryside, Napa is bold and exciting, and Sonoma understated and peaceful. Can other wine regions emulate their appeal and wine tourism success? Wise planning and sustainable development are required.

LESSONS FROM NAPA VALLEY

Nowhere else in the world has wine tourism been developed (and without a strategy) to the size and prominence as it has in Napa. The visitor to this scenic area north of San Francisco can choose from over 240 wineries to visit, find unique accommodation, enjoy fine dining or picnics based on deli food, ride hot-air balloons, or take the Wine Train. Some visitors like this level of activity and choice, others prefer to head over the hills to a quieter, more rural Sonoma Valley to escape the crowds and commercialism. But anyone seriously interested in wine and/or tourism knows that Napa is a must-experience destination.

A number of important observations can be made about success factors and the related problems this wine region faces. Napa is within easy driving range of millions of Bay-area residents, and these people have a very high level of disposable income. The climate is favorable to all-year visitation, and California in general, as well as San Francisco in particular, are very popular tourist destinations. Add beautiful scenery, high-quality, award-winning wines, substantial advertising budgets, and a long history of winery involvement with visitors and you obtain high levels of visitation. The Robert Mondavi winery alone attracts over 300,000 visitors annually.

Napa also has problems—with congestion, urban encroachment, high costs, and a gradual diminishment of authentic ruralness. Their approach has evolved from one of developing wine tourism to managing it. To many people, the less developed Sonoma Valley is more appealing, even though (or because) it has less tourism infrastructure. Is Napa a model for other wine tourism destinations? Further insights are provided in the interview with Daniel Howard.

Interview With Daniel Howard, Executive Director, Napa Valley Conference and Visitor Bureau

Daniel Howard is a graduate of the Harvard Business School and was raised in the San Francisco Bay area. His job as Director of the Napa Valley CVB puts him in a unique and important position to understand, and contribute to wine tourism planning and marketing. The Bureau itself was established only in 1990, and while it is based in the city of Napa and must promote that center as a conference and meetings venue, partnership with the wine industry is essential.

Q: Daniel, why is Napa the most developed and well-known wine tourism destination in North America, if not the world?

A: The bottom line has been producing the best wine, otherwise why would people be interested in the first place? Napa's appeal is closely dependent on the reputation of its wines. Beyond that, we have a critical mass of wineries here, in a fairly compact, easy-to-reach valley. There are 240 wineries to choose from, close to a big market and tourist gateway, San Francisco. California has a great climate so visitors can tour comfortably all year round. The scenery is beautiful and offers something different in all four seasons. We also have an industry that has, for many years, seen tourism as a good way to sell wine. Another factor is that Napa wineries have been leaders in demystifying the whole wine business, to make wine more accessible to everyone. Now other wine areas try to copy some of these elements and send their professional people here to learn how.

Q: What role did the Robert Mondavi winery play in putting Napa on the map?

A: It opened to the public in 1966 and they have been leaders ever since. Mondavi promoted wine and the Napa, not just his own brand. Wineries here are very marketing savvy, which makes my job easier.

Q: What are your markets?

A: Eighty-two percent of visitors to the Napa valley are here for winery tours, according to research we commissioned. Overall, about 11% of tourists are international, and 30% are regional—from the Bay area. We get the bulk of our visitors from all over North America, are very popular with Canadians, and are attracting more and more Europeans. Repeat visitation is high, especially for weekend getaway breaks. We used to have a low-demand winter season, but now there is strong demand all year. It is not really a family destination, is definitely upscale and somewhat expensive.

Q: And what are your main marketing activities?

A: We market aggressively throughout the US and Canada, trying to sell Napa as a romantic destination. We spend the most money on attracting meetings and conventions for mid-week business. In fact, 30 wineries cater to this group business, particularly attracting meetings and retreats from Silicon Valley high-tech companies. Personally, I go to Europe annually on promotional visits, and all through the US, with a special objective of luring incentive tours.

Q: So Napa is a niche-market destination? That seems at odds with the large volume of tourists coming here.

A: People here want to preserve the rural, agricultural atmosphere. Mass tourism is actually feared and rejected, in large part because we can see the negative side of it all around. So higher prices, catering to up-scale niche markets, will generate higher yield with fewer visitors. Wine promotes a very focused market.

Q: Congestion is certainly an issue here, at least at peak times along the highway, is it not?

A: Car volumes get very high, particularly on weekends. Tourism has to be managed in the Napa, especially to protect the resource base. Management includes appropriate marketing as well as physical development planning. We have strong county ordinances covering land use and winery developments, all of which was radical in the 1960s and was definitely fought over. I would say the wine industry was saved from excessive urban and tourism-related developments by these measures.

Q: Does Napa work with Sonoma and San Francisco?

A: We have a good working relationship with their industry associations, and there have been specific cooperative initiatives. In part, I think

Sonoma is envious of Napa's success, but also they want to be different—less developed. We could certainly work more closely with the San Francisco Bureau, though. It is the major gateway to Napa. In fact we are a corporate member of their Bureau. We joined to make sure that Napa was covered well in their literature, and not promoted just as a day-trip but a real destination. About 30 Napa wineries are also members.

Q: How is your Bureau funded?

A: We have in 1998 a budget of $600,000 plus a lot of leveraged money through joint promotions. Wineries and the wine industry are major partners, plus we get 30% of our budget from the hotel tax. We are a member-based organization and most wineries are members. Also, Amex is a big partner in our promotions.

THE DESTINATION CONCEPT

Eric Laws, author of *Tourist Destination Management* (1995) distinguishes between several types of destination: major cities; resort communities and purpose-built resorts; touring areas with service centers. Wine tourism destinations can be individual wineries in cities and resorts, but for the most part we are talking about a touring area with one or more service centers that provide accommodation, information, dining, and other services vital to the attraction and hosting of visitors. Most wine tourism destinations are rural and include small villages and towns, although the relationship with nearby cities is important in terms of markets, accessibility, and packaging.

All destinations have development and marketing elements in common, namely the relationship with visitor origin areas, accessibility issues, competition, development of attractions and services, and marketing to different styles of visitation. Most visitors will come from nearby cities, and most tourists will use cities as gateways or service centers for part of their wine tour. Key cities and regions can be identified in which target markets must gain awareness and a positive image of the nearby wine country. Research should be aimed at these major origin points and relationships with them must be cultivated. For interstate and international visitors, cultivate relationships with tour companies and other elements of the travel trade.

Time, cost, and comfort factors must be considered in connecting the destination with its markets and with other destinations. Any number of inhibitors, or barriers, can influence travel, including legal requirements (e.g., visas), conditions of roads, location of airports, scheduled air service, and packaging. Other inhibitors include language or cultural differences, and the absence of hospitality.

Competition can include other wine-related attractions or leisure and cultural opportunities in general. Sometimes it is merely the knowledge or image of competitors that influences travel patterns. All destinations must develop market-positioning strategies to deal with competitors.

Wineries are the core attraction, but a range of wine-related and general-purpose attractions and services is needed to create a destination image. Touring routes, events, tour companies, fine dining, unique accommodations, and a range of essential visitor services are all required.

Wine tourism destinations can expect a variety of styles, or patterns of visitation, each of which results in unique planning and management challenges and requires a different marketing approach. The bulk of winery and wine country visitors (except in very remote areas) will be day-trippers from nearby cities. They are usually in a family group or with visiting friends or relatives and travel by personal car. Their proximity makes them potentially frequent and therefore knowledgeable visitors, so they will likely get off the beaten path. Some of them might decide to invest in wine country businesses, or purchase a second/retirement home.

Independent travelers are mostly car-based tourists who usually plan their own routes, engage in spontaneous activities, and often make their own arrangements for accommodations. But a degree of packaging might be desired, especially by those coming from longer distances. Fly/drive packages in particular should be provided: the car comes from, and goes back to, a nearby airport or city center. Packages offering local accommodations, meals, and tours or events should also be popular with some of the FIT segment.

Two types of group tours are common: the small, dedicated wine tour, and larger, general-purpose tours that include wineries as part of a broader itinerary. Small groups can have flexible itineraries, whereas large coach tours generally have tight, prebooked visits to wineries and restaurants. A large number of coach tours can cause traffic and parking problems at peak times, and many wineries will not cater to them.

People visiting resorts, owning second homes, or visiting local friends and relatives constitute an important market. Their patterns of visitation are likely to be different, especially in terms of seasonality (less in the peak periods) and frequency (likely to be repeaters). They are based in the area and therefore have different needs and interests.

Business and meeting travelers staying in an area can be induced to stay longer, or to spend part of their time and budget in wineries. They do not come to the area mainly because of its wine attractions, but wine might play a part in winning the convention or event.

The marketing implications of these different visitation styles are discussed in a later chapter, but it is important to realize that "destination" means something different depending on the type or style of trip and the origin of visitors. The destination might be perceived as:

• a place to stay in for a holiday, incorporating a variety of activities;

• a place of business, with leisure options;

• a place to pass through, with one or more stops;

• one's home area, with permanent ability to visit its attractions and events and to use various services.

PLANNING AND MANAGING WINE TOURISM DESTINATIONS

The model presented earlier of the wine tourism system (Figure 1.1) provides the framework for a wine tourism strategy. Basically, there is a supply side that much be matched with current and desired market segments (i.e., demand). The wine and tourism/hospitality industries plus one or more marketing and development organizations in the destination must provide the infrastructure and sustain the resource base. Figure 6.1 outlines a planning process for developing wine tourism destination strategies and products.

Stage One: Research and Evaluation

Figure 6.1. Destination wine tourism planning process.

Evaluate and Protect Natural Resources

Although wineries are the core resource for wine tourism, providing the lure for wine tourists and many of the ancillary services wine tourism needs, it is wise to begin with the natural resource base that supports viti-culture. Erosion of soils and pollution of water through environmental abuse, or depletion of viticultural land through urban development or even too much tourism development, will ultimately restrict or harm wine tourism.

Planners should determine the existing scale of grape growing and wine production, as well as assess its potential for growth. Input from viticultur-alists and agricultural agencies will be necessary. Some questions to ask:

• Is there potential for expansion and what will be needed to foster or per-mit growth (e.g., water supply, zoning to protect agricultural reserves)?

• Will viticulture or construction of wineries interfere with other resource users? Can conflicts be avoided or resolved?

Evaluate Landscape Conditions and Scenery

Most grape and wine areas combine attractive natural scenery with cultural landscapes of fields and buildings. All too often, however, the beauty and rural atmosphere are threatened by careless developments and a failure to anticipate how growth will impact on this precious resource. Creation of a legal agricultural reserve (as in Napa Valley) will go a long way to preserving rural atmosphere, but attention should also be paid to the design of wineries and tourism infrastructure, and the aesthetic impact of roads, power lines, and water schemes.

Inventory and Map Wineries

Probably guide books and maps already exist that show the wineries and how to get to them, but a field study might be required to obtain the details needed for a computer database:

- types and numbers of facilities (e.g., visitor centers, art galleries, restaurants, tasting rooms, picnic areas) and their visitor capacities;
- services provided to the public (e.g., tours, interpretation and education);
- events and functions (monthly calendar);
- accessibility and parking for cars and buses; wheelchair provisions;
- special features.

Questions to be asked:
- Are the wineries visitor oriented?
- What is the quality level of facilities and services?
- Is there a critical mass within easy access of market areas, roads, or service towns in the region?
- What private sector initiatives are committed, planned, possible?

Perform a Winery Audit

The audit (covered in Chapter 4) examines the winery's attractiveness and service quality. Wineries might be reluctant to share their internal audits, but a more general audit can be conducted at the regional level.

Evaluate Other Attractions

Only a few wine tourists will spend time in an area without other attractions. In particular look for partnership opportunities with cultural and heritage attractions, agricultural producers, and appropriate recreational activities. Evaluate the portfolio of community and especially wine-themed events.

Services

Are all essential and desirable visitor services available nearby? Inventory wine tours, restaurants, accommodations, and information services in particular. Does the region have a wine interpretive center? What about "wine villages" combining attractions and services?

Evaluate Accessibility, Signage, and Potential for Wine Routes

A separate section is devoted to this important subject later in the chapter.

Traffic Volumes, Flows, and Cycles

Determine road adequacy, hazards, congestion points, and necessary improvements to facilitate touring and formal wine routes. Where do tourists go on their own, and when does recreational traffic peak?

Stage Two: Demand Assessment

Analysis of Available Tourism Data

Unfortunately, most tourism research has neglected this niche market, so only general patterns and trends are documented. The destination management or marketing organization (DMO) should partner with wineries and other attractions to conduct special wine tourism surveys for specific wine regions. Area-wide surveys are needed to determine overall reasons for visits to the area, interest in wine, and patterns of travel and spending within the area. This information can be combined with data from winery visitor surveys.

Visitor Surveys at Wineries

Wineries and the DMO should employ the same or similar surveys, to maximize the value of research. Wineries might add their own questions and keep results to themselves, but a core of common questions asked at all wineries would reveal a great deal about visitor motives, activities, spending, preferences, and reactions to their experience.

Market Area Surveys

Visitor surveys conducted in the wine region do not provide information about why people are not visiting. Select the primary target market areas (especially nearby cities) to assess awareness and interest levels, desired products and services, and the best ways to reach target segments.

Travel Trade Contacts

Conduct surveys or use more informal contacts with the travel trade for their business needs and expert knowledge of what kinds of wine tours and packages will work best. Key targets are coach tour wholesalers, incentive tour consultants, and inbound tour operators. Travel agents in target cities will have good advice on how to retail wine tourism products.

Segmentation and Identification of Key Target Groups

Details on segmentation were provided in Chapter 4. Following analysis of existing and potential markets, one or a few segments should be selected for concentrated market development. Communications are expensive, so trying to reach all potential wine tourists is likely to be impractical.

Forecasting of Demand by Segments

Without baseline data on the segments this cannot be done except through guesswork. At a minimum, information is required about winery visitor numbers and trends, combined with general area tourism patterns and trends.

Marketing Audit

How well has the destination been doing in attracting wine tourists? Similar to the winery audit, the DMO should evaluate its marketing and especially its communications efforts as a prelude to formulating a wine tourism strategy. Feedback from visitors and nonvisitors will form an important part of the audit, plus professional advice from the travel trade, wine industry, and local services. Also appraise past and current strategies and developments pertinent to wine tourism.

Stage Three: Consultations and Identification of Issues and Positions

Planners will want input from key stakeholders:

• industry input (wine, tourism/hospitality, travel trade);

• public input (especially from special interest groups that will sooner or later pay attention to all tourism promotions and developments);

• other stakeholders (e.g., agencies dealing with environment, culture, leisure, sport, heritage, agriculture, soils, water, electricity, roads, etc.).

Visioning and Goal Setting

• Craft a vision for wine tourism: what should this sector be, and what should it achieve in the future?

• Identification of distinctive competence (i.e., competitive strengths).

• Specific goals derived from the vision.

• Strategies to achieve the goals.

Visioning can be a time-consuming process, involving all the key stakeholders in one or more rounds of discussion, consensus building, compromise, and editing. Many different visions are likely to arise, so common ground has to be identified. Eventually, strong leadership might be required to pull things together.

A vision must be based on sound knowledge of the destination, its strengths and weaknesses in a competitive context, and a combination of realism and dreaming. Here is a sample:

> Our wine region will offer the best in wines and wine-themed experiences for diverse market segments, all year round. We aim to outperform competitive regions through creative product development, packaging, and aggressive marketing. We will become the dominant wine tourism destination for short breaks, incentive tours and international wine tourists.

A more modest vision, and more realistic for most wine regions, could be as follows:

> Our vision is to develop wine tourism attractions and services, and to promote wine tourism as a major theme, with the aim of becoming a successful, all-year destination. We will emphasize high-quality visitor services, wine-themed events targeted at key segments, and wine themes in all out communications.

Generic Goals for Developing and Marketing Wine Tourism

When setting goals, develop general statements that will guide subsequent actions but leave room for interpretation and flexible implementation. Goals should be formulated for each of the following subjects:

- attracting high-yield, special-interest wine tourists to stay multiple nights in wine regions;

- generating cellar door and ancillary sales for wineries;

- developing accommodation and dining services to meet a range of visitor needs;

- developing a range of recreation attractions, special events and visitor services with wine as the theme;

- theming of the destination, based on wine and related products;

- achieving brand name recognition for the wine region;

- establishing well-signposted wine tour routes;

- providing adequate information and education for visitors.

To support goals, specific objectives must be set, usually on an annual basis within the context of marketing and action plans. Objectives contain specific performance measures so that their fulfillment can be accurately determined. For example, to meet the goal of developing wine-themed events, a pertinent objective might be: "Provide financial and marketing assistance to create a new wine festival for the spring season, commencing in (date)."

Stage Four: Formulate Strategies and Action Plans

To implement the wine tourism strategy a number of basic actions are required:

- partnership between the wine industry, destination marketing organizations, and suppliers of essential and augmented visitor services;

- leadership in planning, product development and marketing;

- conservation of the natural resource base and rural ambiance;

- a comprehensive and sustained research program.

More specific action plans can be developed for annual or periodic review. To be effective, the *action plan* should specify target dates for accomplishment of the action, responsibilities (who does it?), resources to be provided (budget), and other pertinent information to help ensure the job gets done as planned. Specific areas for destination-level action planning include:

Attractions Development

• visitor and wine interpretive center,

• new and improved events,

• create wine routes; sign posting.

Services Development

• hospitality training,

• wine tourism awards.

Infrastructure Development

• improve roads.

Organizational Development

• committee tasks,

• liaison and lobbying efforts.

Marketing Plan

• more and improved visitor information,

• a new wine country video,

• sales trips.

In the following sections major destination developments (i.e., "products") for wine tourism are discussed in detail, namely visitor and interpretive centers, wine villages, wine routes, signs, and tours and awards.

WINE TOURISM PRODUCTS FOR DESTINATIONS

Wine-Themed Visitor and Interpretive Centers

Visitor centers typically provide information about their regions, but so much more can be done with the wine theme. Several examples are profiled to illustrate how visitor centers can also do the following:

• educate visitors about viticulture and wine;

• provide a sales outlet for regional wines;

• direct visitors to wineries and other services or attractions;

• host functions and special events featuring regional food and wine;

• sell regional, wine-themed souvenirs and other products to visitors;

• contribute to viticulture and wine research.

Two notable wine visitor and interpretive centers are profiled in the next chapter, and in addition read the material later in this chapter on Barossa Valley regarding its visitor center.

Wine Villages

A major part of the appeal of European wine regions is the combination of beautiful rural scenery featuring vineyards, and the quaint, architecturally and culturally unique villages and towns that service the industry. For example, Davidson (1998), writing in *WineX Magazine*, raved about the medieval hamlet of Montalcino in southern Tuscany, one of many hill towns in wine country. With wineries just outside town, it offers plenty of good wine and food, and no snobbishness. Many are centuries old in their wine traditions, including outstanding restaurants, wine bars, and annual wine festivals.

Wine villages of this type have not developed in the New World, mainly owing to the modernity of the industry. But there are examples of villages within wine country that provide the same services to the wine industry and tourists, and many of these have their own special character; some are heritage attractions in their own right. Several examples in California easily come to mind, including Solvang in the Santa Ynez Valley, north of Santa Barbara, which is Danish themed and a popular shopping destination. It is the logical base for touring the surrounding wine country. In Napa, the historic spa town of Calistoga fits the description of wine village, as does historic and charming Sonoma.

Regions without wine villages should seek to create them by encouraging heritage conservation, architectural theming, wine-related signage, and the holding of wine events. Private investors are likely to respond to concerted public efforts.

In many ways, planning a wine village is similar to what has called the "tourist shopping village" (Getz, 1993). These small population centers seem to develop naturally in response to tourist traffic, especially in close proximity to cities, along touring corridors, and in resort destinations. Often a major investor is responsible for providing the core commercial attraction and services, followed by others who see a good thing developing. At some point civic intervention is required—to ensure consistent theming, to prevent overcommercialization, or to deal with traffic and other problems caused by too many visitors!

A number of strategies can be suggested. First and foremost is to gain recognition of the value of the wine village concept to wine tourism development. Without public discussion and formal planning and development efforts, the potential of wine theming might easily be lost. The leadership of a winery (see the case study of Hillstowe winery in Hahnsdorf in the next chapter) can be the catalyst for related progress. Public infrastructure, such as development of a wine visitor and interpretive center, can also get things moving, or creation of an annual wine festival might be the trigger.

What should the wine village contain or look like? Conservation and adaptive reuse of old buildings with distinctive styles should be a top priority, emulating Old World charm. But modern villages can succeed by adhering to design and signage themes, streetscaping, and other beautification efforts, and by obtaining the right mix of products and services. Visitors will be delighted to find the following:

• information and wine interpretive center;
• wineries, or tasting rooms of wineries located elsewhere;
• wine bars and restaurants with good cellars featuring local wines;
• a range of other shops, including art, collectibles, and antiques;
• a range of accommodations, especially up-market bed and breakfast;
• ongoing entertainment programs, such as street performers;
• periodic wine festivals and related events.

Here are a number of planning principles for creating and enhancing the wine village:

• Inform and consult with the community regarding wine tourism and the impacts of tourism in general. What are the residents' fears and goals?
• Conduct research on resident and visitor attitudes and preferences
• Evaluate potential costs and benefits; discuss these in an open forum.
• Implement a planning and control process to ensure that goals are met, particularly with regard to protecting heritage resources and avoiding

traffic problems in the village.

• Establish architectural design standards to reflect the local/regional theme.

• Incorporate wine-related themes into local events and entertainment.

• Ensure the availability of wine-related information throughout the village. Is there a need for an interpretive center? wine retail outlets? a museum of wine? special tour-bus parking?

• Begin and end wine routes in the village.

• Determine if the village is pedestrian-friendly and safe.

• Formulate an action plan, including priorities for public and industry funding.

• Encourage local investment in the wine village concept and related themes

• Improve local knowledge of area wines and wineries.

• Foster a customer orientation in all local businesses and services.

Wine Routes

Wine Routes (or roads or trails) have existed in Europe for over 50 years, and are an essential ingredient in wine tourism strategies. They offer the destination an opportunity to make tangible the wine theme; the consumer benefits from better information and accessibility to attractions and services, and wineries should see increases in traffic.

The European Council of Wine Routes *(Europaische Weinstrassen),* based in Bordeaux, is part of the European Council of Wine Regions and was set up under the European Community. Their goal is to promote wineries and improve the quality of service they provide. Cooperation among key stakeholders is fostered, including government at all levels, industry, and associations.

According to researchers on theme trails in general (Silbergh, Fladmark, Henry, & Young, 1994) they can be defined as "a route for walking, cycling, riding, driving or other forms of transport that draws on the natural or cultural heritage of an area to provide an educational experience that will enhance visitor enjoyment. It is marked on the ground or on maps, and interpretive literature is normally available to guide the visitor" (p. 124). A continuum exists from highly educational trails to those stressing visitor enjoyment.

Drawing on Silbergh et al. (1994), theme trails should embody the following general planning and design principles:

• continuous traffic flow along the route (i.e., easy to navigate);

• provision of maps/guides and sign posting;

• appropriate facilities connected to enhance visitor satisfaction (i.e., toilets, restaurants, accommodation, interpretive centers, attractions);

• facilitate discovery and enjoyment by both visitors and residents;

• linkages between national, regional, and local trails should be made (and confusion avoided);

• integrate their planning with that of the attractions and facilities along the routes;

• involve public and private stakeholders;

• trails should be part of a visitor management strategy that helps to protect sensitive resources and areas, avoids congestion, and spreads benefits widely;

• consider the capacity of the route and the area to absorb traffic and tourists;

• marketing potential of the trail must be considered at the beginning of the planning process, including identification of target market segments;

• a permanent monitoring and maintenance system is needed, including visitor and facility feedback.

Creating a wine route might very well help establish a new wine region, or bring together the necessary partners for the first time. It can be a project that in itself attracts publicit, or stimulates research and planning for wine tourism in general. Individual wineries and services along the route can be induced to improve their quality or to expand. As to costs and problems, Silbergh et al. (1994) have identified a few. Sign posting and the necessary maps/guides can be expensive, and must be regularly updated. The collaboration among organizations that is required can become strained over time, or partners might pull out. A long "shelf life" has to be contemplated to get the benefits, and measuring impacts might be difficult.

Care should also be taken to avoid too many trails, or too many themes within one region. If theme trails already exist, should they be replaced, merged or otherwise integrated? For example, many tourist regions already possess "scenic routes" and the stakeholders might have to decide if greater advantage could be gained by adopting or converting to a more targeted wine theme. There is no inherent reason why several themes cannot be pursued, but visitor confusion is a risk.

Displacement and concentration of visitors is another potential problem. Once a route has been publicized, there might be a shift in traffic and sales from one area to another, leaving some owners or communities unhappy and other areas congested. Can this be avoided? Here are some strategies that can be followed, all of which depend on a regional planning assessment:

- Connect all wineries and attractions in one circular route (in some areas with many facilities, or very dispersed attractions, this might be impossible).
- Connect major nodes in one circular route (such as communities with services—wine villages—and subareas with a critical mass of wineries or related attractions).
- Suggest multiple touring routes categorized by length of trip, type of attractions to be experienced, or other criteria, to highlight as many wineries and services as possible.
- Encourage travelers to move in both directions, to avoid congestion.
- Avoid circular tours altogether and encourage base-camp tours (i.e., visitors base their tours in communities or resorts with many services, then use guides/maps to range into the countryside on their own).
- Linear routes might be more appropriate in some regions where wineries and services are concentrated along a valley or road.

Route planners should also start out with the assumptions that visitors easily get lost, often deliberately stray from suggested itineraries, frequently like to do something spontaneous, and enjoy surprises. Monitoring actual visitor behavior and getting their feedback will help improve the wine trail experience.

Another factor to consider is that wineries, attractions, and services all compete for business and the wine route will not stop owners from attempting to gain competitive advantages. The routes have to be sold on the premise that the region must first be perceived to be an attractive destination, then individual businesses must attract customers.

Trails and wine events also go together. A typical wine festival involves movement from winery to winery, and this can be done by way of the formal wine route (to publicize it) or deliberately away from it (to avoid congestion).

One of the most famous beverage-themed trails is the Malt Whisky Trail of Scotland, having existed since the early 1970s. It receives financial support from both the distilleries and public agencies and aims to provide high-quality visitor attractions and retail outlets. There is extensive promotion throughout the United Kingdom and abroad, as whisky and Scotland are almost synonymous. The Wine Council of Ontario, Canada, has created a sign-posted wine route for its Niagara and Lake Erie appellations. Tourists can obtain the Wine Regions of Ontario: Winery Tours Map, which clearly shows roads and 39 winery locations, including several in Toronto and Kitchener. Each winery is described briefly, with information on tours, hours and times of operation, tasting, and contact details. British Columbia, Canada, has its Wine Trails. A booklet-style guide with maps is provided by the B.C. Vintners Quality Alliance.

In Victoria State, Australia, the Great Southern Touring Route connects several wine regions and encourages visitors to and residents of Melbourne to hit the open road. Although the touring route is generic, the route association has published a Great Southern Food and Wine Trail guide to explicitly encourage wine and food tours, specifically "a culinary voyage of discovery." The guide adds: "discover the taste-tempting offerings of fine regional produce and wines, exciting restaurants, breath-taking scenery and other attractions which make this an unforgettable journey." Departing Melbourne, tourists can connect in a circular route the Geelong, Grampians, Pyrenees, and Ballarat wine regions, together with experiencing the natural wonders along the Great Ocean Road and in the Grampian Mountains. The guide has beautiful and tempting photos of scenery, food, and wine, plus details on many dining establishments, food specialties and local produce, wineries, and events. International visitors will, however, want more information covering accommodations, distances, and travel times. The guide profiles only one accommodation place: the Warrenmang Vineyard Resort.

The New Zealand's Heritage Inns Wine Trail encourages touring of New Zealand's wine countries and staying at members' Heritage Inns properties.

Visitors can put together their own tour and rest at many unique accommodation places along the way. Maps show inn locations and driving times between them, while information is provided on the wine regions (Web site: www.heritageinns.co.nz/wine-trail.htm).

From San Francisco north to Crescent City, following route 101, California's Cheese Trail passes through and complements several wine regions. According to Jay Stuller (1998), there is a strong parallel between the development of premium wines and the more recent emergence of premium cheeses as a tourist draw—especially when featured together! Focal points of the cheese trail are several cheese factories open to visitors, and restaurants that offer fine cheeses. Wine and cheese certainly come together in the historic town of Sonoma, which is home to the Sonoma Cheese factory and the Vella Cheese Company. On Sonoma's charming town square is situated Freestyle!, a restaurant featuring so-called "artisanal" cheesemakers, including some without any public facilities. Sonoma is also the perfect place to pick up wine, cheese, and specialty meats at the deli and head off to the town square or one of the nearby wineries for a picnic.

Signs

With or without a formal wine route, sign posting is critical in wine country. The basic objectives and elements of a signage policy should include the following points.

- **Direct visitors to all wineries, attractions, and services**. Even along a formal touring route, signs should give visitors the means to visit all the region's attractions and services. The main resulting problem can be confusion arising from too many signs, or confusion between the suggested route and optional side-trips.

- **Manage traffic.** It might be desirable to steer traffic away from sensitive or congested areas, or towards clusters of services. Some roads might be inadequate for certain types of vehicles.

- **Develop a consistent theme and messages about the area**. Signage is part of branding, so it should reflect the regional theme and all its visual manifestations.

- **Be as clear and easy to use as possible.** Drivers have limited ability to see, read, and comprehend signage. Expert advise should be taken on the design, size, situation, and sequencing of signs for motorists. At key points a pull-over will be preferable to roadside or intersection signs.

• **Make an entry and exit statement.** Something special is required when visitors first enter the wine country, and then again when they depart.

A world-class wine region should also have its own wine routes and world-class, wine-themed signage. This was the thinking behind the Hunter Valley scheme that yielded some truly unique, functional, and attractive sign posting. A Commonwealth grant of $40,000 made to Cessnock City Council helped pay for the improvements, although individual businesses included on the new signs also had to pay up front. All components of the signage were designed and produced locally.

The Hunter Valley system is fully integrated, encompassing maps and "fingerboard" signs that provide a much better impression and more information than the previous mix. "With the new system visitors know, just from the style of signs, that they are still within, or that they've now entered, the vineyards district. It has changed what was previously a hit or miss arrangement into a district with a distinct identity," said Ken Phelan, Senior Strategic Planner for the city (quoted in Australia, Department of Industry, Science and Tourism, 1996).

Forty-three strategic sites were involved in the project, 13 for district maps and 30 for fingerboards. Identical maps show the entire wine district and are located at entry points or hub points (e.g., major intersections) along highways. The principle criterion is that visitors will naturally focus on these points and will want to make decisions at that spot. At least one or two maps will be visible to every visitor arriving by car or coach. Alongside the maps are alphabetical listings of businesses, coded to numbers on the map. Solar panels provide electricity to light the maps at night.

"Fingerboard" signs provide direction to individual wineries and services. Standard symbols are used, including bunches of grapes for vineyards and the crossed spoon and fork for eateries. Accommodations are identified by a bed. The construction of these fingerboards allows for adding and removing signs, as needed. Reflective lettering is used so that night drivers can read the information. The road name is also prominent.

Wine Country Tours

There is a mutually beneficial, but often uneasy, relationship between wineries and wine tour companies. Some winery owners fear inundation from large tour buses full of swilling, unsophisticated, low-spending sight-seers. But most wineries are nevertheless dependent to a small or large extent on visitors. Wine tours require access to attractive, receptive wineries, and hopefully special treatment for their customers. Clearly, effort must be expended by both parties to reach the right balance.

Why do people choose an organized wine tour? Journalist D. Berman (1997) observed: "Since the 1980s, Australia's wine industry has emerged as a world contender—which has made tours of the country's winemaking regions wonderfully alluring to wine enthusiasts." The appeal is heightened by the fact that many wines are simply unavailable outside the country. Specific benefits of a wine country tour include the following:

- no other options exist (for many tourists, there is no real or perceived option but to take a tour, as they lack a car, knowledge, time, or energy to go it alone);
- convenience (even with the ability to tour alone, the operator makes a package of elements very convenient);
- price or perceived value (operators can make the whole package cheaper than the prices customers must pay; perceived value relates to the impression customers have of getting extra value);
- uniqueness (on their own, customers cannot always gain access to certain wineries, to winemakers, or premium wines and food; the tour can offer a unique experience unavailable to most tourists);
- knowledge (a knowledgeable wine tour guide can add greatly to the experience of the area and its wines);
- luxury (e.g., riding in a comfortable limousine, staying in the best accommodation, enjoying great wines and meals, being pampered);
- safety (fear of drinking and driving, or of driving under unknown conditions);
- socializing (wine touring with a group of similarly motivated strangers can be fun and rewarding; going with an affinity group, like a club, can provide a new way to socialize; touring with a friend or spouse can be romantic!).

Organized wine tour experiences will vary to a degree, but should always consist of a number of basic elements derived from the above list of motives. At its core, the experience must be convenient, educational, fun, and safe. To this short list can be added the options of luxury, diversity (i.e., mixing wine with other attractions), surprise, humor, and even challenge. Delivering more than is promised is a sure way to generate satisfied customers and repeat business.

There is a clear distinction to be made between scheduled, large-coach tours and small, flexible guided tours. A third major type is the customized group tour related to corporate outings, affinity groups, or incentive tours; these can be designed more like a special event.

Corporate, incentive, and affinity group wine tours are likely to involve different motivations and requirements. Incentive tours are actually rewards to high performers, and therefor the experience should be special, memorable, pampering, and luxurious. Incentive tourists are having someone else pay for their fun so they expect the tour operator to design something unique, not just escort them to wineries. Incentive tourists want to be treated like Very Important Persons, if only for a while.

Accordingly, it might be appropriate to include one of more of the following elements:

• high-standard accommodation, meals, and transport (use limousines);

• banquets, theme parties, or mini-food and wine festivals;

• meet the owners, winemakers, and chefs;

• receive gifts, especially premium wines;

• be surprised with elements not publicized in advance.

Corporate functions might very well have a business component in the form of a meeting, awards presentation, or socializing between people who otherwise do not meet regularly. These special considerations have to be planned with the clients. Affinity groups, like seniors clubs or sports teams, might very well have only a secondary interest in wine and wineries, so care has to be taken to maximize their socializing and not overdue the wine interpretation; unless, of course, they are wine clubs!

A partnership has to be negotiated for successful winery tours; winery managers and tour operators will have to resolve a number of potentially divisive issues.

Access and Reservations

Many wineries literally do not want to see a tour pull up, and their reasons are certainly compelling:

• cannot handle crowds;

• do not want visitors who are there for the purpose of drinking, not learning and buying;

• do not have the expertise to cater to special visitor needs;

• resent the (perceived) fact that tour companies make the profits while wineries provide the attractions and consumables.

Consequently, many wineries require advance reservations, while some exclude tour groups altogether. On the positive side, being selective can ensure that mass tourism is avoided, inappropriate visitors are not attracted, and special-interest tours get the best treatment.

Large group-tour companies *need* large winery attractions, complete with toilets, guided tours, retail sales outlets, and food services. Small tours want to meet owners and winemakers, sample premium wines, get an exclusive look at the facility, and receive special knowledge from experts. So tour operators make arrangements with a select group of wineries to schedule (or at least phone in advance) visits, making arrangement with some for food or special samplings, and build the winery's costs into the package price. These can all be negotiated for mutual satisfaction.

Free Samples Versus Tasting Fees

Why should wineries give away expensive product, especially when they are usually taxed on the "free" samples? There are, in fact, a number of good reasons for free tastings:

• Why else would visitors come to unknown, out-of-the-way wineries?

• How else can the winery get people to try new products?

• Tastings frequently lead to on-the-spot sales, and satisfied tasters can become loyal customers.

• Keeping the visitor at the winery as long as possible helps sell other items and food.

• Competition among wineries can be intense, so free tastings can be essential in some environments.

Many winery owners, on the other hand, would probably like to charge for all tastings. Their reasons are equally good:

• to recover costs (especially the damnable taxes!);

• to discourage binge drinking and inappropriate visitors;

• to ensure that visitors can sample all the wines, including the expensive ones;

• to meet different preferences, as sophisticated tasters usually focus on the best wines.

A number of variations in tasting fees have been observed, and these are options for wineries to consider:

• A formal tasting fee is posted for all visitors to see, but it is frequently waived at the discretion of the owner or manager (this ploy can discourage undesirables).

• Fees are charged, but refunded with a purchase (this seems to satisfy most customers).

• Tasting can be "free," but the costs hidden in the retail price (which can make wine seem more expensive relative to the competition).

• Fees can be charged to tour operators and hidden in the package price (enabling the operator to accurately proclaim that all fees and charges are included).

• Fees can include a souvenir (especially the tasting glass), which offers the customer something tangible.

• Fees can be charged only for premium wines, preferably in a separate tasting room (most people understand this principle, which is like first-class versus economy travel).

Chapter 7

CASE STUDIES OF WINE TOURISM DESTINATION DEVELOPMENT

McLAREN VALE & FLEURIEU VISITOR CENTER, SOUTH AUSTRALIA

Although vines were first planted here in 1839, McLaren Vale has only in recent years developed as a premium wine region with its own brand name recognition. In part this has been attributable to the predominance of the Barossa, and in part to the fact that it was mostly a grape-growing area with little wine actually produced there.

There is much going for it from the perspectives of both premium wine-making and wine tourism. Adelaide, the state capital (population over 1 million) is very close by, ensuring a large day-trip market, and the country-side is both attractive and unspoiled. Nearby beaches are also popular.

This wine area has about 230 independent growers and about 55 wineries. It accounts for almost 9% of the state's grape production, which translates into 4% of Australia's. The area is corporate headquarters for the wine giant, BRL Hardy, situated at its attractive home winery, Chateau Reynella. Another corporate giant, Southcorp, owns the Seaview Winery, which boasts the largest selling brand in Australia.

Winemaker Scott Collett of Woodstock Winery is past chairman of the winemakers association and was involved in securing the new visitor center. He has also worked hard for developing the regional identity, which includes securing an approved geographical indication for the McLaren Vale Wine Region and actively promoting the wines of this region. Brand awareness is developed through the McLaren Vale Wine Show and "Meet Your Maker" shows that take the area's wines to large markets such as Sydney and Melbourne.

An Australian benchmark in wine tourism was created with the opening of the A$1.6 million McLaren Vale & Fleurieu Visitor Center in 1997. While visitor centers are in themselves commonplace, this one features viticulture and wine like no other. The center's first manager, Rod Hand, said "It will provide the first physical focus for a region which has already won awards for its tourist attractions and its premium wines" (personal communication).

Along with the usual information and accommodation booking services, its unique elements include:

- an operational, 6-hectare demonstration vineyard that will produce the center's own Shiraz for sale;
- interpretive gardens featuring an olive grove and almond orchard;
- wine tasting, education, and sales area;
- offices for the local wine and tourism industry associations;
- lecture theater and display areas suitable for art exhibitions, meetings, and other functions;
- shop featuring local crafts;
- café and wine bar.

Development of the center emerged from recognition that the tourism potential of this region, and particularly the McLaren Vale Wine Region, was not being fully realized. Being very close to Adelaide, considerable pleasure traffic was already being experienced, but there was no entrance statement or visitor information at McLaren Vale itself. Although wine is a central feature of the center, it also serves the peninsula's other communities, which enjoy a great deal of countryside and beach-oriented tourism and day-use recreation.

The center was financed by a combination of state, Commonwealth, local authority and local wine industry money, plus community support through goods and services. Its formal goals are to contribute to development of tourism in the region and be a focal point for tourism operators and associations. It is intended to become self-sufficient, especially through eventual sale of its own Shiraz label.

In its first year of operations approximately 50,000 visitors were recorded, and Rod Hand hoped that would reach 100,000 very soon. Inquiries at the desk came mostly from South Australians (34%), then interstate visitors (25%) and international tourists (15%).

The center relies on the wine industry for managing the vineyards. Indeed, partnership with the wine industry was and remains fundamental to the center's success. To bring wine and tourism even closer together, Rod became Chair of the McLaren Region Tourism Association, placing him in a pivotal position (figuratively and literally) to coordinate tourism and Center activities.

CALIFORNIA WELCOME CENTER, SONOMA COUNTY

Located in Rohnert Park, this welcome center was specifically situated and designed to introduce visitors to Sonoma County's wine country. Car- or coach-based travelers heading north from San Francisco on US 101 will find it rewarding to stop here first. The attractive building also houses the Sonoma County Visitor and Convention Bureau, while the site features a vineyard and lake. In close proximity is a resort hotel with golf course.

It is unique in several ways. First, it contains a demonstration winery to educate visitors on the entire winemaking process. The Sonoma County Grape Growers Association planted a vineyard on site in 1993, which demonstrates trellising and other viticultural techniques.

Displays include a topographical relief map of the county, and a video presentation. A touch-screen computer allows guests to plan a self-directed county itinerary using information on wineries, hotels, restaurants, and other activities. Direct phone lines are available to over 100 are wineries.

A tasting bar features three Sonoma wines each week, and the large retail area offers over 200 local wines plus a range of other products, many of which are wine themed. The Welcome Center caters to coach tours as well as independent travelers. Group programs are by appointment and four packages are offered for groups of 25 or more. The basic package includes a welcome packet and tasting of three wines, at $7.50 per person in a half-hour time frame. Other options include an educational tour, wine appreciation with a professional instructor, lunch, and dinner. The top-end dinner package was priced at $75.00 in 1999. The facility has a complete commercial kitchen and is also available for private rentals.

HAHNDORF IN THE ADELAIDE HILLS, SOUTH AUSTRALIA, AND HILLSTOWE WINES

The Adelaide Hills provide a lush, picturesque backdrop to the capital of South Australia, and at the same time form a distinct wine region. One of its gems is the historic village of Hahndorf, which, although popular for its heritage and shopping, is also becoming a center for wine tourism. Adelaide Hills claims to be Australia's "premier cold climate wine region" (Adelaide Hills Grapegrowers and Wine Makers Association, undated brochure). The Mount Lofty Ranges have an altitude of 400 meters and higher, close to the Southern Ocean, and contain distinct microclimates. Visitors will discover that winemaking dates back 150 years or more, but the area was "put on the map" by winemaker Brian Croser who, in 1978, established a vineyard and attracted considerable attention to his successes. Croser's Petaluma wines are now internationally acclaimed, and his historic Bridgewater Mill establishment, containing cellars and a fine-dining restaurant, is a must-visit landmark.

In the 1998 Adelaide Hills Visitor Guide (Adelaide Hills Regional Tourist Association, undated brochure), Hahndorf is described as the state's "most popular tourist attraction, an historic German village with many original buildings still standing." It boasts tea rooms and cake shops, gourmet stores and gift shops, plus pubs, accommodation, and the Hahndorf Academy of arts. Being close to the city (30 minutes or so by car), the village also attracts meetings and conferences. The village also hosts a number of festivals annually.

Walking the pleasant, leafy main street of Hahndorf can transport the visitor to the Old World, or back a century into pioneering days. Conservation of the built heritage is an absolute priority, and within that framework many visitor-oriented establishments have creatively adapted old buildings. The charming Hillstowe Winery complex blends in perfectly, yet the complex includes mostly recent recreations.

Hillstowe is run by the father and son team of Chris and Hamish Laurie. Their ancestors planted vines in South Australia in 1853, so they have roots and traditions to match those of the village. Their McLaren Vale vineyard dates back to 1980 and the Adelaide Hills vineyard was established in 1984. The Hillstowe label was created in 1991 together with the slogan "better vines better wines." In 1995 the Lauries opened a cellar door in Hahndorf, followed in 1997 by a barrel hall and winery in the old cheese factory at nearby Mount Torrens.

In 1998 they were busy moving the cellar door to Thiele's Cottage, one of the oldest buildings (circa 1845) on the main street of Hahndorf. Both Adelaide Hills and McLaren Vale wines are available in the new cellar, plus light meals. Down a side street is a group of new but authentically designed cottages in the style of German pioneer villages, providing the visitor with an historical, wine-themed experience. As they put it: "Hillstowe's complex of stone cottages nestles amongst trees and gardens in this historic township."

The basic concept is to separate the cellar door operation, which now has maximum exposure to passing tourists, from other functions. Visitors can purchase light meals, have a picnic and buy souvenirs. The previous cellar door has become a function room for promotional tastings and private events.

Bus tours from Adelaide visit the Hillstowe complex, plus several smaller limousine and coach tours of the Adelaide Hills stop there. The Lauries promote their wine tourism attraction through joint marketing with tourist organizations. The classic Hillstowe truck is frequently seen in front of Adelaide's smart wine bars.

GRAPEVINE—WINE CAPITAL OF TEXAS

As the name might suggest, the City of Grapevine has positioned itself as the wine capital of Texas (also see the Texas profile and interview with Dr. Tim Dodd in Chapter 2). But their wine tourism strategy did not evolve from a successful local grape or wine industry—the strategy came first! Their Convention and Visitors Bureau played a lead role in developing and marketing wine tourism.

Interview With Paul McCallum, CEO, Grapevine Convention and Visitors Bureau

Q: Why and how is your bureau involved in wine tourism?

A: About 12 years ago the Grapevine Convention and Visitors Bureau became involved in product development by necessity. Being located by a major international airport, Grapevine had great full-service meeting hotels that catered to the corporate client Monday through Friday for about 8 months of the year. Weekends, summers, and holiday periods, business was nonexistent. Grapevine was determined to build a leisure market for these down times and thus began development of the downtown historic district, festivals, and special events. From this early success it seemed logical that a town named Grapevine should have vineyards and wineries. A little research showed that some vineyards and at least one winery existed here before the turn of the century.

At the same time, the Mayor and City Council were concerned that with Grapevine farms succumbing to housing additions the town's rural flavor might disappear. Vineyards and wineries were seen as a way to keep farming in the community while at the same time building a tourism product. Grapevine City Council adopted the most wine-friendly ordinances in the state and encouraged wineries to move to Grapevine through zoning, promotional, and marketing assistance.

Over an 8-year period six wineries have located in Grapevine and the goal is to eventually have 12 to 15 wineries. The small wineries also act as greenbelts and buffer zones between highways and residential areas.

The Convention and Visitors Bureau produces and promotes the wine-related festivals, provides assistance to the Texas Wine and Grape Growers Association, now headquartered in Grapevine, and produces promotional literature for the wineries, restaurants, and art galleries.

As an outgrowth of its involvement in the wine industry, Grapevine has developed two sister-city relationships. One is with Parras de la Fuente in Mexico, home to the oldest winery in the Americas (Casa Medero is 402 years old!), and the other is with Krems, Austria, the premier wine region of that country.

Q: How is wine marketed as the "branded" experience for Grapevine?

A: Wine and vineyards are perceived as romantic, spiritual, family-oriented experiences. They are places where one can get away from it all, a safe haven from hectic, everyday life. Wineries and vineyards also conjure up thoughts of fine dining, peaceful inns, quaint B&B's, art galleries, antiques, etc. Grapevine has built its tourism product over the last 10 years around all of these facilities, and the town's very name, Grapevine, is enough to make the connection between the wine experience and the shopping/dining getaway experience. Promotional materials that are focused around the leisure market, weekends, holidays, and festivals and events carry this branded image of Grapevine as the center of the Texas wine industry.

It is important that the focus is on the growing of wine grapes, the harvesting and crushing of grapes, and the whole process of turning grapes into wine. The focus is not on drinking wine but rather on wine as the medium that brings people together.

Q: What do you think are critical success factors in the wine tourism market?

A: Presuming there are wineries and vineyards within your area you could consider the following programs:

- Develop events that celebrate the various cycles of the vineyards (flowering of the vines, harvest and crush, bottling and new releases, art and wine events, themed tours).

- Package accommodations, restaurants, and wineries into getaway programs.

- Have wineries host authors, artists, etc., that will draw niche markets.

- Develop a wine trail system that routes people through scenic, historic, shopping, dining, and winery areas.

- Help wineries develop newsletters and activities that draw people to the wineries from far enough away that they need to overnight in the area.

- Promote the increased economic benefits of wine tourism through employment, business growth, and increased investment.

Grapevine's Tasting Rooms and Wineries

The newest local winery is CapRock, which features an 11-foot bar where patrons can order 2-ounce samples, and discuss wines and grape growing while enjoying murals of the winery, which is located in West Texas. The tasting room also features many gift items for the wine connoisseur, and extravagant gift baskets.

Delaney Winery and Vineyards (on Champagne Boulevard!) is designed in the classic French style, has a grand barrel room with antique vats, tasting area, gift shop, and beautiful grounds for enjoyment. Visitors are invited on a guided tour through the vineyards, tank room, bottling room, and lab as they are told of the winery's history, concept behind the facility, and methods of the winemaker.

Homestead Winery and Tasting Room is situated in one of Grapevine's many historic homes. Homestead enjoys a solid reputation for its excellent Muscat Canelli, Chardonnay, and Cabernet Sauvignon wines. If you are lucky you might catch the tasting room manager, Janeye McCallum, on site, belting out unbelievable Patsy Cline tunes, no charge!

La Buena Vida Vineyards is one of the state's oldest producing wineries and has its own winery museum, native Texas gardens, fountains, herb gardens, and picnic tables under a wisteria-covered arbor. This family-owned winery takes pride in being Grapevine's first winery and tasting room.

La Bodega, in addition to offering their own wines, sells the best wines from select Texas vineyards. Wine is available after noon daily. La Bodega is the first (and likely only) airport winery in the world.

New in 1999 will be Northstar Winery, to be located on Main Street adjacent to the Train Depot. Owner Dale Bullough was planning to open in late summer after renovations are complete.

VICTORIAN WINERIES TOURISM COUNCIL

In 1993 Victoria Wineries Tourism Council (VWTC) was the first organization in Australia to be established specifically for wine tourism, in the form of a Ministerial advisory body. As its name suggests, the focus has been on wineries as the core product, but the Council does have a destination-wide mandate and roles that are supported by members drawn from tour companies.

The State Tourism Commission had identified wine and food as key strategic tourism strengths for Victoria in its 1993 Strategic Plan, and so impetus for establishing the Council came from the top, not the wineries. The point of having a separate council, according to Jack Rasterhoff, CEO of the Victorian Wineries Tourism Council, is that it is industry driven and therefor responsive to the needs of wineries and wine areas.

Vision Statement: "For Victoria's wine regions to become a first choice tourist destination for both Australia and international visitors."

Mission Statement: "To increase the economic benefit and yield in the wine regions of Victoria through winery tourism by developing and implementing, in conjunction with stakeholders and strategic partners, strategies which maximise the tourism product strength."

Positioning Statement: "Discover Victoria's wines through the winemaker, not the grapevine."

Goals for the VWTC

1. To enhance Victoria's competitive advantage in wine tourism.

2. To develop and implement marketing and promotional strategies to increase tourism activity, visitor numbers and yield to Victoria's wine regions.

3. To develop closer links with regional wine and tourism organizations

4. To take a leadership role in the wine tourism industry, both in Victoria and Australia.

5. To ensure that Victoria's wineries involved in winery tourism adopt customer service standards accepted as best practice in the tourism industry in the state.

The Scale of Wine Tourism in Victoria

Research conducted every 2 or 3 years by the Council on Cellar Door Activities (the survey includes 1500 interviews at cellar doors) provides estimates of visitation and impacts: 1994–95: 1.6 million visits, 1995–96: 1.9 million visits, 1996–97: 2.3 million visits.

Factors explaining this growth, according to Jack Rasterhoff, relate to both supply and demand. More wineries have opened to the public and existing wineries have added visitor facilities, notably restaurants. Over 50% of the state's wineries now have restaurants or other eating facilities. There is also better signage in the regions. Demand stems from increasing interest in lifestyle experiences, lots of promotion, and special events. Wanting to learn about wine and food is a major motivator.

Winery tourism is high yield, as they found that over half of the visitors do so as part of a short break including accommodation. The economic benefit of winery tourism is estimated to be around $183 million annually, with 51% of that being spent on non-cellar door activities including food and accommodation.

VWTC Activities

One major success in Victoria has been the establishment of 32 wine festivals, up from an original 12 in the days before the Council. VWTC has an events grant scheme that draws on $100,000 in funding to match event budgets. The scheme has concentrated on getting new wine events started, rather than providing operating funds. Growth in attendance at wine events was reported to have increased by 19% since 1993. The Yarra Valley Grape Grazing alone attracts over 30,000 visitors annually. So successful has this program been, drawing on enthusiasm in the regions, that it is now a real question as to how many wine events the state can successfully support. VWTC has produced quality guidelines for events receiving their assistance.

Planning and Coordination

The Council has a 3-year strategic plan that ties into the state's tourism plan, and these two organizations work closely together on marketing as well as planning. VWTC also cooperates with the Melbourne Visitor and Convention Bureau, especially with regard to food, as Melbourne has the catering expertise and numbers needed for the state's growing number of wine and food festivals. As well, there is recognition that Melbourne is the major source of winery visitors and the gateway for interstate and international wine tourists.

Jack Rasterhoff believes that critical mass is needed to create an effective wine tourism destination. Victoria has more designated wine areas from the Geographic Indicators Committee (16) than any other state in Australia, and only a few of these have brand recognition. In some there are currently too few wineries or related attractions and facilities to support much tourism. In addition to sufficient numbers of wineries, one or two "icons" are highly desirable (i.e., famous brand names or major wineries).

Marketing

There are too many wine areas in Victoria, and Australia in general, for every one of them to achieve brand recognition outside the immediate area. Focus groups in Sydney, for example, revealed that even the Yarra Valley — arguably Victoria's preeminent wine region — lacks consumer recognition. While special events and continued promotion of specific wine regions will help, other strategies are needed.

The top priority of the VWTC is to raise awareness of Victoria as a destination where a wide range of top quality wine tourism experiences can be enjoyed, for both the domestic and international markets. Wine tourism will also be stressed through foreign wine sales, and more use can definitely be made of wine trade shows and even the bottles as tourism promotion tools. Specifically, foreign wine consumers need a reference map to locate Melbourne and Victoria, plus "call to action" material. Small wineries have been slow to make use of their labeling as tourist promotional material.

VWTC has an active visiting journalist program to bring domestic and international writers to Melbourne and into the wine regions. Wineries cooperate willingly in hosting these important visitors. Accreditation of cellar door operations is another initiative, aiming for high-quality facilities and visitor experiences. The state tourism awards competition, held annually, recognizes "tourist winery" as a distinct category.

Packaging is a vital marketing activity for wine tourism. VWTC has noted that nearly 40% of people visiting Victoria wineries do so as part of a short break, so its packaging has emphasized this type product (see the Marketing section of this chapter for details).

Other marketing activities include:

• Production and distribution of the guide book "Wine Regions of Victoria" (a comprehensive, 100-page booklet that has become one of the state's most popular tourism publications); its aims were to increase regional awareness and translate that into interest and desire to make wine tours; the guide serves as a planning tool and handy reference.

• Production and distribution of the Calendar of Events and Festivals.

• Development of the Wine and Foodlovers Short Break program, designed to increase winery visits and tourism yield to the regions (discussed in the next chapter).

• Product development in conjunction with the wine regions, tourism operators, and Tourism Victoria.

• Providing financial support to assist wine regions in staging quality wine and food festivals.

• Participation, in conjunction with Tourism Victoria, in interstate and overseas advertising campaigns and promotional activities.

• Review of regional winery signage guidelines; research revealed that one third of winery visits were made as a result of tourists seeing road signs.

Research

Several references have already been made to research funded by the VWTC. These studies have provided valuable data on wine tourism trends, consumer behavior, segmentation, and economic impacts. In the future they want to interview people in the regions, not just at wineries, to determine more general patterns of travel and reasons for not visiting wineries.

Issues

Is wine tourism mostly for the small and medium wineries? Jack Rasterhoff is convinced that the dollar value of cellar door sales at the large, corporate wineries is also quite significant, and he notes that the profit margins on wine sold at wineries is at least twice that of sales through other distribution means. While the large companies might not promote the regions, their various wineries are often operated as independent business units, and as such they tend to behave like other wineries that participate in regional promotions.

Contacts: E-mail: vwtc@wineries.tourism.vic.gov.au; Web site: www.visitvictoria.com/wineries

WINE TOURISM IN THE HUNTER VALLEY, NEW SOUTH WALES, AUSTRALIA

The Hunter Valley is Australia's most developed wine tourism region, based on its location within a 2-hour drive of downtown Sydney and its reputation for quality wines. Unlike the Napa Valley in California, however, the Hunter still preserves its very rural atmosphere and country-town feeling. Its attractive scenery and pleasant climate make visits appealing all year round, but as yet development and traffic levels are not excessive. That might be changing fast.

Several Commonwealth tourism grants have contributed to wine tourism development in the Hunter. A grant of $90,000 was provided to the Singleton and Upper Hunter Business Enterprise Centre, in 1993–94, for preparation of a regional tourism plan. It allowed a register of tourism assets, attractions, and services, development of a marketing strategy and overall plan for the Upper Hunter zone. Videos and brochures were also produced. One beneficial outcome noted by Cathy Parsons was the connection of wine businesses to general business support assistance in areas like training, business planning, benchmarking, and network facilitation.

Signage improvements benefited from two separate grants, resulting in the planning, design, and installation of directional signs and information bays. The cooperative approach to signage development, according to Cathy Parsons, involved Cessnock City Council, local vineyard associations, and local tourist associations. New and better signage raised awareness by tourists of the Upper Hunter subarea and tourism operators.

Interview With Gus Maher, Director of Tourism, Cessnock and Hunter Valley, Australia

Q: Are you worried about excessive tourism development, or losing the rural atmosphere of the Hunter?

A: It is not at that scale yet, although a number of major developments are on the drawing board. We have a marketing plan, but we will need a general tourism plan to regulate and shape the growth, otherwise it could pose a threat.

Q: What are your primary markets?

A: Research found that Sydney accounted for 70% of our visitors, but 10% are from interstate Australia, outside New South Wales, and fully 20% are international tourists.

Q: What does a typical visit to Hunter consist of?

A: Structured day tours are very big, and growing. There are a lot of tour companies in Sydney bringing out tourists for a few hours, stopping at a small number of wineries, doing a lunch plus some sightseeing. We also get a large number of car-based tourists, and a growing proportion of them are staying overnight, especially on weekends. We also have specialty golf markets developing.

Q: Who do you target?

A: We are aiming specifically to attract more international tourists, particularly mid-week, and niche markets like golf. Wine tourism is very compatible with the resorts and golf courses we have.

AUSTRALIA'S NATIONAL WINE CENTRE

Central to implementation of the national Australian Wine Tourism Strategy will be completion in the year 2000 of a National Wine Centre in Adelaide. The State of South Australia has allocated $20 million and the federal government committed $12 million to the project. Its purpose is to serve as a national and international focus for an industry that continues to grow as a major source of wealth and prestige. It is to serve as an icon for the industry, and will therefore have implications for wine tourism.

Interview With Anne Ruston, Chief Executive

Q: What is the tourism connection of this project?

A: The Centre will provide both the wine and tourism industries with a new and exciting marketing tool. There is growing international awareness of Australia as both a tourist destination and a world-class wine producer, so the two naturally go together. Specifically, the Centre provides a platform for delivery of the National Wine Tourism Strategy. The Centre will help make wine a global brand for Australia.

Q: How will it look and what will it do?

A: It will be headquarters to the national wine and grape industry bodies, so research and marketing functions will be on site. Wine education standards and policy will be concentrated here. Wine tourism will have a good home. Certainly trade visitors to Australia will want to pay it a visit, but tourists will equally be attracted and welcomed. Architecturally the facility will be eye catching and sophisticated, reflecting quality and the big picture thinking that is the Australian wine industry. The image will be state-of-the-art, international, and highly competitive. Australia's wine industry may not be as old as its European counterparts, but our ancient continent and the rich environment it provides gives Australian wine a great advantage. It is this unique environment with its clean air, brilliant sunshine, and its rich and fertile soils, which when driven by cutting-edge technology, produces wine that has earned the highest respect in world markets.

It is going to be built within Adelaide's beautiful Botanic Garden, close to the center of the city, with very good access to visitors and residents alike. The site will include a new rose garden of international standard and a working vineyard to demonstrate best practices.

Inside, visitors will receive an interactive, educational experience about grapes and viticulture, winemaking, climate and soils, and wine styles. This should appeal to all age groups because of the interactive technology and entertainment approach. It's an exciting story to tell! And of course there will be an opportunity to taste and smell the products.

Wine appreciation, vocational education, professional development, and Master Classes are all scheduled to be conducted from the Centre. It will also be a venue for wine tasting functions and wine sales.

Q: Why Adelaide?

A: It has to be in a major wine-producing state and a capital city, and South Australia is the nation's leading grape and wine producer. In fact, South Australia accounts for nearly 70% of the half million bottles that leave this country every day, earning nearly half a billion dollars annually. So the state takes wine and wine tourism very seriously—they were the first to commit serious funds to the project.

Q: Some critics have said this Centre will actually hurt wine tourism in South Australia's regions by satisfying visitor curiosity and taking up their time in Adelaide. Is that a risk?

A: I think just the opposite will occur. The Centre will be a logical starting point from which visitors can access information about all the many wine regions. It will be a springboard to travel outside Adelaide and South Australia. The regions will have exhibits, and there will be a wine tourism information office including a booking center.

Q: Wine and food are marketed together in Australia. Where does gastronomy fit in?

A: While wine will have star billing, food is an essential accompaniment. And by presenting food in the context of its relationship with wine, the Centre will not aim to compete with restaurants and wine bars. In fact it is going to be very close to Adelaide's most recognized restaurant and wine bar precinct, so it should encourage outside business.

Q: What is it modeled after?

A: This is the first! Australia is building the first national wine center anywhere, so we are setting the pace. That makes it unique, and an added incentive for a visit to Australia and Adelaide.

WINE TOURISM IN THE BAROSSA, SOUTH AUSTRALIA

Barossa is a brand name, representing a must-visit wine tourism destination in South Australia covering the Barossa Valley and Eden Valley. While a certain amount of wine tourism will occur regardless of planning and marketing, it takes a major effort to position a region at the forefront and sustain its competitive advantages.

The Barossa Visitors and Wine Interpretation Centre in Tanunda was the first of its kind, attracting $400,000 in federal government funding towards the total cost of $1,200,000. It was completed in 1996. Cathy Parsons (1999) noted that the Centre improved service to visitors, helping 66,000 in 1997—up from 55,363 in 1996. A number of important lessons were learned from its development:

• the vital importance of the community and especially local winemakers;

• need for a marketing plan before it opens (12–18 months in advance to get included in wholesaler itineraries);

• a range of promotional materials is essential (they developed a new video to screen in the Centre plus a 2-minute promotional video);

• the value of strategic alliances (working links with, and referrals between, other centers);

• materials for visitors to take away (e.g., cellar door notes on tasting wines);

• use of technology to reduce staffing and operational costs (e.g., they developed an automatic video display when people enter; use of touch-screen information display);

• position the center as the starting point for tours.

Public consultation was part of the project from its inception, plus representation from a variety of conservation and industry groups. Meticulous design standards were set and implemented.

A Commonwealth grant of $39,000 was received by the Barossa Regional Economic Development Authority in 1995–96 to assist in a tourism audit for the region. This supported development of a motivational brochure focused on food, wine, and cultural attractions in Barossa. Each town produces its own town walk brochure, directing tourists through a chosen theme trail, detailing points of interest. It draws together information on regional history, culture, and wine. The South Australian Tourism Commission uses the main brochure in its promotions nationally and internationally.

Barossa Dining

German influences are strong in South Australia's Barossa Valley, both in the wines produced and themed dining. Green-and-white road signs give tourists advance notice of approaching dining establishments, festivals feature food and wine in wonderful, exotic combinations, and picnickers fabricate their own culinary delights to enjoy in the countryside.

The Lyndoch Bakery and Restaurant promises fresh pastries baked on the premises, authentic German brezen, bienenstich, and blackbread amidst Bavarian décor. The local tour company Fruits of Inheritance promises a lunch of wursts, saure-gerken, kuchen, and traditional Barossa food. Maggie Beer, writing for the Barossa Wine and Tourism Association (1996), argued that "No region in Australia has a food and wine culture of such richness and true regionality as the Barossa." Here it is rooted in history. She goes on to say: "From the beginning these settlers . . . planted kitchen gardens of herbs and vegetables, followed by orchards for fruits such as apricots, pears, figs and nuts. They grew cereal crops, cut hay, grazed animals and foraged for wild foods that abounded on the flats and hills." The result? Special meats and smoked sausages, a range of pickled vegetables, dried fruits, whole-grain breads. The changing of the seasons plays a role in determining what is on the menu or available in shops: apricots, almonds, olives. Local freshwater crustaceans called "yabbies" are available fresh in summer and autumn. In winter, it is wild mushrooms, and in spring try wild currants with hare, rabbit, kangaroo, or quail.

Interview With Barry Salter, G.M. Barossa Wine and Tourism Association Inc., and Marketing Manager "The Barossa," South Australia

Q: Why is your position unique?

A: We have a truly special organization here, combining tourism, wine and events all in one organization and office. Its was an amalgamation of three separate groups: Winemakers, Tourist Association, and Barossa

Vintage Festival, so my job is also very unique. It took a couple of years to make that happen but it now gives us a lot of strength and potential.

Q: What is your mandate and scope?

A: BWTA is the voice of Barossa for wine, tourism, and events, all of which are vitally important to our economic health. We provide services to members and visitors, market the region to domestic and international markets, and organize major events.

Q: What are your main marketing actions?

A: We produce regional guides, a calendar of events, regular newsletters, brochures, and other collateral, and do electronic publishing on our Web site (www.barossa-region.org). As well as organizing festivals we do promotions in selected market areas.

Q: You have a new visitor center?

A: Yes, we are proud of our new home, right on the main street of Tanunda in a former restaurant. Government grants helped our association build offices, Australia's first wine interpretive center, and the information center. The Barossa Wine and Visitor Center is open 7 days a week, and it provides information on accommodation and attractions, ticket sales, merchandise sales, and plenty of advice. The center includes an auditorium and boardroom for meetings, kitchen and toilets, and an outdoor garden. Over 65,000 visitors came into the information center last year for information or assistance.

Q: Do you run it all alone?

A: Not a chance! We have a great professional staff consisting of me—the general manager—a tourism officer, administration officer, full-time clerical officer, and a casually employed tourist information staff. Plus, the Barossa Vintage Festival has contracted the services of a full-time manager who works with us, and the winemakers have contracted for a full-time marketing consultancy.

Q: How do you define wine tourism?

A: It's been in existence for over 50 years, but not called wine tourism until recently. To me, wine tourism centers on a key idea, namely: it's not only a great wine, it comes from a special place. And Barossa is a special place because it is one of this country's richest and most famous viticulture and winemaking regions. So people want to see where the great wines are produced, soak up the atmosphere, and experience the lifestyle.

AUSTRALIAN NATIONAL WINE TOURISM STRATEGY

Australia is the first country to develop a comprehensive wine tourism strategy. The federal Department of Industry, Science and Resources has funded a number of wine tourism developments (see Figure 7.1) and in 1997 provided $70,000 to the Winemakers' Federation of Australia for development of the strategy. According to Cathy Parsons (1999) of the Regional and Environmental Tourism Branch of the Department, "it reflects the government's commitment to spreading the economic benefits of tourism to regional and rural Australia and to encouraging the development of linkages between the tourism sector and other industry sectors." Strong financial and organizational support was also obtained from state and regional wine tourism organizations, wine industry organizations, national state and regional industry development organizations, and the Australian Tourist Commission.

John Morse, Managing Director of the Australian Tourism Commission, spoke on the Strategy at the first Australian Wine Tourism Conference, held in Margaret River (at Leeuwin Estate) in May of 1998. He noted the importance of tourism to the nation, as it was the leading export, worth $16 billion a year and accounting for 10% of the gross domestic product. Forecasts suggested that international arrivals would double within 8 or 10 years, partly benefiting from the Sydney Olympics in 2000.

In terms of the country's image, Australia always ranks as highly desirable, but actual conversions into trips are not high. Consequently, the nation's tourism image must be improved and expanded. This is where wine tourism fits in, not only because it adds to product diversity but particularly because wine symbolizes the Australian lifestyle. Wine could become the first global, generic brand for Australia.

John King of Global Tourism and Leisure was contracted by the Winemakers' Federation to develop the strategy. He and his task force assembled available research, visited wine regions for consultations, inspected specific wineries, and identified issues.

- Upper Hunter Tourism Development Plan including promotional material ($90,000) (1993–94)
- Signage for Vineyards, Cessnock City Council ($80,858) (1993–94 and 94–95)
- Barossa Visitors and Wine Interpretation Centre, Tanunda ($400,000) (1993–94)
- Fleurieu and McLaren Vale Visitor Information Centre ($320,000) (1994–95)
- Mudgee regional tourism signage ($35,300) (1995–96)
- Upper Hunter Signage ($61,000) (1995–96)

Grants Made Under the Rural Tourism Program:

- Legends, Wine and High Country wine and food trail, Albury Wodonga ($128,400) (1994–95)
- Barossa Food, Wine, and Cultural Experience theme brochures and map ($39,000) (1995–96)
- Opening the Cellar Door to Tourism, Margaret River ($35,000) (1995–96)

Figure 7.1. Funding of wine tourism projects by the Australian Department of Industry, Science and Resources (1995–1998) under the Regional Tourism Development Program.

The national Wine Tourism Strategy was released as a Green Paper (draft) in October 1998, with the intent of obtaining further stakeholder input prior to the end of the year. It was produced by Global Tourism and Leisure for the National Wine Tourism Strategy Task Force, and released at the Wine Industry Outlook Conference in Melbourne.

> The National Wine Tourism Strategy has been designed to generate clear commercial benefits to the partner sectors in wine tourism development by identifying Key Objectives in the development of wine tourism in Australia, and the Key Strategies to achieve those objectives. (p. 2).

Most important of its recommendations was the formation of a national body to be the focus of implementation of the plan: a National Wine Tourism Council.

The Vision: "By 2008, Wine Tourism in Australia will be worth $1.5 billion, annually; a major source of profits for the wine and tourism industries; a key driver of economic, social and identity development in regions; the enjoyment of wine, food and other associated activities will be an integral part of the Australian tourism image and experience."

The Mission: "To promote wine tourism by creating a diverse range of quality visitor experiences, built around visitation to wineries and wine regions."

Key Objectives

1. Developing a Wine Tourism Industry:
   - develop wine tourism as an integral part of the wine and tourism industries;
   - develop a national identity and culture for wine tourism;
   - establish active partnerships between wine and tourism;
   - identify and eliminate barriers;
   - undertake research to grow the value of wine tourism.

2. Building Wine Tourism Products and Services:
   - develop products and services to meet existing expectations and create future demand;
   - identify investment opportunities;
   - establish product and service standards.

3. Implementing Wine Tourism Marketing Initiatives:
   - develop powerful brand imaging and promotional programs to stress the lifestyle experience;
   - better coordinated marketing;
   - better delivery of information to consumers.

4. Generating Regional Development Benefits:
   - increase economic and social benefits to regional communities through stronger regional identities.

Key Strategies and Actions for the Recommended National Wine Tourism Council

1. Developing a Wine Tourism Industry:

- establish clearly defined responsibilities vis-à-vis national, state, and regional industry bodies;
- the National Wine Centre to provide the secretariat;
- encourage all state tourism authorities to develop wine and food tourism strategies.

2. Interindustry Communications:

- implement a wine tourism awareness program targeting the wine and tourism industries;
- ensure that wine tourism is a key element in the National Domestic Tourism Strategy being developed by the Tourism Council of Australia;
- coordinate the dissemination of products and services to tour wholesalers and tour operators;
- utilize the annual wine tourism conference and Wine Australia for networking and education;
- identify barriers and work to remove them (specifically aim to eliminate the tax on wine samples at cellar doors and other events).

3. Industry Research:

- undertake and disseminate research on: product and market opportunities, product linkages, strategic partnerships, and cooperative marketing;
- work with the Bureau of Tourism Research to expand information on wine tourism collected by the National Visitor Survey and International Visitor Survey, including regional visitation levels and visitor satisfaction.

4. Investment in Management Expertise:

- facilitate improvements in wine tourism management, including establishment of a Wine Tourism Trade Show in association with the National Wine Tourism Conference; develop case studies and cost–benefit analyses of the successful integration of wine and tourism.

5. Skills Development:
  • promote the adoption of wine tourism education;
  • develop and promote the "Aussie Host" customer service training program with the wine industry.

6. Visitor Monitoring:
  • provide consumer research guidelines to assist wine tourism operators;
  • disseminate a wine tourism newsletter and develop a Web site.

7. Building Wine Tourism Products and Services:
  • facilitate the development of touring packages between states including wine and food trails;
  • facilitate wine dispatch systems to allow for efficient international forwarding from wineries;
  • facilitate development of wine and food touring programs and itineraries linked through a common national system of symbols and sign posting;
  • work with state tourism bodies to develop interstate and interregional links including interstate touring, transportation between wine regions, and the networking of wine events;
  • establish a register of wine-related events.

8. National Industry Standards:
  • facilitate the adoption of consistent national wine tourism product and service standards (refine and adapt state-based quality assurance programs);
  • work with state and regional organizations to offer regional industry workshops to promote high-quality service, linked with a national accreditation system;
  • work with the Australian Tourism Commission to establish minimum standards for "export readiness" for the inclusion of enterprises in international wine tourism marketing programs.

9. Implementing Wine Tourism Marketing Initiatives:
  • implement complementary international marketing strategies in partnership with the ATC and Australian Wine Export Council;

- encourage the ATC to incorporate more wine tourism imagery in overseas promotions;
- help develop an international sub-brand for promotion of Australia wine tourism overseas;
- help ensure that wine tourism is being effectively promoted to international tour wholesalers and in-bound tour operators;
- help ensure more effective use of visiting media;
- use "larger-than-life" characters in the wine industry as promotional champions;
- facilitate creation of joint wine tourism marketing committees for key export markets;
- encourage adoption of regional and winery links on wine packaging and promotions;
- facilitate provision of wine region trip planning information to the tourism trade and consumers in key foreign markets.

10. Extension Into New Markets:
- maximize opportunities for wine tourism arising from the Sydney 2000 Olympic Games and other major events;
- extend the conventions and incentives markets into wine regions;
- encourage the pursuit of the corporate meetings market as a key part of future wine tourism development.

11. National Promotion:
- encourage state and regional tourism bodies to provide consumer wine tourism product and trip planning information to tourism operators;
- ensure the proposed national wine tourism Web site contains wine tourism trip planning information linked to state and ATC sites;
- develop a network of regional wine interpretive/information centers, linked with the National Wine Centre.

12. Generating Regional Economic Benefits:
- commission research into the regional economic and social benefits of wine tourism;

- work to achieve the active support of regional communities and government for wine tourism development;
- develop at least two major case studies in wine regions;
- work to encourage establishment of regional wine and food industry networks to focus on branding and promotion of regional wine, food, and produce.

Issues

Who will implement this ambitious national wine tourism strategy? Initial reactions within the country pointed out that no financial resources had been committed to the proposed national wine tourism agency, and to the fact that some of the states were already taking action on recommendations of the plan. Given that states are already highly competitive in the wine tourism field, can they be expected to share the costs of a new agency, especially if it is perceived to lessen their competitive advantages?

Competition among wine regions is at the heart of the problem. The roles of region, state, and nation have to be coordinated carefully to avoid duplication and to maximize cooperative planning and marketing efforts that benefit the entire sector.

VICTORIA WINERY TOURS

Barbara Nixon, founder and Director of Victoria Winery Tours (VWT), delivered a well-received presentation on wine tours to the first Australian Wine Tourism Conference in 1998. To many in the audience, her advice for wineries and destinations interested in developing tourism was very practical, based as it was on experience in several of Victoria's wine regions. Barbara's expertise has also been recognized through her appointment to the Victorian Wineries Tourism Council and induction as Life Member of the Victorian Tourism Operator Association.

The company was founded by Barbara in 1991 as a "cottage industry" based on personal interest. It is now a full-time business for her, with several full-time and part-time employees. Prior to moving to Australia she worked in Chicago and met her husband Bob in an elevator. Now they have their own vineyard in the Macedon Ranges appellation north of Melbourne.

The VWT philosophy is to stress fine wine, good food, enjoyment of the countryside, and a friendly, small-group experience. "We are experts at discovering what the tourist is looking for, and then fulfilling that desire," says Barbara. "Our company owns and operates a small vineyard in the Macedon Ranges area, so our knowledge and passion for Victorian wines, and the understanding of the hard work of our winemakers, is literally from the ground up. We offer informed and entertaining commentary in each of the winery areas, as wine region tours is our business."

Itineraries are flexible, both large and very small wineries are visited, and all the state's wine regions can be covered. As well as small-group tours in two minibuses, they offer exclusive limousine tours with private guides, and programs for larger groups including conferences, corporate functions, and incentive tours. She prefers that wineries provide tastings at no charge, believing that wineries should be able to convert visits to sales. A tasting fee can be appropriate for social clubs or large groups, but not small, dedicated wine tours.

Other products are offered, including a Country Gourmet Tour featuring a master-class cooking hour conducted by Louise Fergusson at the Fergusson winery in the Yarra Valley, combined with a ride on the Puffing Billy steam train in the Dandenong Ranges. Two-day tours are available to more distant wine areas in Victoria, such as Rutherglen or the Pyrenees. The company also does tours of the large, historic Melbourne Wholesale Market where it operates the people-mover system.

Sample Tours

Daily Wine Region Tours

These tours are personalized, small-group tours. A flexible itinerary allows for additional stops at places of interest. All minibuses are air conditioned with uniformed driver/guides. There is a minimum of two persons, with the price set at A$95 all-inclusive through March 1999, covering hotel pickup and return, lunch and morning tea, all wine tastings and entrance fees. The Yarra Valley, Macedon Ranges, and Mornington Peninsula are all regularly covered as these three lie closest to Melbourne and offer both a range of wineries, other attractions, and pleasant countryside.

Yarra Valley Wine Tour

Discover the beauty of this premier grape-growing region. Visit a combination of small and large wineries, including Domaine Chandon and DeBertoli winery. Other wineries may include Yarra Ridge, Eyton-on-Yarra, and St. Huberts. Enjoy morning tea at beautiful Badger Weir where we feed the native parrots. An optional morning stop at Healesville Sanctuary can be included. Lunch at Fergusson Winery is always exceptional, choosing one of the many dishes from our special menu. Lunch and morning tea are included.(Victoria Winery Tours brochure)

A Magic Day in the Macedon Ranges (Large Group)

The Mount Macedon region is an area of gracious living, of remarkable private gardens, an area steeped in history and, of course, the mysterious Hanging Rock. Our tour will take you on a journey of discovery—discover a private garden in its spring glory, view the Port Philip basin from atop Mt. Macedon and the Memorial Cross, learn the facts and fantasy of Hanging Rock, then taste some wine at Hanging Rock Winery. Follow all of this with a regional produce lunch served with local wines at The Grange Restaurant at Glen Erin Winery. Enjoy a three-course lunch, each course served with a specially selected local wine from the Macedon region. This is a tour of the good things in life: good food, fine wine, and the Macedon countryside. Tour includes: entrance to private garden (weather permitting), entrance to Mt. Macedon State Park (Memorial Cross), wine tasting at Hanging Rock Winery, three-course lunch at The Grange Restaurant at Glen Erin Winery, three glasses of local wine, five-star coach, Victoria Winery Tours guide/host. Duration: full day, 9:00–4:30. Price: A$95 per person, based on 20 minimum (valid through March 1999).(Victoria Winery Tours brochure)

Farm Gates and Cellar Doors

VWT is the official tour operator for this new food and wine trail in the Yarra Valley. The local produce has been a passion of Suzanne Halliday of

Coldstream Hills, and the tour was her brainchild. It operates daily and visits four regional producers and a winery for lunch. Among the farm gates included are U-pick berry farms, honey producers, a lavender farm, gourmet mushrooms, venison farm, and orchards. While self-pick farms are more appealing to locals, salmon and trout farms add a new dimension to wine tours.

Marketing

Because so many of our passengers are international, this has a great impact on the marketing strategy. Very little paid advertising is used for VWT. Instead, I prefer to work through local wholesalers who display my product in their color magazines. These color A4 size brochures are branded with the travel agency name. In the case of New Zealand, I work through all eight of the major wholesalers, who offer products to their different chain of travel agencies who are affiliated with them. These wholesalers have started to charge a product inclusion price of approximately A$300 per wholesaler. I still consider this extremely good value.

The breakdown of tour passengers is 65% international, 25% interstate, and 10% from the group/corporate segment. International customers of VWT are 60% from New Zealand, 20% United States, 15% Germany, and 5% other (including Singapore, United Kingdom, Sweden, and South Africa). Approximately 40% of the tours are prebooked, and these are mainly through New Zealand and Qantas (North America). Those from New Zealand who do not book receive a 10% discount voucher that is stamped with the travel agency identification, and it is included with their travel documents. The client receives a 10% discount off the tour price, and we then rebate another 10% to the wholesaler. This is the equivalent of the 20% commission normally charged by the NZ wholesaler. It is a win–win situation, and we still get the passengers on our tours, the wholesaler and the travel agency get some commission, and the traveler has the brochure in hand to read while on the airplane. This is reinforced once they arrive at their hotel, as the brochure is stocked in 120 Melbourne hotel brochure racks via Brochure Distribution Management.

Another form of promotion is through inclusion in the Yarra Valley Wineries Brochure. This has a print run of 200,000 per year, and is widely distributed through BDM as well. However, it also lists three other winery tour companies.

"Fly-Buys" is a loyalty program, used initially for consumers in general to be redeemed for air travel. As many people were losing points (they have a 6-month life), Loyalty Pacific needed more products requiring less redemption points to be included. VWT joined the program in late 1998 and within a few months was averaging about 20 new passengers a month. This is the local market, and one that Barbara was having trouble reaching, as a local couple will not pay $190 to be taken to their own backyard wineries. She deliberately describes the tour as "a day of indulgence" in Fly Buy brochures. Inclusion in this program is used as a point of differentiation from other tours, and she uses this fact in the Yarra Valley brochure.

In North America advertising would be fruitless for VWT, so Qantas Holidays is used as the distribution mechanism. Relationships have been developed with a number of wholesalers in North America who do send clients, but it has proved to be a difficult market to capture. Most Americans who travel with VWT book only when they are in Australia, and most do so the day before they actually want to tour.

Barbara's "in house sales team" consists of hotel concierges and front-desk staff in Melbourne. They provide specific recommendations to VWT, so they are a high priority for further development.

The Internet (www.winetours.com.au) is a good address, but Barbara feels it is not listed with enough search engines. For 1999 she was participating in a trial program with World Travel Net and will monitor the results carefully. Many contacts do come from her e-mail address and about one in ten results in a booking. Her next brochure will have a much bigger pointer to her homepage, and she plans to make improvements to it.

The tour desk at Melbourne Information Centre (at the town hall) accounts for approximately 15% of spontaneous tours booked to VWT. AusRes receives a 20% commission, and it is not resented. Repeat business is increasing from visitors coming back to Melbourne. Referrals are important, but difficult to build.

VWT participates in many overseas and national trade shows held in conjunction with Tourism Victoria and the Australian Tourism Commission. They belong to a number of industry groups, including the Victorian Tour Operators Association, Melbourne Convention and Marketing Bureau, Macedon Ranges Tourism Association, and Macedon Ranges Viticulture Association.

VWT's display-rack brochure features "Winery Tours" at the top and the company name and telephone number at the bottom. A small photo of a wine bottle and food displaying the countryside is accompanied by text under the heading "Daily Wine Region Tours." Also featured is Melbourne Wholesale Market Experience. Inside, a photo and column are devoted to the Yarra Valley, Macedon Ranges, Mornington Peninsula, and Other Activities, with two columns and two photos for the Melbourne Wholesale Market Experience. The fold-in panel provides a "Welcome to Melbourne" and a larger photo of the team—Barbara Nixon and five driver/guides. The back panel provides detailed contact information and space for a travel agent stamp. International commissions are provided for bookings made outside Australia.

Quality assurance is stressed in their promotions:Says Barbara: "Accreditation is the buzz word these days, and yes, we are fully accredited. This means we have a commitment to quality and professionalism, and have passed all the stringent tests of the Victorian Tour Operators Association."

Gift certificates are sold (and mailed) on fine parchment paper. Bottles of wine can be provided with personalized labels for gifts or corporate souvenirs.

Competition

Barbara admits that "competition is good, and it makes me work harder and smarter." Wine tourism is a small niche market, she says, and there are only so many tourists who will dedicate a day in Melbourne to visit wineries. She feels she still has the lion's share of the market, as she gets feedback from the wineries on competitors, but is always looking over her shoulder as competition has increased. The latest newcomer is an operator (an off-shoot of an established tour operation) who started out with considerable paid advertising in print and radio and provides a very similar product.

The tour industry is heavily regulated in Victoria—all operators must be licensed, and safe, high-quality vehicles are required. VWT was having a difficult time renting vehicles on a casual basis, so Barbara led a campaign to get regulations changed. As of January 1, 1999 amendments came into force that now make it possible for VWT to get more vehicles without the cumbersome restrictions that had been in place. However, this improvement might also bring on more competition.

Alliances

Barbara was trying to organize an Australian network of wine tour operators. However, in early 1999 she was deferring that activity in order to see if participation in an alliance called Encounter Wine Tours Australia would pay dividends.

Chapter 8
WINE EVENTS

THE ROLES OF FESTIVALS AND EVENTS IN WINE TOURISM

The wine festival and feast are traditions going back to antiquity, but today they are more popular and numerous than ever. Hardesty (1997) reported that most California wine festivals sell out in advance, and the number keeps increasing! The majority are fund-raising affairs for charity, but festivals and special events can play a number of important roles in tourism and economic development, and all of these are applicable to wineries and wine tourism destinations.

Events as Attractions

Most importantly, wine festivals attract tourists to wine regions and wineries who might not otherwise be tempted, or to make return visits. This can broaden the market for wines and the destination, especially in slow or shoulder seasons, and in rural areas without appeal to all market segments. There are risks, such as attracting people to wine events who are not prime target segments of the wineries, and crowding associated with large events that might reduce the satisfaction of dedicated wine tourists.

Once a wine region develops accommodations, attractions, activities, and services, the pressure to attract visitors all year round will increase, and new events are then seen by the industry as a major goal. Not all of them have to have a wine theme, of course. A balanced portfolio of events will include one or more wine festivals and shows, food, music, and other sport and entertainment. Wineries hosting such events can still realize their objectives, or they can become sponsors and suppliers to events held elsewhere.

Animators

Wineries, for the most part, remain the same for every visit. It is true that new wine releases change the visit somewhat, but that in itself is a great excuse for a special event! Wineries also have to compete with each other as fun, always-different places to visit, and need events for both competitive advantages and to make more money through sales. So wineries are into concerts, food and wine events, meetings and retreats, and many other events that bring people back. Events can also make a theme come to life, such as ethnic cultural themes, or the "good life."

Image-Makers

Every company and destination engages in image building, and events offer a particularly good tool to attract attention, convey positive messages, and foster good word-of-mouth communications. Some destinations can become best known for their wine events, in which case it becomes their "hallmark event." Every destination wants one or more hallmark events that achieve high profile and in the consumer's mind become inseparable. Some wine estates have created their own hallmark event.

In addition, wine-related events frequently occur in cities, resorts, and hotels, which can serve to promote wineries and wine regions, and international wine trade events are an underexploited tool for promoting wine tourism. Sponsors can also be attracted to wine events to communicate with their target market segments. Events designed as platforms for sponsors to gain prestige, make sales or develop mailing lists, host important people, or get media exposure will do better.

Catalysts

Communities attract or create major events for multiple reasons, including using them as catalysts to develop infrastructure that might not otherwise get developed, or to get it done quicker and with external funding. A major wine festival or wine trade show could, for instance, help justify new facilities, or attract a grant. Getting the community and industry groups involved in events can also improve cooperation and organizational and management skills.

WINE FESTIVALS

A number of distinct types of wine event can found. Wine or Food and Wine Festivals have become very popular in the last decade in all wine-producing areas, and these come in several styles.

Community Festivals in Wine Regions

In many areas, especially Europe, the community hosts an annual wine festival to celebrate the harvest or the "nouveau" vintage. Traditional wine festivals have become tourist attractions, but in many other parts of the world wine festivals have been created especially as tourist attractions.

When held in a town, or perhaps at a major wine estate, the problem is to ensure benefits for all other grape growers and vintners in the region. This can be achieved by having them as sponsors or exhibitors, and by selling everyone's wine brands at the one site. However, it will be perceived by many in the industry that multisite events are preferable. One example is the Oregon Wine and Food Festival (www.oregonwine.com/festinfo). This is a midwinter celebration held every year in mid-February since 1983 by the Catholic Schools of Salem, OR, as a fundraiser. It attracts over half of the state's 100 or more wineries and vineyards, plus microbreweries, artisans, and culinary suppliers. At least 10,000 visitors attend from all over the Pacific Northwest. The Oregon State Fairgrounds provides the indoor venue. The program features music and cooking demonstrations.

The Napa Valley Mustard Festival (www.mustardfestival.org) is produced by a local nonprofit, community service organization with a dual purpose:

1. attract visitors during January through March —"a beautiful time of the year when wild mustard carpets vineyards with brilliant hues of green and gold," and

2. promote national and international businesses that participate and sponsor the event .

Visitors are encouraged to explore the arts, culture, and agriculture. Prior to this festival's inception in 1994, a mere 7% of visitors came to Napa during this season, but this has risen to 27%—second only to summer. Some of the festival's attractions include fine art auction; exhibitions; concerts; Savor St. Helena (a downtown wine and food fest); special menus at area restaurants; competition for recipes featuring mustard. Their "signature event" is the "Marketplace" at the Napa Valley Exposition grounds.

Multiple Wineries

The so-called "grazing," "movable feast," or "continuous picnic" event consists of multiple sites at which entertainment, food, and beverages are provided, thereby encouraging visitors to move around. Wineries are the main attraction, of course, although other sites can be used. People are expected to move around on their own, or shuttle busses can be provided.

City and Resort Based

Cities and resorts can and do host wine and food events, and while these constitute competition for wine regions, they also present opportunities for wineries and wine regions to promote their products and attractiveness.

SPECIAL EVENTS AND FUNCTIONS AT WINERIES

Increasingly, wineries and wine estates are being initially designed for, or expanded to become, special event venues. This goes well beyond the hosting of traditional functions like restaurant banquets, cooking classes, or barrel-room tastings, all of which are important. Wineries can be host to small and large indoor and outdoor concerts, festivals involving the host community or a group of wineries, and more innovative forms of entertainment, meetings, and even incentive tours.

McIntosh (1997) argued that the captive audience at winery-based special events is not being fully exploited for boosting tasting room sales. A survey in 1997 of 84 wineries, by *Wine Business Monthly,* found that of those holding special events 40% said they did not view them as ways to make tasting room sales—they were valued for public relations instead. The goals of these events and functions should include attracting more visitors, making them feel at ease and comfortable, and taking the mystery out of wine and wine purchases. Having knowledgeable, helpful staff on hand is vital.

Obviously, some direct connection between the event and retailing must be made if increased sales are an objective. The winery could offer its event guests samples with coupons for additional purchases, or offer otherwise unavailable wines. One-day-only price discounting can be effective. Educational programs and demonstrations might be employed to get visitors into the tasting room or retail outlet.

Wineries planning events and functions must consider their seasonality, as events offer a great way to attract customers in slow periods. Another important consideration is the timing of community and multi-winery festivals, and the activities of competition. For some events it is best to cooperate, while at other times it is useful to differentiate and compete.

Many event and function opportunities for wineries can be identified by examining event calendars and winery promotions. Some of them are more a promotion than an event, but that distinction depends on how it is managed from the visitor's perspective. Many will have a fee attached, while others are free. Most wineries and events have limited and often preset capacities, so tickets might be required, or access and parking restrictions imposed. Major categories and examples follow.

Educational

Cultural tourists want to learn, and the trend is definitely to hands-on, participatory events:

• cooking classes, seminars by chefs, guest chefs;

• winemaker presentations; learn how to make wine;

• demonstrations of viticulture;

• wine appreciation courses; educate your palate or nose;

• lectures on how to develop a wine cellar or buy wine;

• guided tours with interpretation (usually "behind the scenes");

• exhibits (art and crafts, with or without the artists/artisans; winemaking artifacts; antiques; rare autos);

• blend your own wine;

• star gazing at night;

• vertical and comparative wine tastings.

Entertainment

Everybody wants to have fun, so many events feature wine with entertainment or use entertainment to attract new and repeat customers to the winery or destination:

• concerts (outdoors; in cellars and barrel rooms)

• meet celebrities; autograph signing;

• drama;

• dance or ball;

• "buskers" or street performers;

• animal shows;

• karaoke;

• private parties (birthdays, anniversaries, weddings, etc.);

• period or traditional costumes.

Dining and Drinking

Even wineries without restaurants can hold catered events:

• outdoor picnics or barbecues;

• feasts and banquets;

• theme parties (e.g., ethnic foods, wine regions of the world, holidays);

• celebration and tasting of new releases; tastings from the barrel;

• cigar and wine nights.

Business/Trade Oriented

These events are targeted at investors, shareholders, suppliers, and buyers. The tourism trade and hospitality sectors also love to be entertained!

• special retail opportunities (restricted or rare offerings);

• shareholder meetings;

• familiarization tours and functions for media, tour operators, etc.;

• wine competitions;

• free samplings or gifts (by invitation or open).

Recreational

• wine country tours (involving a visit to the winery);

• hiking, bicycling, wagon rides, airplane and balloon flights, cruises;

• sports and competitions;

• nature study;

• scavenger hunt.

Profile: Special Events at Tyrrell's Winery, Hunter Valley, Australia

Many wineries produce their own special events and package them with local attractions and accommodation establishments. Several examples from Tyrrell's follow:

Vintage Weekend: Held in February during harvest, this package includes sampling of fresh juice and newly fermented wine, a tutored sneak preview tasting of new reds, and a Vintage Banquet in their cask room. The 1998 price was A$295 per person (twin share), with two-night accommodation at The Hunter Resort, light breakfasts, escorted winery and vineyard tour, bus transfers between accommodation and winery, and tastings.

Private Bin Members' Hunter Escapes: A range of packages has been offered to members of this private wine-buying club. The "Golf Day" in May involves golf at the area's newest course, Portofino, escorted winery tour and tastings, banquet in the cask room, and two-night accommodation.

THE WINE EVENT VISITOR

As with most festivals and special events, most demand for wine events will be from day visitors within a close driving distance. Those located in or near big cities can expect the largest audiences, although events in resort areas and popular touring regions will be able to tap the visitor market. The biggest marketing challenge faces small events in remote wine regions.

Research in Victoria, Australia, determined that those aged 18–24 years and blue collar workers showed a higher interest in attending wine and food events, but these findings might only be relevant in that one area. Because wine consumption in general is highest among older, higher income groups, there is every reason to expect that wine events can attract the same people. However, the primary target market for the New Zealand Food and Wine Festival, held in Auckland (see the profile in Getz, 1997), consisted of young, upwardly mobile professionals. Their format appeals to those looking for contemporary food, music, and wine in a party setting.

Depending on the key variables of price, entertainment, location and promotions, a variety of segments can potentially be lured. Although families are not frequent visitors to wineries, the right event should have family appeal. A program with entertainment and activities for children will be essential, and the venue will have to cater to the needs of children and parents. So too will the menu.

One of the few published surveys of wine festival visitors is the Barossa Vintage Festival Visitor Survey 1991 by Tourism South Australia, so a detailed examination of this festival is warranted.

The Barossa (South Australia) Vintage Festival

South Australia promotes itself as The Festival State, so it is fitting that one of its best-known wine attractions is the biannual Barossa Vintage Festival. To set the context, an overview of South Australia and the Barossa region is provided.

Internationally, the Barossa is perhaps the best known of Australian wine regions (Fuller, 1997b) owing to its renowned Shiraz, and famous brands like Jacob's Creek and Penfold's Grange (formerly Grange Hermitage). It is also part of the home turf of Southcorp wines, the largest producer and exporter of Australian wine, although the corporate HQ is in Adelaide at the venerable Magill Estate. Other "big names" of the industry, Orlando and Wolf Blass, also claim the Barossa as home.

Located just an hour's drive north from the center of state capital Adelaide, it is easily accessible and offers a pleasant scenic and historical experience. The area's Germanic heritage and Old World, rural charm have helped, as has the high priority the state gives to wine and wine tourism. Wine production in the Barossa dates from the mid-19th century.

According to Ioannou (1997), author of *Barossa Jouneys,* "festivals are an indivisible part of the life of the Barossa community," which today can boast at least seven annual cultural events. The Barossa Music Festival (created in 1990) includes concerts in wineries and churches and helps strengthen the association between culture and wine. The semiannual Essenfest (literally, "eat festival") features regional foods, beer, and wine, and alternates with the larger, more tourist-oriented Vintage Festival. In 1986 the Barossa Winemaker's Association inaugurated an annual Barossa Classic Gourmet Weekend over the last weekend in August. In 1996 it attracted 15,000 visitors for gourmet dining and premium wines at 27 wineries (Ioannou, 1997, p. 159). Live music is featured at each venue.

In 1947, just after the war ended, existing winery events were first combined into a Festival of Bacchus—renamed to the more sedate Barossa Vintage Festival in 1949. Right from the beginning its tourism potential was stressed, and Ioannou (p. 223) credits local winemaker Bill Seppelt with borrowing the idea from the national wine festival in Colmar, France. In 1997 the Vintage Festival celebrated its 50th anniversary, although since

1965 it has been held every second year to avoid clashes with the semiannual Adelaide festival.

Beginning on Easter Monday, this festival sustains the German tradition of celebrating the grape harvest, although in Australia the seasons are reversed. Ioannou also commented upon the increasing commercialization of the event through the 1960s and 1970s when its style became more Bavarian in the belief that it would attract more tourists. The festival also evolved from a broadly based community organization into its contemporary format whereby it is run by a "festival committee" of the Barossa Wine and Tourism Association.

The program is varied and large, involving a number of valley communities and organizations. The event now employs a full-time manager, Barbara Storey, and is well supported by corporate sponsorship.

In 1999, the Festival celebrated 150 years of winemaking in Barossa and combined the best of Barossa heritage—fine wines, abundant food, joyful music, and visual art. It is the largest regional wine festival in Australia with over 100 events in 7 days. These include "Classics in the Quarry," town days with traditional activities, harvest markets, a grand parade, themed lunches, and balls.

Festival Visitors

The Barossa Vintage Festival Survey was conducted in 1991 by Tourism South Australia. It involved interviews with 750 visitors and local businesses and yielded an estimated attendance of just over 24,000 adults. Of these, 7% were international visitors, 15% were from out of state, and 42% were from Adelaide. In total, 84% were not residents of the Barossa. Even though the Barossa is an easy drive from Adelaide, 18% of visitors from the city stayed overnight in the valley. A total of 26% of the visitor trips were overnight or longer (one or two nights being most frequent). Most of the South Australian visitors were regulars, having visited Barossa three or more times during the previous year.

The audience was quite diverse. Twenty-eight percent of survey respondents (all adults) were attending in family groups, only 6% were alone, 36% were couples, 10% were part of a group of friends, 16% were with family and friends, and 4% with a packaged tour group. Those visiting friends and relatives were an important group—local events are a popular social outing when people have visitors to their homes.

Twenty-two percent of interstate and overseas visitors gave the festival as the reason for their trip to South Australia, so it is a proven attraction for the state. This segment is most likely to use commercial accommodation, so their economic impact (or yield per visitor) is high. In total, the festival itself was the main trip motive for 64% of those interviewed and was one reason mentioned by 84%. It is very important to determine trip motives when estimating economic impacts of events (see Getz, 1997), and these data prove that the Vintage Festival generates very high local impacts.

Research revealed that visitors to the festival had spent $1.6 million during the week, mostly on local food, drink, and specifically wine. South Australians spent less than other visitors. The majority of accommodation owners recorded full occupancy, but because commercial accommodation in Barossa is limited, the most popular form of accommodation was private houses. Benefits were spread over a period longer than the festival itself, showing that it generates a major tourism impact.

An important conclusion of the researchers was this: "The Barossa Vintage Festival is one of the State's most significant and widely recognized regional festivals." It has "particular strengths in the State's key positioning attributes of festivals, heritage, food and, of course, wine." "For many, the Vintage Festival is synonymous with the wine experiences, the festive opportunities, the food, the culture and the lifestyle offered by the Barossa Valley and by South Australia" (Tourism South Australia, 1991, p. 15).

WINE TRADE EVENTS

Regions, countries, and industry groups regularly hold small and major trade events, many of which combine "doing business" with a strong consumer orientation. The larger ones tend to be held in major cities, either in the wine-producing country or in important target market areas. The overall goals are to foster sales, and especially exports of wine, through establishment of consumer interest (by way of direct tastings), building trade links (e.g., producers with retailers and wholesalers), and generating positive media coverage. Many wine trade events add a specific tourism component by including tour companies, wine country promotional organizations, and even travel writers.

Wine Australia

The wine industry in Australia established Wine Australia Pty. Ltd. with a mandate to promote the unique aspects of Australian wine and wine regions, to both domestic and international markets, by holding a major event held every 2 years (Sambidge-Mitchell, 1999). Its specific goals are:

- be a high-profile "shop-front" for the promotion of wine and wineries from all the regions (over 40);
- offer visitors a "taste" of each region, including wine and food, tourism products, and geographical differences;
- demonstrate to winemakers the advantages of working together within their regions to develop the region as a single product;
- facilitate linkages between the wine regions;
- allow consumers to "meet their makers" in a relaxed atmosphere.

According to Sambidge-Mitchell (1997), Wine Australia embodies those elements that would presumably form part of a wine tourism strategy: regionality; diversity; unique characteristics; value for money; and fun-filled, interesting experiences.

In 1996 the Sydney event attracted over 25,000 qualified visitors. The venue was an exhibition center themed to replicate a vineyard with real vines, a winery, and cellar environment. Their total budget is approximately A$5 million. The 1998 event in Melbourne had between 350 and 400 wineries participating (maybe 40% of the entire number in Australia!) from all parts of the country, under the auspices of the Winemaker's Federation of Australia. Over 480 winemakers presented more than 8000 labels.

The 1998 event in the Melbourne Exhibition Centre attracted over 28,000 visitors (over 3 public days plus 2 trade days), with particularly good representation from younger adults and female consumers—two important target segments. Some 5000 trade visitors and 1000 international visitors were also attracted. Two of the United Kingdom's top wine magazines, *Wine* and *Decanter,* also had booths.

Marketing of Wine Australia includes appointment of a travel operator with proven success in special event packaging, followed by promotion domestically and abroad. A special committee brings together state tourism offices, the airline Qantas, and state wine and wine tourism associations/councils to increase marketing effectiveness. Some specific marketing actions include:

• Wine Australia tour packages distributed to the regional tour operator network in key overseas markets;

• contacting special-interest groups that might be interested in the event;

• pre- and postevent tours for groups and individuals to the wine regions;

• linking wine, food, and tourism providers in the regions to increase business and trading opportunities with Wine Australia as the catalyst;

• provision of tourism product information leading to tour brochures and packages being assembled in several foreign countries, including Japan.

Related Japanese activity is particularly interesting. Two major tour operators, JTB and KNT, formulated special packages for Wine Australia for both trade and leisure segments. JTB prepared advertising for women's magazines to promote their tours to several countries, with Wine Australia 98 as the catalyst for the Australian tour. Value-added items were part of some of the packages, including a bottle of wine per person for those on the Wine Australia tour who shop in the Gemtec (Japan) store in Melbourne.

Tasting Australia

Tasting Australia is a major food, wine, beverage, and media festival held every 2 years in Adelaide, South Australia. It was inaugurated in 1997, when it attracted 150 international and national food media people, hundreds of industry professionals, and over 30,000 customers. Some of its key goals are:

• provide a forum to present Australia's finest foods and beverages to the world's food professionals, the media, and amateur gastronomes;

• promote Australia as an emerging center for premium food, wine, and associated culture;

• foster media interest with a view to making the nation an attractive destination for international and domestic travelers who enjoy the pleasures of the table.

One of the unique features of Tasting Australia is the World Food Media Awards, a competition among food and wine media. The awards, called The Ladles, are given to such productions as the best television food show, wine book, and wine magazine. Another innovative highlight is the Food and Wine Writers Festival, which showcases Australian and international writers of cookbooks, wine reviewers, and others who write about wine and food. It is held in the Botanic Gardens (future home to the National Wine Centre) and integrated with Feast for the Senses—Tasting Australia's regional wine and food expo for the public.

Other interesting elements of the Tasting Australia program:

• master classes in food and wine, featuring many industry personalities and experts;

• cooks in concert;

• wine tunnel (an interactive, educational experience involving all the senses);

• rare wine auction;

• dinners and wine tastings.

The October timing of Tasting Australia allows it to be packaged with the International Barossa Music Festival and the McClaren Vale Continuous Picnic. Pre- and postevent tours to wine regions are also offered.

Contact: Tasting Australia, Terrace Towers, Level 7, 178 North Terrace, Adelaide, South Australia 5000. Fax: 61-8-8303-2339; Web site: www.tasting-australia.com.au

CASE STUDIES

Festivals of Grapevine, Texas (Visit Their Web Site: www.ci.grapevine.tx.us/)

GrapeFest

Billed as the largest wine festival in the southwest, this annual 3-day celebration is the city's hallmark event, though it honors all of the wineries in Texas. GrapeFest occurs each September over the second weekend of the month.

It began in 1987 as a promotional event highlighting Grapevine and its historic preservation programs. As the festival continued to grow it quickly became the showcase for Texas wines. Some observers actually credit GrapeFest with elevating the industry to prominence, in terms of both quality and credibility. Texas wines were once considered to be tart or flat, but as vineyards matured and sales grew, so did the quality.

Each year the festival begins with the Champagne Cork Shoot-Off, a media event that tests the bottle-shaking, cork-popping expertise of local celebrities, current world/state record holders, and media, as they shoot champagne corks for distance (attempting to beat the 177-foot, 9-inch record). Throughout the weekend, festival-goers experience entertainment and activities galore. Some of the highlights include:

• live music on three stages featuring nationally acclaimed acts;

• the GrapeStomp, a competition where teams of two stomp grapes, "Lucy-style," to produce the most juice within the allotted time;

• the Vintners Live and Silent Auction, benefiting the Texas Wine and Grape Growers, offering domestic and international trips, crystal decanters, cases of wine, art, kitchen appliances, grills, etc.;

• international wine tastings, from more than seven countries;

• boutique wine tastings, from Texas wineries that produce less than 1200 cases annually;

• arts and crafts; food; midway and carnival; children's play area;

• the Texas Wine Tribute, a black-tie gala featuring a silent wine auction and seven-course meal paired with award-winning Texas wines.

One of the most popular events in GrapeFest is the People's Choice Wine Tasting Classic, which offers the opportunity to taste and vote for your favorite Texas wines from over 25 vineyards.

Grapevine New Vintage Wine and Art Festival

This spring festival is dedicated to three of Grapevine's most distinctive pleasures: wine, food, and art. It is held the third weekend in April. The festival begins with the Blessing of the Vines, a centuries-old tradition to ensure robust vines and luscious grapes in which a priest offers a blessing and sprinkles holy water over the vines. The Blessings of the New Releases ceremony serves as the official debut for Texas' new releases. Afterwards, visitors can join a wide variety of activities that include visits to the residential vineyards in the city. They can also enjoy reserve and barrel tastings at a number of local wineries, an elegant chef's brunch, informative seminars, delicious food, and sensational music.

Festival-goers enjoy browsing through the outdoor art galleries and exhibits that are located throughout the grounds, visiting with the artists, and even have the opportunity to commission works for personal collections. Many of the artists are creating their works on site in a number of media, everything from poetry to bronze. You can check out the wine label competition as artists create artwork specifically designed for wine labels. The works will later be offered to the wineries of Texas to use for their new vintages in the next year. For those who are artistically inclined, the festival grounds house three public canvasses, complete with paints and brushes, encouraging everyone to express him- or herself.

Toast Martinborough Wine, Food and Music Festival (New Zealand)

Toast Martinborough is one of the most successful of New Zealand's regional wine festivals. It demonstrates the importance of the community and local wine industry working closely together to set and attain common goals, and it admirably illustrates a distinct form of wine festival. Martinborough is a small town within an easy driving distance of the capital city of Wellington. It boasts 24 smallish wineries that produce a number of varietals, and over a dozen establishments serving food. Not all wineries are regularly open to the public.

Toast Martinborough was created in 1991 to celebrate the area's premium quality wines, together with cuisine from many of Wellington's finest restaurant chefs and caterers.

The basic concept is simple enough, but requires a shared vision and a great deal of planning. For one weekend day a year the town of Martinborough (population 1200) is effectively closed to visitors without a ticket to the event.

Demand for tickets regularly exceeds availability. Tickets are sold nationally, by telephone, through a commercial ticketing agency—and they inevitably sell out very fast. In 1998 the 9000 available tickets were sold out within an hour! On the festival days visitors arrive by car, coach, or train/coach package and pass through security cordons to gain entrance to the town square where they are issued with a Toast Martinborough wine glass and ribboned holder, which act as passes to wineries and the buses. For most of the day festival-goers walk or use the shuttle-bus system to move among the participating wineries where food, wine, and entertainment are provided on a continuing basis. Before departing, visitors can purchase bottles and cases of the local wines in the town square, which features its own entertainment. Discussed below are some of the special planning and management features of this event.

Access and Car Parking

At the security cordon, upon entering the town, visitors in cars are shown which streets or lots to park on. The town square is kept free of cars because of heavy shuttle-bus traffic.

The Wine Glass

This glass comes with a ribboned holder and is the visitor's ticket for buses and venues. Replacements can be obtained for cash, subject to returning the broken pieces.

Festival Francs

Cash and cards are not used at the venues. Rather, visitors purchase "festival francs" at one for a dollar, both in the town square and at seven other outlets at wineries. Sponsorship by a commercial bank facilitates this process, the advantages being:

• security provided by the bank;

• venues do not need to handle cash;

• some visitors might keep francs as a souvenir, which is profit for the organizers; francs cannot be changed back into cash;

• visitors might be tempted to spend more freely, having purchased lots of francs in advance;

• organizers can take their full "cut" when venues exchange francs for real money at the day's end.

Sponsorship by a credit card company (in return for exclusive use of one card) is also facilitated by this process.

Shuttle Buses

Initially buses go to specific vineyard venues, each departing from a sign-posted place around the town square. As venues fill, the shuttles begin making round trips to both drop off and pick up passengers "doing the rounds." Some venues are close enough to encourage walking along streets and roads that are closed to unauthorized traffic. Buses run in both directions and the schedule provides for a stop at each venue every 10 to 15 minutes. The most remote winery (7 km out) is serviced by its own shuttle.

Retailing

Wine bottles and cases may only be purchased in the town square from 3:00 to 6:00 pm, and not at wineries. This regulation relates to the fact that visitors' cars are all parked centrally and it would be difficult to carry more than a few bottles from the wineries. As well, wineries are thereby freed to concentrate on their entertainment and hospitality services. Furthermore, each winery has an equal retailing opportunity in the centralized town square setting.

Officials

Pink-capped festival officials are posted at every venue for customer service, and their uniforms make them clearly identifiable.

Essential Services

First aid and information are available in The Square at the control tent. Washrooms are available in the town square and at every venue.

Venue Activities

Venues compete to offer the best food and entertainment, thereby attracting continuous sales and achieving satisfied customers. The author visited in 1994 and noted that one venue had allowed its entertainment program to lapse for a period, resulting in a total loss of visitors to other sites. Some wineries have earned excellent reputations, so savvy festival-goers head to them first and stake out preferred viewing or picnicking spots where they might remain all day.

Food Service

Food is not merely an essential service, it is an integral part of the attractiveness of Toast Martinborough. For the most part, unique cuisine is provided by Wellington-based restaurants. Local wineries are small and do not have full-service restaurants. The festival program specifies available wines (for tasting by the glass or part-glass) the restaurateur/supplier, the menu (which offers more than one course and several choices of gourmet foods), and entertainment (one or more performers, plus special items like exhibits).

Summary

Toast Martinborough succeeds for several reasons. It is close enough to Wellington and other North Island cities to be a day-trip destination. The town is small enough to permit its effective closure during the festival day each year. The area has a critical mass of boutique and estate wineries, enabling sufficient capacity and choice for a large number of visitors. Industry and community work closely together to achieve their goals. And, certainly not the least factor, area wines have gained a reputation for excellence and reliability.

This format is transferable to many other wine regions, although variations are likely to be necessary. It is essentially a "grazing" style in which visitors are encouraged to sample more than one winery, and while the centralized town square elements allow for efficient control and easier shuttle-bus transport, the involvement of a town is not really essential. Cooperation among the wineries benefits them all through exposure and sales, but competition encourages excellence. (Web site: www.toastmartinborough.co.nz/)

The Leeuwin Concerts

Leeuwin Estate has established an international reputation for the quality of its wines, and for its innovative concerts and other special events. Situated in the heart of Western Australia's premier wine region, Margaret River, the Estate under ownership and direct management of the Horgan family employs events to publicize both the winery and the region, and to generate revenue.

Vines were brought to Western Australia by 1834, but it was not until 1967 that the first vineyards were planted in the Margaret River area. In a very short time span this region has gained a world-class reputation, to the point where it accounts for around 20% of Australia's premium bottled wines (Hardy & Roden, 1995), despite yielding less than 1% of the volume of grape production (The Winemaker's Federation of Australia, 1998).

Wine experts Hardy and Roden (1995) have attributed the wine quality to the area's long dry summers, high rainfall, and great soils, plus the skill and hard work of the wine industry. They also acknowledged the role that Leeuwin Estate and its events have played in marketing the region: "The stature and value of these events for Margaret River are inestimable. Margaret River is a vinous paradise, virtually without equal in the world, and its wines are indeed truly world class" (p. 300).

The Margaret River area can boast a superb climate year round. In fact, Leeuwin Estate has made a specific effort to position Margaret River as the Bordeaux of the New World, with Leeuwin its premier brand. But the region is also blessed with great surfing beaches, unique forests, caves to explore, and natural beauty. Access from the gateway city of Perth is easy, involving something of a 3-hour car or bus drive, and it is also possible to fly into nearby Busselton. Leeuwin Estate has its own airstrip into which it operates daily charter flights to and from Perth. Proximity to the city of Perth (metro population 1.2 million) ensures that weekend and holiday visitation is high, and there is a growing demand for second homes in the area.

Leeuwin Estate was one of the founding five wineries in the region, commencing planting in 1974 and creating its first commercial vintage in 1979. The Horgan family had operated a cattle farm, among other business ventures, and along with others realized the potential for viticulture following state-sponsored research. Denis Horgan formed an association with California's legendary Robert Mondavi, whose advice and profile proved highly beneficial in attracting publicity and ensuring that the Horgans' goals were met. From the beginning, the plan was to produce distinctive wine of the highest quality. Artists were also commissioned to produce paintings to be featured on labels, with the originals on display at the Estate, attracting visitors interested in fine food, wine, and art. By the early 1980s this relatively new wine Estate was attracting over 100,000 visitors annually and this has subsequently been complemented by their special events, with the concerts proving a major attraction from 1985 onwards.

The Horgans are fifth-generation Western Australians. They operate Leeuwin Estate as a family business, with each member playing an important role. Denis has assumed the role of "Founder," and is the catalyst for long-term, strategic planning, promotional activities, and development. Spouse Tricia is Managing Director and is responsible for the day-to-day management of the operation. Their four children manage the activities of Financial Controller, Public Relations, Concerts and Major events, and Direct Marketing. They are an extremely cohesive and closely knit group.

The Synergy of Wine, Art, Food, and Music

The connection with art was developed in conjunction with wine marketing. The top range of Leeuwin's premium wines is known as the "art series," and each year contemporary Australian artists are commissioned for new paintings that are miniaturized onto labels for the varietals. The one exception is the green frog featured on Riesling bottles—they proved so popular that "froggie," in four variations, became an enduring logo. The original paintings of all the art used on the labels are on display in the winery public areas, including the restaurant, but the collection is so big that rotations are required. Longer term plans incorporate the building of an art gallery/function center that will allow for more of the artwork to be on permanent display. The Estate also hosts resident artists from time to time.

The Horgans have developed an overlaying theme for Leeuwin under the heading "The Art of Fine Wine." A specific 2-minute video highlighting the above has been produced and is used extensively in promoting the complimentary aspects of Leeuwin's ultra-premium winemaking activities.

Wine and art make a good combination, especially in light of the up-market orientation of Margaret River, but fine food and wine are inseparable. Leeuwin's award-winning restaurant provides the perfect place for appreciation of the wines with food, and visual enjoyment of the beautiful Estate. Gourmet-quality food is the norm, meaning that discount coach-tours are not an appropriate customer segment. Skilled chefs are also employed to handle the food at functions like weddings, incentive tours, and the concerts. Cooking classes and demonstrations are regularly held at the Estate and are conducted by Leeuwin's own chefs and visiting culinary experts from interstate and overseas.

Music is the third element in creating Leeuwin's unique image and flavor, and this leads into the story of the concerts.

The Leeuwin Concerts

The Leeuwin Concerts evolved as a means to promote the Estate's wines to the broader market, and have grown to become a successful entity on their own. The Horgans comment on the underlying strategy:

> In Australia twenty companies produce 97% of all wine while approximately 1000 others account for the balance. Leeuwin sits amongst this second group as a small boutique producer of ultra-premium wine. As a young vineyard by world standards we could easily have become lost in the crowd. Concluding that we could not justify an advertising budget that would go anywhere near that of the large producers, we decided that as a matter of policy Leeuwin would NOT advertise, and instead would use creative means to establish our identity. Tourism, art, and especially the concerts, have played an effective role in marketing the wines, exposing them to a large audience and generating a sense of familiarity with our product.

First held in 1985, featuring the London Philharmonic Orchestra (and an unrehearsed group of accompanying Kookaburras), these annual concerts have become something of a social pilgrimage for Western Australians. Having tried repeatedly and unsuccessfully to attract local opera, ballet, and symphony orchestras to the Estate, the Horgans finally succeeded in securing the London Philharmonic by sponsoring the orchestra's Australian tour, including performances at the annual Festival of Perth.

The first concert instantly appealed to the Australian psyche, with an audience of adventurous enthusiasts delighting in the picnic atmosphere. The incongruity of witnessing a performance by one of the world's leading orchestras while sprawling on the grass in the Estate's natural amphitheater and sipping fine wines attracted front-page reviews and international press coverage. The idea was an overwhelming success and a tradition was launched.

Following performances by four international orchestras and international stars, such as Ray Charles, Tom Jones, Dionne Warwick, James Galway, Dame Kiri Te Kanawa, Diana Ross, George Benson, and Julia Migenes, the demand for tickets at a repeat performance by Dame Kiri Te Kanawa and the Western Australian Symphony Orchestra in 1995 was so great that consideration was given for both Saturday and Sunday performances the following year.

The decision to expand to two nights was not made lightly. Not only logistics had to be considered, but also marketing issues, accommodation requirements, impact on the district, staffing availability, and the effect on the concert's well-established image. The decision was assisted by the existence of a huge waiting list and a popular performer in Shirley Bassey. Notification to the media of the Estate's intention to hold a second concert was extremely well received and an immediate effect on tourism into the district was witnessed.

At Saturday night concerts two somewhat distinct groups of patrons are to be found. The majority are picnickers who find their own patches of grass, many of whom spend hours on site before and after the concert. They can bring in food, prepurchase Leeuwin picnic hampers, or book into the restaurant. Wine and other food/beverage outlets are available. Musical entertainment is always held after the main event, aimed at encouraging patrons to join in and dance.

A substantial number (about 1600) are corporate guests—the black-tie and evening gown crowd. These sponsored guests enjoy preconcert, afternoon tea/wine in a special enclosure, reserved seating area with short-legged lawn chairs, and a postconcert, lavish banquet with dancing into the wee hours inside a huge, magically decorated marquee. Saturday has been a sell-out at 6500, with slightly smaller demand for the Sunday concerts.

A second major concert has been held every Australia Day since 1990. In large part it is more family and locally oriented to provide an alternative for the comparatively expensive Leeuwin Concerts. This event features top Australian performers. In 1996, 5500 guests were attracted.

Objectives of the Concerts

"To provide entertainment that would appeal to a cross section of the public thereby exposing as many people as possible to Leeuwin and its wines as well as generating substantial media interest."

"To successfully market and stage an 'Australian' concert at Leeuwin to celebrate Australian music on the Australia Day long weekend."

In terms of artistic talent, the aim is to present a variety of entertainment styles in order to appeal to a cross section of the population, each of whom is expected to become a word-of-mouth ambassador for the Estate. To accomplish this, the Horgans aim to "knock the socks off" their guests with stunning quality.

Organization and Staffing

The Horgan family takes direct charge of every facet of event production. This is the responsibility of the youngest daughter, Rebecca, who is supported by the unique and varied skills of each member of the family. Eldest daughter, Simone, is responsible for media and publicity; Justin, administration of contractual arrangements; and Christian, product marketing. An overseeing role is taken on by the parents, Denis and Tricia.

On concert days, some 350 workers are required for numerous specific tasks, including parking, security, staging, lighting, amplification, grounds preparation, signage, portable toilets, bus driving, ushering, catering, serving, retailing, and the clean-up. Many are dressed in distinctive Leeuwin Estate T-shirts, appropriately designated as "Production Team," "Security," etc., with those involved in the corporate guest area wearing crisp, white uniforms to reflect the formality of the patrons' apparel. Some of the details that require attention include:

- special seating for elderly and disabled guests; wheelchair ramps;
- 6000 raincoats purchased in 1996, in case of (rare) rain; shawls available for ladies;
- assistance in locating local babysitters;
- shuttle bus service from nearby towns;
- 1600 low chairs purchased for corporate guests;
- "drink driving" messages are broadcast;
- picnic hampers and discounted Leeuwin wine for sale;
- temporary toilet blocks erected.

A number of community groups (such as sporting teams, church groups, fire brigade, ambulance, etc.) contribute volunteers to the concert, and receive cash donations in return. This policy ensures a supply of local workers while contributing something tangible directly back into the community. As well, some tickets are given to local charities to support their money-raising efforts.

Staff training is given priority, as high-quality service is required. A personal development course is available to all permanent Estate staff and their families. Frontline staff have been through the "Aussie Host" program. Casual concert staff are provided with a tour of the Estate, wine tastings, and detailed briefings. Senior event staff also visit other major events in Australia and overseas, to help make continuous improvements.

In order to provide a unique educational experience, Leeuwin hosts on site up to 20 students at the Year eleven level, and two supervising teachers, during the week of the Leeuwin Concerts. Many students return in later years as casual workers and have benefited in their employment searches from this experience. A quote from Tricia Horgan underlines their philosophy:

> Keeping staff at the forefront of new industry developments breeds continued enthusiasm and vigor into the business, allowing the company to maintain its leadership in respective fields. With competition for top quality staff in a small town we aim to generate not only the best but also the most exciting work environment.

Special events certainly add to the excitement of work at the Estate and throughout the area. Leeuwin keeps on top of event trends, and was a founding patron of the W.A. Events Industry Association.

Tourism Impacts

The annual Leeuwin Concert was planned specifically to attract visitors in an otherwise low period of tourist demand in Margaret River. The concert weekends attract large numbers from Perth and beyond, resulting in sold-out conditions for most of the area's accommodation operators and brisk trade at other attractions and wineries, restaurants, and shops. Some corporate sponsors bring in guests from Asian countries, and many fly in from eastern Australia specifically for the event.

Leeuwin works closely with the Augusta Margaret River Tourist Bureau to coordinate accommodation requests, with the Estate actively finding accommodation blocks for its corporate sponsors. They also organize activities for corporate groups over the weekend so that enjoyment of the district can be maximized. Most area accommodation operators require a minimum two-night booking over the concert weekend, thereby ensuring that event-goers have additional time to spend in the area.

The enormous local, national, and international publicity generated by the annual concerts also reflects the attractiveness of the Margaret River area as a tourist destination. Leeuwin is very proactive about this connection, ensuring that any story about the concert or Estate also covers the area and its attractions. Visiting media people are given tours of both the Estate and district. Few wineries have the ability to generate the enormous media coverage that results.

Wine lovers around the world know the Margaret River appellation and associate it with both quality wines and the warm, sunny attractions of Australia. This is the kind of branding that all destinations try to create, and Leeuwin Estate and its concerts have certainly helped to create and continuously reinforce positive images that lead directly to tourist visits.

The Horgans' philosophy has been to act as a catalyst for wine tourism development in the area. Their efforts have included work to establish a wine tourism group, hosting the first Australian Wine Tourism Conference in 1998, initiating an annual wine dinner to bring key people together, and supporting the annual Margaret River Wine Festival in which a number of wineries host events over the same period. The first Global Wine Tourism Conference is to be held on the Estate in March 2001.

Promotion

More than 10,000 names are on the Leeuwin Concert mailing list, permitting direct marketing for upcoming events and for wine sales. A separate list of some 200 media is used, encompassing national and international press corps who help shape the event's profile. As mentioned, little or no paid advertising is done, or needed. Requests for information pour in all year, growing the mailing list. Many requests are from Western Australians who want distant friends and relatives to plan a visit coinciding with the concert.

A commercial quality video entitled "Philharmonic Safari" was produced the first year, telling the story of the London Philharmonic Orchestra's journey to and performance at the first concert. This was distributed widely and broadcast in a number of countries. Hotels show it on their in-house channel. Produced in conjunction with the Western Australia Tourist Commission, the video also highlights tourist areas throughout the state.

Leeuwin maintains a photo library and broadcasts quality film covering all of its concerts, and copies are regularly distributed to food-, wine-, and tourist-related representatives, along with a comprehensive media kit. Qantas, for example, has used Leeuwin concert footage on its in-flight entertainment. Feature stories have appeared in numerous magazines and television shows.

Journalists and film crews are frequently hosted at the Estate, especially at the concerts themselves, and often in cooperation with the W.A. Tourist Commission. Leeuwin generates frequent press and radio interviews, and works closely with the concert performers to coordinate the best possible publicity for performers and the Estate.

Each year a concert program is produced as a souvenir, featuring the concert, Estate and its wines. Its design corresponds with that of tickets and the T-shirts and windbreakers available at the event (about 3000 are sold annually). Art posters are also distributed throughout the district and in Perth to promote each concert. Postcards of the estate and the concerts are available for sale, plus they are used in the hundreds by the Horgans to directly communicate with potential customers around the world.

Two brochures are produced by Leeuwin for wide distribution. One features the Estate facilities and the other gives an overview to its wines and concerts. A separate souvenir brochure is produced for concert patrons.

Ticketing/Sales

Tickets to the public are sold through direct mail. As the concerts are held over two nights, patrons have a choice of Saturday or Sunday. They are also provided with the opportunity to book on shuttle buses to and from the Estate from various destinations, order picnic hampers, or make restaurant bookings. The ticket price in 1998 was $90. However, this varies with the cost of securing performers.

Corporate group sales are a major element of the Saturday night events. These packages incorporate dedicated bus transfers to and from accommodation houses within the district, or parking, with afternoon tea upon arrival, seating in a specified area on chairs, and an after-concert banquet and entertainment. Participants dress formally and the facilities available tend to attract the community and business elite and lend an aura of formality to the event, while providing an excellent vehicle for entertaining visiting dignitaries and other important clients. A waiting list for participation in this area exists and continues to expand after every concert.

The physical capacity of the site results in a limit of 6500 tickets. While some expansion might be feasible, it is considered this would result in a loss of intimacy and potentially harm the event's perceived quality. The Australia Day Concert is priced at around A\$25 for adults and \$10 for children.

Evaluation

The Horgans do not judge the event's success by sales or profitability alone. Rather, they are viewed as self-replenishing promotional vehicles for the Estate, enabling Leeuwin to reach its target markets in a unique and appealing manner.

As with everything in relation to the Leeuwin Estate, the Horgans have taken a very long-term view. The facilities for the concert are outstanding and have been described by many of the artists as the best outdoor facilities at which they have ever performed. The establishment of both the concert and facilities came at a considerable cost and had generated in the past a cash flow deficit well in excess of A\$1 million. Sales, however, have grown substantially over the years and the concerts now achieve a surplus.

The Future

In 1996 the Estate's new strategic plan focused on wine tourism, setting ambitious goals such as development of the airstrip and the establishment of private dining and boardroom facilities. Specific areas have been designated for vineyard expansion and for tourism developments, including chalets and short-term accommodation, an art gallery, natural flora and forest propagation, and restaurant expansion. Increased wine production is to be sold through the cellar door and exports, requiring increased international promotion.

Consideration is being given to doing two types of annual Leeuwin Concerts, one for classical music and the other popular. There seems to be unlimited scope for expanding the events program in general, including more conferences and incentive tours, corporate events, themed parties, and private functions. The provision of high-quality accommodation on the

Estate is a real prospect, with the orientation being peace and quiet in a unique natural environment combined with access to excellent food and wine of the Estate.

In 2000, Leeuwin Estate celebrates the 25th anniversary of its founding and the 21st of its first commercial vintage. A festival year of events is planned, and although targeted at the local Western Australian community, it will also place a strong emphasis on appealing to Eastern Australian and offshore visitors. The year's program will focus on "The Art of Fine Wine" and will incorporate events to complement the unique environment of Leeuwin Estate and its excellence in the area of wine, food, and the arts. Leeuwin Estate maintains a comprehensive Web site (www.leeuwinestate.com.au/).

Chapter 9

MARKETING
WINE TOURISM

WINE TOURISM DECISION-MAKING PROCESS

To influence the wine tourist, or other visitors who might become interested in the wine tourism experience, a knowledge of the consumer decision-making process is required (see, e.g., Morrison, 1996, p. 91) The basic process as applied to wine tourism is outlined below.

Stimulate Awareness and Interest

• Make potential consumers (including the travel trade) aware of the product, which will include the destination, individual wineries, events, other attractions and services, and packages available.

• Image-fostering advertising is important, especially at the destination level, to sell the IDEA of wine tourism and winery visits.

• Potential consumers require some form of stimulus to identify a need that can be met through wine tourism (e.g., for romance, rural and cultural experiences, getaway short breaks, sophistication).

• It will be easier to stimulate interest among the core segment of dedicated wine tourists, but broader segments must also be stimulated.

Facilitate the Information Search

• Destinations must provide for a variety of information-searching behaviors, including Web sites, toll-free numbers, brochures, travel guides.

• Word-of-mouth recommendations are vital. Positive word-of-mouth communications can be created by satisfying and exceeding customer needs and expectations.

• Go to extra lengths to inform the travel trade, writers, and tour companies. Techniques include familiarization tours, direct sales, promotions, special events, packaging and advertising of specific opportunities.

• Influence the media through ongoing public relations efforts to feature the area and its attractions.

• Advertise effectively by learning how to reach prime target segments.

Combat the Competition

• Consumers have many choices. Direct competitors exist at the level of destinations, individual wineries and services, or specific events.

- Competition should focus on value for money and quality experiences, but might also include price advantages (especially through packaging).
- Cultivating a positive destination image and keeping that image in the minds of target markets is vital.

Make the Sale

- Interest in a product might be high, but the marketer must convert interest and positive attitudes into decisions to travel and buy. Rather than wait for this to happen, marketers learn how to "make the sale," whether it is with tour companies or special-interest groups.
- Make the selection of your product easy, through packaging and eliminating perceived risks (financial, social, psychological).
- For events, cultivate a sense of urgency (e.g., a once-only opportunity).
- Many steps can be taken to facilitate the act of visiting a destination or winery and making a purchase: improving accessibility, signage and specific information to travelers; designing and maintaining attractive properties; providing quality service; offering quality products.

Reduce Post Purchase Anxiety

Consumers often feel anxious after a purchase and during a trip; this is a normal emotion that can be partially managed:

- Provide information that confirms the wisdom of the purchase/trip.
- Exceed visitor expectations.
- Deal effectively with all visitor problems and complaints.
- Monitor visitor expectations and satisfaction.
- Continuously improve service and product quality.

According to Morrison (1996, p. 93) some consumer decisions are routine, made frequently, and require little effort. For example, taking trips to certain areas can become habitual—little perceived risk is involved, and information is already available or unnecessary. Wineries and wine destinations have to spend considerable effort to attract first-time visitors, satisfy them, and turn them into loyal, repeat customers. The concept and tools used in "branding" will help this process, generating tremendous rewards for successful brands covering wine labels, wineries, and wine destinations.

THE ROLE OF "BRANDING" IN WINE TOURISM

According to Fattorini (1997), three major factors in satisfying modern wine drinkers are consistency of quality and taste, branding (easily recognizable and consumer-friendly brands), and brand loyalty and identity. In this section branding is defined and its relevance to consumer decision making—especially to the wine tourist—is examined.

What Is Branding?

Lockshin (1997) provided this definition: "A brand is really a shorthand description of the various attributes that a specific product provides to the buyer. These attributes are perceived by the buyer and may not be objectively measured" (p. 386). According to Miller (1994), brands are more than commodities or products. They are "unique and sought after repeatedly by consumers by name" (p. 284). Brands can be a company's "face," setting them apart from competitors (Bentley, 1998, p. 34).

Consumers are often willing to pay more for their preferred brand, to select it without thought because it is a familiar, risk-free decision, and to choose a recognized brand name over generic or unknown labels. This gives high value to known, trusted brands. Branding helps in differentiating one product, company, or area from competitors. All wines compete, to a degree, because substitution is generally easy—of white for red, French for Californian, cabernet for zinfandel, or one company and its brands for another's. The more recognizable and trusted the brand, the more advantage it gives. Branding also keeps managers and destination planners focused on long-term strategies, whereas numerous day-to-day problems tend to get in the way of strategic thinking.

To create a brand requires a blending of functional and emotional values. It must not only signify quality or value for money, but also generate feelings of familiarity, trustworthiness, or tradition. The preferences, attitudes, and needs of target market segments must be understood before sophisticated branding can succeed, so market research is essential. For example, some segments will react better to a mature, sophisticated appeal and others to a more youthful, popular appeal. A brand will have to be crafted for each of these segments, because they are after quite different emotional benefits. On this point, Fattorini (1997) said that "people attribute certain qualities to their peers on the basis of their wine choice" (p. 30).

"Brand equity", according to Lockshin (1997), "describes a set of assets (or liabilities) linked to a brand name and symbol that adds (or subtracts) value to a product or service" (p. 386). These assets must be managed, and require investment. To the firm, brand equity translates into efficiency and effectiveness in marketing, brand-loyal customers, higher prices and profit margins, brand extensions (adding new labels and products), trade leverage (in dealing with wholesalers and retailers), and overall competitive advantage.

Lockshin (1997) said it is now expensive to launch a brand within crowded categories. There are numerous wine regions, companies, and varieties of wine in the marketplace, so achieving brand name recognition among consumers requires a major effort. For many small wine producers it will be easier to work cooperatively to create a regional brand (or appellation) that will help sell individual wines from the area.

Steps in branding can be summarized as follows:

1. Producing a quality product or service.

2. Devising a competitive strategy to differentiate your product/service.

3. Formulating a concept or idea and a name or symbol to represent it to the public; legally protecting your names and symbols.

4. Projecting the idea through use of the names/symbols in all communications in all markets; be consistent and insistent in their use.

5. The total image of the wine, winery, or wine destination must be packaged.

6. Develop brand extensions (or "spinoffs") to capitalize on successful brands.

7. Protect against counterfeiting and inappropriate uses of brands.

8. Monitor consumer reactions and effectiveness; keep the brands fresh and relevant.

Branding the Winery

Winery owners and managers will understand the necessity of creating attractive brands for their company and wines, but the winery itself must be branded to achieve the benefits of wine tourism. To a certain extent the wine and company brands will sell wine tourists, just as a successful destination brand will bring visitors. But suppose wine tourists arrive and find that the winery does not reflect their expectations as shaped by the wines and company advertising?

Following the branding steps identified previously, here are the necessary actions for developing and sustaining an attractive brand for winery tourism:

• The winery conveys the image of quality wines (not necessarily expensive wines).

• It reflects the positioning strategy of the company (younger target segments will be impressed more with a fun lifestyle than with a sophisticated lifestyle); the winery experience is differentiated from competitors.

• It reflects the branding strategy of the destination (this might require some degree of compromise).

• Symbols and/or names are used to represent the concept (i.e., theming).

• Visitors are educated about the wines; interpretation can be fun.

• Package the wines and the winery visit; be a destination.

• All imagery (wine and winery) must be consistently communicated.

• A well-branded winery can "extend" its product range beyond wines (e.g., programming, events, merchandising).

• Guard against competitors copying your branding and imagery.

• Evaluate effectiveness with target segments.

Southcorp Wines Ltd.

Southcorp is Australia's largest wine company, formed through acquisitions and expansions to encompass many famous brands including Penfolds, Lindemans, Seppelt, Wynns, and Seaview. Major brands like these naturally attract interest from wine consumers and other travelers, leading to winery visits, but does a large company heavily committed to globalization truly gain from wine tourism? What are the costs and benefits?

Until recently, Southcorp was not particularly interested in cellar door sales, as they contributed little to overall corporate income. The cellar door operations had been neglected, while numerous boutique wineries provided most of the impetus for development of wine tourism. However, after the latest major acquisition in 1991, attention focused on finding identities for all the company's brands—a process that led to a new emphasis on wine tourism.

Each of the company's 13 active cellar door operations must now support and reflect its own brand proposition. Brands, such as Lindemans, each have their own highly visible home base in an identifiable wine region, even though all of its wines might not come from that area. Drawing from consumer research, Southcorp's brands are targeted to the preferences of different market segments and consumers are steered towards the appropriate brands.

Cellar door operations are the new public face of Southcorp Wine's brands in the wine regions. They generate profits as separate business units, and integrate the brand proposition into all facets of design, tastings, events, and sales. Each cellar door therefore aims to project the quality, culture, and heritage of the wine and wine region.

Cellar door managers and staff seek to educate their customers, and the focus is not on making immediate sales. While Southcorp has always provided special hospitality to the media and wine trade, now private rooms and access to all wines is available to those willing to pay for the privilege. Functions and events are taking a higher priority, and partnerships with international tour operators are being forged.

Southcorp has a dedicated Cellar Door Management Team. Staff at wineries had to adapt to the new tourism orientation, with a greater focus on customer service and education. Liaison with regional, state, and national wine and tourism agencies is part of management's job, while the company has played a leading role in helping to develop the national wine tourism strategy.

As a direct result of the new branding strategy and tourism orientation, investment in winery facilities has increased. Several have received facelifts and major renovations are being made to the historic Lindeman's Ben Ean Winery in the Hunter Valley, and to Wynns Coonawara Estate in South Australia. Magill Estate in Adelaide remains the company showcase, having undergone a $10 million renovation since 1994, including a world-class restaurant featuring a wide range of Penfold's best wines.

Branding the Wine Tourism Destination

The goal is to use branding tools to position the destination as a highly attractive "wine country," or in the case of a city like Grapevine, Texas, as a "wine capital." "Positioning" is the science (or art) of placing a desirable image in the minds of target markets, relative to competitors. To do so requires market research, segmentation, and consistent communications. Image making for wine country can be accomplished in several key ways, including event marketing, theming, and advertising. Let's look more closely at "theming."

While the term "wine country" in itself appears to have positive connotations in the public's collective consciousness, at least in North America, competitive destinations might want to develop a more specific theme based on unique natural features, heritage, or aspects of their wine. Suitable themes might be:

- sophistication (e.g., the image Napa Valley coveys through its large, impressive wineries, fine dining, art, and charity events);
- rural, small-town ambiance (Sonoma County comes to mind);
- ethnic (traditions and tastes);
- historic (wineries plus wine villages);
- action oriented; "cool" (go after the next generation).

To implement the theme requires use of consistent symbols, messages, and events that celebrate the theme. The choice of a name for the destination or campaign, and a logo, can be important. The entire market mix can be used (e.g., the creation of up-market packages for the sophisticated, and down-home events for other segments). Remember that positioning strategies are aimed at specific target segments. However, incompatibility of messages and visitor segments has to be avoided—groups can be kept separated in time or place.

The successful destination brand will engender the following consumer responses:

- **Familiarity:** they know your name/logo/slogan and what it stands for; word-of-mouth recommendations are very high.
- **Trustworthiness:** your destination delivers consistent quality; problems or complaints are dealt with effectively.
- **Tradition:** events are worth attending every year; heritage is brought alive; ethnicity and regional cuisine are celebrated.

Brand loyalty at the destination level means attracting repeat visitors who prefer your destination above competitors. Events are certainly one way to bring people back, but quality of products and services is the most important attribute the destination can offer. When conducting market research, identification of repeat visitors and those likely to visit frequently should be a high priority.

Brand extensions can also work for destinations. A visitor bureau in wine country, for example, can use wine themes for merchandising (as at the Sonoma visitor center), or attracting meetings and conventions (with pre- and posttours and wine-themed banquets).

RELATIONSHIP MARKETING

As noted in the earlier discussion of sales and distribution options, building and sustaining relationships with customers is an essential marketing process. Relationships are also required with key industry partners, tourism organizations, and suppliers, but in this section we will concentrate on customers. Relationship marketing is based on the facts that intense competition exists for every one of your customers, and that it is easier and cheaper to keep a customer than to acquire a new one. People are more likely to become repeat buyers of brands they know, identify with, and provide the expected level of quality and service.

Every Visitor Is a Potential Loyal Customer

A primary rule for cellar door managers is to never let a visitor leave without attempting to establish a relationship. At a minimum, secure a name and address, either by way of the sales slip, by inviting visitors to sign guest books or enter a contest, or by offering to send them a souvenir calendar or newsletter. Having made the effort to visit the winery, regardless of whether or not they made a purchase, it should be assumed that they are potential customers and/or potential spreaders of good word-of-mouth publicity.

To facilitate future sales, provide visitors with your price list that incorporates provision for the visitor's own tasting notes. Have staff encourage tasters to make notes, if only general impressions of which wines they like. Otherwise, having visited numerous wineries, the customer will likely forget all but a few. To encourage loyalty, send out periodic newsletters complete with special offers. You can either qualify recipients by sending only to those who make a purchase (this could be short-sighted) or to those who voluntarily sign up for it.

The process of relationship building has several steps:

- **First contact:** Their impressions of your winery, staff, service, and wines must be of a high enough quality to command attention and respect.

- **Recollection:** Customers must leave with a favorable impression and carry with them information that will ensure future sales or repeat visits—do not rely on their memories!

- **Reinforcement:** Loyalty will stem from continued contacts, both in terms of information and good quality wines and service. Making customers feel like part of the family is one strategy, while reinforcing their images of wine country romance and lifestyles is another. As with all loyalty programs (note how airlines and hotels do it), customers expect some tangible benefit as well, such as discounts and special offers or invitations to special events.

- **Research:** Monitor trends in repeat visits and sales in order to determine the effectiveness of your efforts. Over time it should be possible to detect the core (most profitable) segments, then give them extra-special treatment. Remember that relationships are for life, so do not abandon the programs if they do not yield immediate returns.

Researchers have identified critical elements in retail relationship building. Macintosh, Lockshin, and Spawton (1998) specifically studied the role of the wine salesperson and concluded that investment in staff training will pay off. They suggested: "Since customer trust appears to be such an important factor, training focused on enhancing customer trust would be particularly beneficial" (p. 13). To achieve this goal the staff and sales people must be perceived by visitors to be honest, competent (knowledgeable about wine), dependable (to give good advice and service), likeable, and visitor oriented. That's a lot to expect from staff!

The Power of Word-of-Mouth Communications

Recommendations or advice from friends, relatives, peers, and influential persons is without doubt one of the most powerful communications media. It can be controlled only to a degree, but it must be a priority nevertheless.

Staff must be made aware of the fact that even nonbuyers are primary sources of communications about the winery and the wines tasted, with potentially tremendous impact on future visits and remote sales.

The Corporate Customer

An innovative relationship-building example is provided by Chateau des Charmes in Ontario's Niagara wine region. This winery dedicated part of a vineyard to Toronto's Royal York hotel. The winery gets a loyal corporate customer and exposure to the public through sales in the hotel. Royal York gets its own quality house wines (which do identify the winery) and its staff help pick the grapes.

Winery and Destination Partnerships

Wineries and destinations must cooperate in relationship marketing. A very specific tool is "database marketing" in which winery contacts are combined with destination-level research to generate increased knowledge of consumers and enhanced, direct-marketing capabilities. This is vital for identifying and keeping loyal destination visitors. A related tool is that of "loyalty programs," such as airline frequent flyer clubs.

Wineries and DMOs should also cooperate to provide repeat visitors with incentives, such as by the offering of a "passport" that rewards visitors for visiting more wineries in the region. Suitable rewards might be discounts at local accommodation and restaurants, souvenirs, membership in an exclusive wine club (providing access to special offers), or invitations to be special guests at events. The more partners involved, the more effective these programs can be.

Internal Marketing

Without the commitment of owners and staff, improvements in service quality and sales will be difficult to achieve. Internal marketing means "selling" the company's philosophy, positioning strategy, and marketing approach to everyone involved so that a uniform, dedicated effort is made. In family businesses this might occur without thought, but when staff are involved the owners must make the effort to train, motivate, and reward good performance.

Destinations have an obligation to ensure that effective hospitality and wine-specific training is available. Cooperation with local colleges and universities can do the job, but establishment of a new program might also be necessary. "Internal marketing" for destinations also means public awareness of the benefits of tourism and encouraging hospitality and good service towards tourists.

The ensuing interview coves a number of points, but in particular sheds light on the branding and relationship marketing of a famous winery family.

Interview With Murray and Bruce Tyrrell, Tyrrell Winery, Hunter Valley, Australia

The Tyrrells run the oldest family winery in the Hunter, possess one of the most famous winery brand names in Australian wine and one of the best-known labels (Long Flat Red), and have been major players in the development and promotion of wine tourism in this region. Murray is the patriarch, famous for his involvement in the wine industry and establishment of the winery as one of the most visited. Bruce, his son, is currently the managing director responsible for operations.

Q: Tyrrell's offers its cellar door visitors free sampling of all your wines, even the best. Why are you so generous?

A: Murray: Since 1960 we have provided all our quality wines at the cellar door because that was, and remains, the best way to convince people to buy our products. We believe direct contact is needed, namely the personal touch of an expert cellar door manager. Cellar door sales always provide us with good cash flow, although the importance of this has declined as wholesale and exports steadily increased over the years. Also, we get lots of foreign visitors and that helps develop the overseas market.

Bruce: I do not believe in limited, set tastings, like many other wineries provide. It is more important to first find out what the customer wants or likes, then cater to their tastes. We want to encourage brand loyalty through winery visits and quality tastings.

Q: Your winery has been a tourist magnet for decades. What accounts for your success?

A: Murray: Partly it's proximity to Sydney. That's a major factor, especially for large tour companies that bring thousands of visitors to the

Hunter Valley. The Tyrrell name is well known, and we have always been hospitable to visitors.

Q: Your winery produces and participates in special events. Are they important for wine tourism?

A: <u>Murray</u>: Yes, I am a big supporter of events—like the new Hunter Valley Festival, which I helped set up and will commence next year (i.e., 1999). It is to be a month-long celebration. But more support from government and major wineries is needed. I want it to be bigger and better than the Barossa Vintage Festival.

<u>Bruce</u>: For the past 3 or 4 years we have produced our Jazz festival right here on the estate. Last year it attracted 5000. But I think the area needs a monthly events program—something happening all year round.

Q: Other wine estates have added accommodation and restaurants, but not Tyrrells. Why is that?

A: <u>Murray</u>: We really do not want to expand. There are plenty of accommodation places, restaurants, and other attractions already in the area. In fact, the development seems to be proceeding too quickly and might eventually threaten the wineries. The local Council and the state (New South Wales) should look at the overall balance between wine industry needs and tourism, and maybe limits are needed.

<u>Bruce</u>: Because many wineries rely on cellar door sales there has been a lot of support for tourism.

Q: Are there other issues you face related to tourism?

A: <u>Murray</u>: Well, staff in general in wineries need better training—to deal with customers and provide education. And we—the Hunter—lag behind other regions like Barossa and Margaret River. There has not been the cooperation here that is required, nor sufficient government support. The visitors we do attract are good quality and getting better.

<u>Bruce</u>: Loss of land is a threat, which gets back to the issue of perhaps allowing too much development. For us, we plan a better cellar door facility, bigger and more visitor oriented. It should be half educational and half entertainment.

Web site: www.tyrells.com.au (See also the profile of Tyrrell winery events in Chapter 8)

THE MARKETING PLAN FOR TOURIST-ORIENTED WINERIES

Marketing the winery as a tourist attraction and sales outlet involves more than promoting its wines, although quality wines in themselves will attract visitors. The tourist-oriented marketing plan must have a clear vision of what is to be achieved, use of the full marketing mix to attain distinct tourism goals, and a unique set of performance measures.

Situation Analysis and Market Appraisal

All marketing plans start with an appraisal of the company's current position in the marketplace, and accomplishments (measured against preset performance standards or objectives). A SWOT analysis is typically used to summarize the following types of information:

Strengths: What is our "distinctive competence"? (i.e., what we do best); what advantages do we have over competitors? Is tourism giving us (or likely to) competitive advantages?

Weaknesses: What have we done poorly? Is our service to customers as good as elsewhere? Do we meet minimum performance standards in all areas of operations and marketing?

Opportunities: What new or existing market opportunities can we exploit? What forces in the environment (political, social, economic, demographic, values, technology, etc.) will impact on our business in the future? For example, what are we doing to expand our scope to include international wine tourists?

Threats: What are our competitors doing, or what might they do, to capture market share from us? Will environmental forces potentially hurt us in the future? A key question has to be: what will happen to our markets when the baby boomers become a shrinking force? Are we prepared for the next generation?

A regular "marketing audit," as described in Chapter 4, should be part of the situation analysis. A detailed process and checklist has been provided for evaluating tourist marketing effectiveness.

Mandate or Mission

What business are we in? Many winery operators think of themselves as being only in the wine manufacturing business, or perhaps agriculture as well. The starting point is to reposition the winery as a tourist attraction, even a destination, with a statement such as this:

> We are a vineyard and winery devoted to the production of excellent wines. Our business is focused on identifying and satisfying changing preferences for wines, while continuing to educate visitors and consumers on what we do best. Our facility will be an attraction in its own right and will offer friendly, knowledgeable service, a range of wine-related products, fine dining and special events, all in a unique, safe and clean atmosphere. Our philosophy is to be profitable, charitable, and environmentally responsible in all our business operations.

The mandate or mission statement provides the starting point for specific strategies. It incorporates the basic marketing orientation and the notion of distinctive competence, or what the business can do best. It might not be appropriate or possible to be a major destination or to have a restaurant. A good mission statement also identifies the commitment of the company or owners to family, shareholders, staff, community, and environment.

Vision

A vision statement is useful for shaping strategies and identifying goals. Where do you want the business to be in 5 or 10 years? Do you want to grow the business and diversify? Or consolidate and stress cash flow? From a tourism perspective, do you want to be the best attraction in the area? Family businesses have to discuss their collective futures together and arrive at a consensus, while corporations typically retain experts to lead them through the strategic market planning process. Here's a sample:

> Our vision is to become a major wine estate destination incorporating a high-volume winery tour, fine dining facilities, substantial retailing, and exclusive overnight accommodations.

Goals and Objectives

While the mission statement is often proudly displayed for public attention, visions and business goals are more private. The main business goals will relate to profitability, return on investment, and perhaps disposition of the business (especially within families). Goals are general statements of what is to be accomplished in order to fulfill the mission and attain the vision. They provide guidance, but do not set specific targets. Major wine tourism marketing goals should cover the following:

• image and theming of the estate (consistent with its wines);

• branding the wines and the winery;

• positioning for competitive advantages, including identified target market segments;

• development of the site, facilities, and events;

• major communications and promotional efforts;

• human resource development (i.e., staff training) for service quality.

Objectives must be attainable to be useful, and specific—pertaining to measurable results. They should preferably include a time frame. For example, specify how many new database entries are to be cultivated (for direct marketing) over the next year. Based on past performance (or expert opinion) set objectives for cellar door sales, visitor satisfaction levels, or the ratio of first-time to repeat visitors.

Selecting Target Markets

Chapters 3 covered what we know in general about wine consumers and wine tourists, but this should be combined with detailed information about visitors to the region and the specific winery. A wise marketing strategy is based on selection of target segments that will meet the following criteria:

• they are substantial and measurable (there are enough of them to make it worthwhile, and you can measure their characteristics);

• they are durable and loyal, making relationship marketing worthwhile;

• they are defensible against competitors (what advantages do you have in catering to their needs and desires?);

• they are quality, high-yield visitors (they want what you have to offer and spend a lot to get it);

• they are compatible with other segments you attract.

Major variables used in segmentation were discussed previously, so now we can identify some logical combinations that might constitute your target segments. Probably the simplest approach is *geographical*, as most customers are going to be from the day-trip region, and mostly from nearby cities. That tells you where to concentrate, but not how or to whom. Armed with the *sociodemographic* knowledge presented earlier, it makes sense to focus efforts on the better educated, higher income, urban professionals of the baby boom generation (and older). For the foreseeable future they are *the* force in wine consumption and wine tourism. But this should not be done to the exclusion of younger people, for this is a great risk they will not follow their elders into the culture of wine.

Greater refinement in target marketing is going to require some research to identify the following potential sources and how to attract them:

• wine clubs,

• food and cooking groups,

• other affinity groups whose members might be interested in wine or wine country tours,

• corporations looking for something different in a retreat location and experience,

• incentive tour companies who bring up-market tours to your region.

Interstate and international markets are harder to cultivate. Work with tourist agencies and inbound tour operators to develop both group tours and car-based, independent travelers.

Relationship marketing can provide the extra competitive advantage. Your database of customers, including their backgrounds, visiting and spending habits, attitudes and preferences, is a source for refined segmentation. A psychographic profile will require surveys or focus groups, but will inform you on the nature of benefits sought by the best customers, and what products, services, and communication messages will work best for them.

Increasing competition will demand attention to the extra details of sophisticated market research and segmentation. The more you know about your target markets, the better you will be in attracting and satisfying them.

Strategies

The generic marketing literature suggests several strategies for any type of business, and these can easily be adapted for wine tourism:

- **Market penetration:** increase sales to existing customers, or increase your share of their wine and wine tourism expenditures; loyalty programs can be employed.

- **Market development:** cultivate new customers, for the same products; international tourists can be your new markets.

- **Product development:** new products to meet consumer demands (this strategy requires research and entails higher costs and risks); adding tourism infrastructure and services represents product development.

- **Diversification:** diversifying from wine production into wine tourism is an example.

All businesses are faced with competition, and must react or get left behind. A wiser approach is to anticipate and get ahead of the competition, for which the basic choices are as follows:

- **Differentiation:** do not imitate other wineries, make yours unique; ensure that your use of the full marketing mix communicates your unique position within the marketplace.

- **Cost advantage:** being cost-efficient can enable higher profit margins while keeping prices competitive (competing on price works for some, as there is always a demand for the top and bottom ends of the price scale, but it is wiser to compete on value for money).

- **Focus:** if you cannot be the ultimate wine estate destination, concentrate on that which you do best and focus on very specific market segments.

The wide range of tourism-oriented strategies is indicated by the case studies and profiles contained in this book. There is plenty of room for all types of wineries and programs: small and large, grand and modest, remote and centralized, sophisticated and "with it," traditional and pioneering. Creativity and practicality combine to meet the business goals through image making, positioning, and branding. Some possibilities, all based on wineries mentioned in this book:

- the winery as museum, art gallery, and monument to taste and sophistication;
- the winery as fun-filled event venue;
- the wine estate destination;

- the family home and business, at which all visitors are personal guests;
- the winery as retail outlet;
- the winery as an educational institution;
- the winery as living history (i.e., heritage).

Wine tourists will relish diversity and originality within every wine destination, so there is ample scope for new ideas.

The Marketing Mix

All elements of the marketing mix are utilized to achieve goals and implement strategies. We follow Morrison's (1997) eight marketing Ps as the framework.

Product

The wine part of the "product" is obvious, but in wine tourism the winery and wine country *experience* is what is really being sold. Its main elements are: fun, educational, emotional, sensual, and social. Packages, discussed later, are products for consumer purchase, as are special events.

People

A major motivation for visiting wineries is to see or meet the owners and winemakers, so they are a key part of the product. So too are informative, entertaining, and helpful staff (who also know how to sell!). Attention to service quality will pay off in sales and loyalty. We have already discussed relationship marketing and internal marketing, which are two critical elements in developing the "people" element. Our previous discussion of service quality in Chapter 3, and service mapping, is also relevant.

Place

The winery and wine estate are the attraction; they must be designed to entice, inform, and satisfy visitor needs. Also consider the relationship between winery and other wineries within a destination. The concept of "critical mass" is important, as are touring routes or "wine trails."

Price

People spend more money when traveling, when having fun, and when staying overnight. The price of wine is often going to be incidental to the price paid for a wine tourism experience, and it can be packaged in this way. All pricing decisions should incorporate the principle of providing value to the wine tourism experience.

Packaging

Work with the destination and other services to develop and sell wine country packages stressing the entire experience. Only a few wineries can be packaged destinations all to themselves. Details on packaging are provided later in this chapter.

Programming

A winery without tours, interpretation, entertainment, and special events is just a factory, retail outlet, or warehouse. It has to be brought to life through programming all year round. What the winery cannot accomplish has to be done through the destination marketing organization or a group of wineries. See Chapter 6 for discussion of events.

Partnerships

Working with other wineries, attractions, and services is essential in wine tourism. The leadership and coordination of an effective destination marketing organization is essential.

Promotions

Communications is a better term to describe the mix of actions necessary to connect your winery experience with the target markets. The essentials are: advertising; media and public relations; sales promotions; direct sales; event marketing; publicity; and word of mouth. Specific recommendations on each are given in the ensuing chapter.

The Marketing Budget

Without doubt, wine tourism depends on joint or cooperative marketing efforts. It is the role of a strong destination marketing organization to ensure that the destination is popular and all wineries within it get their fair share of promotion. Major companies will always outspend the small wineries, but it is certain that a high proportion of visitors attracted to the majors will also visit the small neighbors on the same or subsequent trips.

Performance Targets and Evaluation of Results

What are the key ways of evaluating wine tourism marketing performance? First, objectives have to be set or evaluation becomes very general and possibly misleading. Targets can be for:

• visitor numbers and related sales;

• satisfaction levels and repeat visits;

• word of mouth and other free, positive communications that result from visitors and familiarization tours;

• visitors or sales resulting from specific expenditures (events, advertising, sales missions, etc.).

Investment in general winery or destination image building is difficult to assess, but some expenditure or personal effort on image building is necessary. So too is an investment in community and media relations, even if a tangible payoff is not immediately apparent.

DESTINATION WINE TOURISM MARKETING

A separate wine tourism marketing plan for the destination is preferable, as in itself it will serve to promote and solidify wine tourism concepts. However, there is plenty of scope for incorporating wine tourism within comprehensive marketing strategies for the destination or the local tourist bureau.

A strategic plan for wine tourism (covered in Chapter 6) will provide policies and general marketing directions. The outline of a winery marketing plan, above, also identifies the elements of a destination marketing plan. By way of comparison, Figure 9.1 examines the marketing mix for wineries and destinations, revealing points of difference and complementarity. In this section we can focus on the special communications actions required by wine tourism DMOs.

Many DMO actions must be in partnership with wineries, the tourism and hospitality sectors, and other agencies. Specific examples are included in the following discussion of packaging.

Marketing Mix Elements (8P's)	Winery	Destinations
Product	Wines: winery experiences; other merchandise; branding the winery and brand extensions	"wine country" experiences; branding the destination; awards for products and services
Place	Winery as attraction or destination; accessibility and visibility; site design	Destinations for short breaks, touring, holidays, meetings and special events Critical mass of attractions and services Foster a unique sense of place
Price	Wine value for money; tasting and touring fees	Positioning and Reputation on price; the cost of related services and packages in the area
Promotions	Education of visitors; relationship marketing; event marketing;	Promoting destination first, then individual attractions and services; provide information and wine-themed visitor centers; signage is crucial; event marketing
People	Owners and wine makers as part of the product; internal marketing; service quality	Destination-wide training programs and resident awareness/attitude campaigns
Programming	Bringing wineries alive through interpretation, events and entertainment	Area-wide wine events; involving the community
Partnership	With other wineries, DMO's and the tourism industry	Provide leadership for wine tourism; formulate joint marketing partnership opportunities
Packaging	Wine estate packages; cooperative wine country packages	For different target segments and occasions, all year round

Figure 9.1: Comparison of winery and destination marketing mixes.

Packaging

Packaging is so important it might be considered a basic wine tourism product. After all, many potential wine tourists will not know what is offered, how to experience wine country, or how to assure themselves of a quality experience. The package is what they will buy, and it will shape their experience.

Especially if sanctioned by a reputable body, a package not only shows how to enjoy wine tourism but gives assurance of quality to the consumer. Properly designed, the package provides perceived added value (through a combination of elements that would individually cost more), and by making available combinations or experiences not otherwise available. It must also maximize ease of purchase and provide all the information a consumer could want.

Industry bodies such as visitor and convention bureaus, tourism agencies, or wine tourism councils are well placed to take the lead in assembling and promoting wine tourism packages, in partnership with individual wineries and service establishments. The involvement of a reservation agency might be required.

A number of basic package types are available, and these should be developed and monitored to determine which work best for specific target markets and segments.

- **Self-designed itineraries with a menu of choices:** Let the traveler select where and when they want to go and do, giving them a selection of wineries and services from which to pick (in different price ranges and locations); this type is illustrated later (Victoria's Wine and Foodlovers Short Breaks).

- **All-inclusive wine country resort packages:** Tourists will spend one or more nights at a single accommodation establishment, with all food and winery visits prearranged; increasingly, wine estates are offering these opportunities, but consumers can be given a selection.

- **Event based:** Consumers attracted by wine events will want a choice of accommodation, food, and event tickets; adding transportation is a definite plus, as some consumers will fear traffic congestion and police checks to counter drunk driving.

- **Meetings and conventions:** Winery visits and wine-themed banquets can be packaged for the business event.

- **Group tour packages:** Provide tour operators options for their multidestination tours; these are especially aimed at interstate and foreign visitors who want a taste of wine country in their tour, or are visiting several wine regions.

An excellent example is from the Victoria Wineries Tourism Council. Victoria's Wine and Foodlovers Short Breaks 1998–99 brochure communicates package details to consumers. It promotes a common package for all the wine regions in the state, consisting of two-night accommodation with breakfast, one lunch or dinner, and three bottles of wine from participating wineries. Events are listed so as to encourage event-based visits.

Travelers can design their own itinerary to include two or more regions or add extra nights to the package. Bookings can be made through any AFTA travel agent, or by calling Capricorn Reservation Services. Hertz rental cars are available in the package, making it attractive for fly and drive visits.

Some of the specifics are important. A $100 deposit is required upon book-ing and terms are given for cancellation and amendments. Rooms only can be booked. Valid dates for the prices are specified, as are responsibilities and limitations of the offer.

OTHER ESSENTIAL MARKETING ACTIONS

Familiarization Tours

Fam trips are vital for travel and wine-related media, celebrities (leading to endorsements), influential VIPs (accompanied by media attention), and the travel trade. Usually the DMO organizes these visits, but a winery can take the initiative. A partnership with accommodation, tour companies, etc., is vital. Wine should also be featured in any general-purpose fam tours with-in the destination, including those for meeting planners. Include winery visits in economic development fam tours.

Some wine writers have loyal audiences and so can be very influential, but the majority of wine tourists are not likely to be influenced by specialists. A pri-mary objective should be to get destination publicity into the popular media.

Event Marketing

Events attract tourists, build a positive image, and involve the community in wine tourism. Many DMOs use events as partnership vehicles, to involve their members, and some are able to generate revenue through booking or package commissions, admission fees, and commercial sponsorships.

Developing a portfolio of events is a wise approach. Occasionally host a mega-event, the kind you have to bid on, for the attention and tourists it brings, but concentrate on growing annual festivals and events that can become a hallmark of the destination. Every wine country needs at least one major wine-themed event. The range of events should include public festivals, trade and consumer expositions, and wine shows involving competitions.

Food and Wine

Destinations, or wine associations, have to work with regional restaurants and accommodation establishments to ensure that the appellation's wines are featured. Partnerships with agricultural producers should also be sought so that a regional cuisine using fresh produce can become an attraction.

Wine and Responsible Behavior

Turn a potential problem into a marketing initiative by being proactive about responsible drinking, anti-drunk driving, and designated driver programs.

Introducing Wine to General Destination Visitors

Numerous travelers undoubtedly visit and pass through wine regions without giving any thought to wine-related experiences. Does every information center promote the wine theme? Are wine routes connected (at least by signs) to the busiest highways, airports, and other transport facilities?

One captive market that should be a priority for every DMO is that of residents. The number one source of tourists in most areas is that of visiting friends and relatives, every one of which is a potential wine tourist. Offer incentives to residents to take their guests to wineries (e.g., frequent visitor programs), and to specifically invite guests at times of wine events. Spending advertising dollars on the local market will positively impact on tourism.

Awards

An awards program can not only generate publicity, it will help encourage wine tourism development and improvement. As discussed previously, Australia has both national- and state-level tourism awards that now include one or more wine-related categories. The following categories of award are suggested:

- tourist-oriented wineries (the most comprehensive and prestigious of all the awards),
- winery restaurants,
- winery tours and interpretation,
- wine tour companies,
- wine festivals (community involvement),
- winery functions and promotional special events,
- wine-themed communication material,
- wine-themed services outside wineries (accommodation, dining, manufacturing, retailing).

Tourism-related awards can be presented alongside wine show awards, thereby stressing the wine and tourism partnerships, or as part of broader tourism awards. The awards should be a publicity-generating event in their own right.

To be credible, the awards should be based on applications made according to standard format and adjudicated by impartial experts from different backgrounds.

MARKETING WINE COUNTRY WITH OTHER SPECIAL-INTEREST PRODUCTS

Any number of recreation opportunities seem to be compatible with wine country experiences. Destinations can find competitive advantage through the packaging of wine and other activities.

Golf Tourism in Wine Country

They definitely go together—golf and wine tourism—for several good reasons. Perhaps the most important factor is the similarity of target markets, as both activities attract high proportions of mature, upper-income, well-educated adults; golf, however, has a somewhat higher level of appeal with males. Second, wine country is typically attractive for destination golf because of its beautiful scenery and wide-open spaces. Increasingly, wine country is a preferred location for golf-based resorts and second-home or timeshare developments. There is a high degree of compatibility, but there is also the risk that too much golf and resort development will impinge on viticulture.

The French have been developing golf courses at an accelerating pace, sometimes in prime wine regions. Pollard (1998) visited several, and was impressed by the injecting of their culinary genius into the game—specifically by taking lavish lunch breaks replete with local wines. In Bordeaux, specifically the Gironde area, Chateau des Vigiers is a self-contained golf resort built in 1990. Being a 1-hour drive east of the city of Bordeaux, it is a good touring base for wine country. The resort boasts a 400-year-old chateau, and hundreds of acres of vineyards and pear orchards frame many of the holes. Pollard found their restaurant to be superb, with a wine list featuring the Chateau's own vintages. At Golf du Medoc, Pollard found that each hole is named after a local vintner (e.g., Rothschilds), and tee markers are shaped like wine bottles.

Accommodation

How do accommodation establishments fit the wine tourism theme? Are there specialty types, designs, or marketing strategies that can capitalize on, and support, wine tourism at the estate and destination level? In earlier chapters we looked at examples from wine estates with accommodation on site. In this section we examine accommodation establishments that are marketed with a wine theme, and unique forms of accommodation which seem to fit the wine country image.

Many wine regions already contain accommodation establishments that use the wine theme in their name or promotions. This adds to the positioning of the area as wine country, but raises the possibility that the image can be cheapened by overuse and inappropriate uses. Just what should "wine hotel" or "wine country resort" provide? What standards are desirable? The DMO might consider trade marking key names, symbols, and logos so that control is preserved.

Bed and Breakfast

There is a strong association between wine country and this form of accommodation. Partly it is the low-keyed, intimate, rural nature of many wine regions that lends itself to small, family-run accommodations. Partly it is the fact that B&B has in many areas moved up-market, encompassing antique-furnished heritage homes, which appeals to the same baby boomer market that visits wineries. This kind of high-yield niche market is preferable to mass markets (large tour groups in particular) in many wine regions.

Country Inns

A larger, more commercial version of B&B homes is the "country inn." While no precise definition exists, it can be described as a distinctive form of accommodation signifying a rural environment, strong sense of place, and a cosy, themed atmosphere. True country inns are not large, are usually expensive, and in wine country can be expected to serve regional cuisine with quality local wines. They might also cater to small meetings and incentive tours, but large tour groups are likely not targeted.

Spas

Spas are associated with healthy lifestyles and romantic getaways, so they thematically fit into wine country. Spas variously focus on one or more of the following: pampering, with luxurious surroundings and premium wines and meals; fitness, with plenty of exercise equipment and programming; health treatments. They are not just for older women, as at one time was the common perception. Spas are tapping into the baby boom market and attracting couples, singles, and groups of both genders and wider age brackets.

Self-Catering

Many wine country visitors like to have a self-contained unit, preferably a cabin, chalet, or condo-style apartment, for weekends and longer stays. The key feature is ability to perform normal housekeeping and cooking. These types of accommodation are more likely to attract families.

THE COMMUNICATIONS (PROMOTIONS) MIX

Advertising

Only large wine companies can afford to employ substantial paid advertising, especially television and radio. Advertising is primarily the responsibility of destination marketing organizations, through partnerships with members. However, individual wineries might find it advantageous to advertise in selected magazines and newspapers, assuming target markets have been properly researched. An example could be the inclusion of a paid ad in a travel magazine known to reach the professional class in a nearby city, but to be cost-effective its results should be monitored.

Public and Media Relations

Wineries should work with the DMO to host familiarization tours from the media. Prepare and circulate a media kit, and be sure to invite individual journalists to your special events. Create media events for free publicity. To maximize good public relations, take part in charity events and contribute to community projects. Host local groups (best during slow tourist periods) and encourage them to return with friends and relatives. Start a wine club for residents, or give them preferred access to new vintages and special offers.

Sales Promotions

These are extraordinary actions designed to increase sales, such as sales (price discounting), special events incorporating sales, and partnering with other businesses for cross-promotions (e.g., your wine and their food product).

Event Marketing

Leeuwin Estate, profiled in Chapter 8, shows how this form of communication can work effectively. Events are great ways to establish an image (part of the branding process), attract new and repeat customers, and increase sales.

Direct Sales

The cellar door sales area is an application of direct sales. The value of "relationship marketing" has already been thoroughly discussed. Every winery visitor should be viewed as a potential repeat customer and a word-of-mouth promoter of your products. Direct sales to the travel trade are also essential.

Printed Material

A range of printed material can be employed, either for paid advertising (i.e., distribution to hotels, attractions, information centers, etc., through companies that specialize in this service) or as free handouts and mailouts. Every winery probably wants their own "lure brochure," and these can range from a single card (front and back) to a more elaborate, folded brochure, depending on the cost and purpose. If they are to be displayed in a brochure rack, the size is usually fixed but the design can be creative. At the very top a single message might stand out and catch the eye. For example, "Wine Country" was used by Sattui Winery in Napa, "Top Ten" (best winery tasting rooms) by Dry Creek Vineyard in Sonoma, and "Wine Tasting and Gourmet Deli" by Viansa in Sonoma. Basic information to communicate in the brochure and in other printed material includes:

- images of the winery,
- unique selling proposition (what is special about it?),
- features (dining, shopping, tours, tasting),
- location and how to get there (include a map),

• times of operation,

• contact details,

• advice: are tour groups welcome? appointments needed?

Resist the temptation to include too much printed information, especially if the type is small. Be considerate of the eyesight of aging baby boomers.

DESTINATION PROMOTIONAL MATERIALS

Wine Tourism Travel Guides

There are quite a few commercial wine tourism guides on the marketplace, and more are appearing all the time as the popularity of wine country grows. Official guides created by tourism and wine agencies or industry groups should be different. They are very likely to be picked up in the region, but it is also desirable to get them directly to potential consumers through coupon redemption and toll-free telephone campaigns. They must convey information equitably about all local attractions and services. They will be looked upon as being authoritative — thereby inviting complaints if they are wrong or inadequate.

The Wine Route Map and Guide

A map is the minimum information required to implement the wine route concept, although the best package consists of map, guide to attractions and services, and signs. Guides can be in the form of pamphlets, books, audio tapes, or combined with the map.

Maps that convey too much information will be as useless as those that show too little. Maps aimed at tourists should be tested in advance. Remember that motorists need enough detail to stay on the route, determine exactly where they are, and make optional side-tours if they so desire. Roads are the most important information, not the attractions and services. Use symbols with numbers instead of numerous names to show where the wineries and services are, and key the numbers to fuller descriptions in the guide.

Essential Elements of the Wine Region Travel Guide and Wine Route Guide

• Wineries: location, facilities, and services (especially tours), wines made and sold, special features (e.g., architecture), opening hours/seasons, address and contact details, events; a little profile of the estate, wine-maker/owner, tasting notes, prices.

• Where to stay, including bed and breakfast, country inns, spas, hotels and motels, and self-catering establishments.

• Dining, particularly those restaurants with good wine cellars featuring local wines.

• Shopping outlets, especially those with a wine or country theme.

• Other agricultural produce (especially cheese, fruit, local specialties).

• Other attractions and activities in the area.

• Events calendar.

• Other information sources (contact names, addresses, numbers, Web sites).

For motorists, suggestions as to driving times and direction of movement will be useful, particularly if the routes are long and services sporadic. Maps have to be clear enough to differentiate between rural and built-up areas and to permit navigation within complex road systems. Maps that are not to scale, or are more of a picture than a proper cartographic rendering, will likely confuse visitors. Getting to some wineries will require detailed directions cued to actual signs and landmarks along the roads.

Lure Brochures

Developed for mass circulation, the "lure brochure" aims to make a good first impression of the destination and invite requests for further information. It is generally found in brochure racks at information centers, hotels, and attractions, so its size and format are limited.

Some practical advice can be given on the design and contents of wine country brochures:

• Unusual shapes and designs will attract attention among all the competing brochures; use the wine theme to advantage.

• Some travelers are looking specifically for wine-related materials, so be certain to stress "wine" at the top.

• Including maps that can be used to navigate by car is important.

• Sufficient information must be provided so that the brochure can be used to direct the tourist to the destination and its key attractions.

• Sources of detailed information must be provided (information centers, toll-free numbers, mail addresses).

The DMO should carefully plan brochures and guides with the industry, because confusion and mixed messages can easily result from uncoordinated efforts. Individual wineries put out their own brochures, as do commercial firms who fill their materials with advertising. Be certain to apply the principles of destination branding to all materials.

Events Calendar and Guide

As discussed in *Event Management & Event Tourism* (Getz, 1997), the destination event calendar should be much more than a list of activities. It is an opportunity to portray an animated, all-season destination through themed imagery (especially color photos), and to sell event packages. Although wine-related events deserve their own calendar and brochure, there might not be enough to warrant it. In those cases, make certain wine events get a prominent place in generic event calendars.

Video

Videos of wine country make great souvenirs to sell in information centers and wineries, leading to word-of-mouth (or sight) communications. They are all essential for trade and consumer shows, distribution to tour companies, and for the travel media.

Too many wine-related videos focus on viniculture, rather than the wine country experience. Concentrate on the sensory experience, use events and animated footage of visitors to the fullest, and describe the appeal of wine country visits to a variety of target markets such as the romantic weekend getaway, day-trip, family vacation, incentive tour, or business retreat.

Videos (and other promotional materials) produced on a partnership basis run the risk of featuring only the participating businesses. This is a mistake, because it gives viewers a limited feel for the area. The DMO has a responsibility to portray the attractiveness of the entire area.

Educational Material

The wine and tourism sectors should cooperate to produce consumer-oriented educational materials to complement the wine country experience.

This material would naturally highlight regional wine styles and advise the user on how to get the most pleasure and information out of their visit.

Web Sites

The Internet (World Wide Web) is now jam-packed, commercialized, and increasingly slow. Wine-related sites abound. So individual wineries and regions are going to have an increasingly difficult time ensuring that their sites can be efficiently reached by interested wine tourists. Basic problems with the Web as a research tool (e.g., searching for wine sites in general or one region in particular) became painfully obvious to this author while writing this book:

- Search engines generate far too many irrelevant possibilities and are in themselves difficult to use.
- There are numerous wine-related sites, all of which steer the "surfer" in many directions, and often on wild goose chases.
- Confusion is easy about which sites are purely commercial versus those placed by legitimate DMOs or government agencies.
- Sites should be coordinated, especially destinations and their individual attractions and services.
- Addresses are frequently out of date (and searchers cannot get to the new site).
- Links between sites often do not function as intended.

In short, only the persistent and experienced Web surfer is likely to find your site within a reasonable period of time; many will simply get side-tracked and give up. If they do find you, they are likely to be disappointed with your site, or receive inadequate information and incentives, for the following (well-researched!) reasons:

- takes too long to load (e.g., large page 1 graphics);
- page one is boring, uninformative, or unclear as to contents and purpose;
- entry to your site occurs through a page that does not give direct access to your home page or site map;
- lack of a site map (so users can steer their own way through it);
- inadequate linkages to wineries, other attractions, and services in the area;
- does not provide what potential wine tourists are looking for.

What should a wine country Web site offer? Generically, the Web has several key functions and these are the starting point:

• **Source of information:** The majority of visitors to your site are looking for something in particular, and have visited on purpose; many are pre-qualified potential visitors.

• **Lure:** Some surfers will get there by accident or out of idle curiosity, and some might be converted into potential visitors; is the site attractive and interesting enough to motivate a trip?

• **Filter:** Users have different needs and interests and the site must enable them to find what they want (e.g., there is a big difference between wanting a phone or fax number to call the DMO and searching for details of wine country festival packages).

• **Sales vehicle:** Internet commerce is growing rapidly, but opportunities to purchase wine-related experiences are few and far between; few Web sites contain the "call to action" that advertising should provide.

When designing Web sites, remember that many users have slow, obsolete equipment (2 years and your home PC is no longer adequate for much of the Web software!). Consider the needs of novice users who do not have technical skills and do not know the conventions.

Essential Web site features for wine country:

• lists, and links to wineries and wine-related attractions;

• accommodations, restaurants, and services; ability to book rooms and reserve tables;

• events calendar;

• a virtual tour (photos, music, animation);

• maps of the destination (that can be downloaded and used for navigation);

• packages for sale;

• contact numbers and addresses;

• e-mail box (you need someone to respond!);

• special offers (write, call, or e-mail for coupons, newsletters, wine clubs, etc.; develop a database).

Providing hyperlinks to area attractions and services is necessary, but do you really want your site visitors to click out of your area? Consider carefully what links to include. Perhaps the most important problem is ensuring that anyone interested in wine will get to your site while searching and surfing the Web. Consider the following scenarios. Someone in Europe is searching Australia out of a general interest in visiting there: will they stumble upon a wine-related site? Another wine consumer is looking for wine festival packages in North America: what are the odds they will find all the pertinent information?

To be effective, wine destination sites must be linked systematically (directly or through intermediary sites) to:

• all general wine sites,

• all sites covering the geographic area,

• all winery, event, attraction, and service sites within the area.

In addition, consider linking to other special-interest sites covering cultural, heritage, industrial, rural, small-town, and event tourism. Be part of state- and national-level systems. You have to get indexed by the major "search engines." Some, like Yahoo, require an application and a waiting period while they process your information. That increases the odds you will get indexed in the way you want. Others index your site through use of "robots" that find key words, and that makes it more likely you will be way down the list of someone searching for your type of product or service. Use experts in Web site design to help you through this baffling process.

Advertising the Destination on Wine Labels

Just as every visitor is a potential word-of-mouth marketer, every bottle of wine is a potential marketer for the destination. The wider the sales areas, the more impact this advertising can have, but it requires the cooperation of all wineries. If the label itself cannot provide destination-specific information, why not try to attach a small information card to the bottles or a special promotion inviting contact with the DMO? Assume your appellation is unknown: what basic information do you want consumers to have about the area? This is an opportunity to apply destination branding.

Chapter 10

SUMMARY AND CONCLUSIONS

This book has defined wine tourism, examined the nature of the wine tourism experience, summarized available research, identified issues, and provided practical advice to the wine, tourism, and hospitality sectors on how to develop and market this special form of tourism. Wine tourism presents great opportunities for destinations and for business success, especially over the next several decades when the baby boomers are at their peak of wine consumption and travel. There are many challenges as well, and these must be met in order to assure the benefits of wine tourism will be realized.

In this concluding chapter we start by reviewing major points covered under the headings of The Wine Tourism Experience, Major Trends, The Wine Tourist, and Major Challenges. The most important critical success factors are then covered, stressing those pertaining to the planning, development, and marketing of this growing niche market. The chapter ends with suggested research priorities.

THE WINE TOURISM EXPERIENCE

Wine tourism is travel related to the appeal of wineries and wine country, a form of niche marketing and destination development, and an opportunity for direct sales and marketing on the part of the wine industry. To the consumer, wine tourism is an experience of wine country in which all the senses are involved. It must be fun, educational, culturally authentic, and romantic. The three critical perspectives on wine tourism—that of the consumer, wine industry, and destinations—must all be recognized as having their own goals and priorities, and partnerships are required to make wine tourism work for everyone.

Understanding the wine tourism system is the starting point for its planning, development, and marketing. The interactions of tourists, suppliers, and destinations—through destination marketing or management organizations (DMOs) —define the system. On the supply side, wineries are the core attraction, but other attractions and services must also be provided for a complete wine country experience. DMOs have a number of critical functions, including resource protection, marketing, and fostering collaboration.

When developed and marketed to be sustainable in the long term, wine tourism offers considerable benefits to the host communities and destination, the wine industry, and to tourism and hospitality businesses. The "value chain" concept illustrates how wine production adds economic value to grape growing, and how the attraction of tourists adds value to wineries and communities. Wine tourism and wine sales—especially exports—are mutually reinforcing. Furthermore, wine tourists can be high-yield, quality tourists who travel particularly for the benefits of wineries and wine country, and spend more money. The normal patterns of seasonality of demand in destinations can be countered in part through the all-year appeal of wine, viticulture, and wine-related events.

MAJOR TRENDS

Wine tourism is well established in Europe, where wine routes and the appeal of traditional wine villages, festivals, and brand name appellations will undoubtedly continue to attract visitors from around the globe. In Europe, the links to cultural tourism, including the close relationships between wine and regional cuisine, are at their best. Elsewhere, a number of areas in the New World with growing reputations for quality wines are already popular, and many more are seeking to be positioned as "wine country" destinations. Napa Valley in California demonstrates how substantial wine tourism can become, along with some of the problems success might generate, while Australia demonstrates how the elevation of wine tourism to high priority at state and national levels can ensure its success.

Numerous small (or boutique) wineries have been established, with many or most being dependent on visitors for sales. Some wineries or wine estates have become destinations in their own right, with the addition of restaurants, accommodations, events, and recreational activities. Large wine companies with multiple wineries have also discovered the importance of wine tourism as a marketing and sales tool, especially with regard to branding.

At the destination level competition for wine tourists is increasing rapidly, although the formulation of policies and plans for wine tourism is just now becoming established. In Australia, special-purpose wine tourism organizations have been created. Wine and food festivals and events have multiplied and are enormously popular, and wine tours to and within wine country are expanding in number and size. Competitive advantage is being sought through creation of wine and food packages, wine routes, and events. Although most destinations are planning to develop wine tourism, the evolution of Napa Valley has demonstrated that management of the wine tourism system is essential and that single-minded promotion can lead to unsustainable growth and related problems.

In the foreseeable future, as wine tourism becomes a major niche market globally, and a very substantial development force in successful wine tourism destinations, this sector will receive the planning, management, and research attention it deserves. At the turn of the century wine tourism remains a novelty, but it will soon become mainstream. Tourism is one of the world's most constant and largest growth industries, and all its culture-dependent niche markets are destined to flourish.

THE WINE TOURIST

Not enough is known about the wine tourist, or about how wine consumers can be motivated to become wine tourists. Little research has been done on the effectiveness of marketing campaigns, the success of winery design and events, or on any other aspect of wine tourist attitudes and behavior. This gap has to be filled through cooperation of the wine and tourism industries.

With regard to wine consumption, several important trends must be noted. Quantity of wine drinking is down in many countries, but everywhere people are drinking better quality wines at higher prices. International and interstate trade in wine continues to grow, exposing more consumers to "foreign" wines. Consumption in some Asian countries is taking off. All these trends bode well for wine and wine tourism. Furthermore, wine is now generally associated with attractive wine country experiences, authentic culture and food, and a healthy lifestyle.

Wine consumers, particularly in North America, are older, better educated, wealthier, and more inclined to favor all forms of cultural and rural tourism. For the next 20 years or more, the baby boomers (who were starting to hit the age of 50 in the late 1990s) will be the primary target market, resulting in a golden age for wine and wine tourism. This "boom" does, however, present several crucial challenges.

Wine tourism is closely related to other forms of special-interest travel. To expand its consumer appeal it must stress its cultural and rural connections, and maintain a healthy-living and healthy-environment image. Wine and food help make "lifestyle" experiences tangible. While an association with art and sophistication has a definite appeal, especially to urban professionals in the baby boomer years, the younger generations must be reached in different ways. Younger people, again especially in North America, are introduced to wine primarily through "coolers," and are likely to be resistant to the high prices now being charged for the ever-better wines on the market.

Some research is available to permit a segmentation of wine tourists, leading to better identification of target markets. Success might depend on going beyond attracting the dedicated, baby boomer wine tourist and appealing to submarkets such as young people, affinity groups, general-purpose tour groups, meetings and conventions, and event tourists. At the international level, it can be expected that wine tourists will travel in increasing numbers from and within countries that both consume and import a lot of wine. The main sources will likely be North America, the United Kingdom, several European countries without a wine industry of their own, Australia and New Zealand, and emerging markets in Asia (such as Japan and Singapore).

MAJOR CHALLENGES FACING WINE TOURISM

The Generational Challenge

Baby Boomers will dominate wine consumption and wine tourism for at least the next two decades, but what then? These are the golden years of wine consumption and wine tourism in North America and the industries must capitalize now, but they cannot take for granted that growth will continue indefinitely. Strategies must be formulated and implemented now, or the next generations of wine tourists will be much reduced. In particular, the trend to increasing "sophistication" (read "snobbishness") of the "wine culture," and increasing prices, must be resisted; these two conditions will likely turn off the next generation.

The Health Challenge

Although the health benefits of moderate alcohol consumption are now widely recognized, with wine in particular being associated with a healthy lifestyle, enough questions and challenges remain to ensure that health will remain a major issue. The industries must continue to educate and lobby for recognition of benefits, and must continue to deal proactively with the potential problems of abuse. Stressing moderate consumption as part of an active and healthy lifestyle will likely work best.

The Environmental Challenge

Organic viticulture and winemaking are spreading rapidly, but many environmental issues remain for the wine and tourism industries to tackle. The basic challenge is to preserve and enhance the resources upon which sustainable wine tourism rests, including soils, land for grapes, water for irrigation, community support, and cultural authenticity. Use the "green" imagery of wine country and environmentally friendly practices as marketing tools.

The Challenge of Mass Tourism

Wine tourism and mass tourism are largely incompatible—perhaps not in cities and highly developed regions, but in most rural areas where wine tourism is the major appeal. Most wine regions do not want to become developed to the level of Napa Valley, and at some point they must engage less in promotion and more in destination management. Attracting high-yield, quality visitors through target marketing is the best strategy.

The Challenge of Cooperation

Partnerships are absolutely vital to wine tourism, as they are to many other forms of special-interest tourism. One of the primary roles of the destination marketing organization is to facilitate necessary partnerships and foster a sense of common purpose.

The Challenge of Demonstrating Benefits

To ensure community and political support, wine tourism must demonstrate its benefits and deal with its impacts. Little research has been done in these areas, and few researchers have paid much attention to wine tourism. That is certainly changing for the better, but a consistent and shared research strategy will be required regionally, nationally, and internationally.

The Legal Challenge

Taxes, trade restrictions, land use controls, environmental regulations, drunk-driving campaigns, and many other legal issues face the wine industry and challenge wine tourism development. None of these issues can be ignored. With increasing priority given to wine tourism it should be possible to gain certain advantages with legislators, but that will depend in part on better communication of the benefits of wine tourism and on public support.

The Competitive Challenge

Wine tourism is a highly competitive specialty market, and competition is growing rapidly: more wineries, more aggressive destinations, and more sophisticated marketing can be expected in the immediate future. All the planning and marketing tools explained in this book will be required for successful competition. The following summary of critical success factors points the way.

CRITICAL SUCCESS FACTORS FOR WINE TOURISM

Many factors that can determine the success of wine tourism for wineries, destinations, and related business ventures have been identified through literature review, analysis, case studies, and the special survey conducted in Australia and in Washington State. The most important of these critical success factors have been selected for final emphasis.

Reputation for Quality Wines

First comes the fine wine, then the consumer and wine tourist. Few people will travel specifically to regions or wineries that are not known to produce good-quality wines, and few will travel on speculation without information about good wines they can expect to find. Regions with reputations for consistent, quality wines will do best, and on this point the industry sample agreed completely. Wine tourism can actually reinforce the communication of quality by drawing attention to new wines and to wineries without the means to advertise widely. In this way, wine reputations and wine tourism grow together.

The Tourist-Oriented Winery

Wineries are the core attraction. They must be designed to maximize visitor satisfaction as well as sales. Winery owners and staff are part of the attraction, and training for service quality is therefore essential. The successful winery attraction will provide for the education of guests, direct sales, and relationship building. Attractive, visitor-oriented design is essential to create the right atmosphere, but large scale and sophistication are options reserved for major wineries and wine companies. Conduct a winery audit to discover how to improve visitor appeal and marketing effectiveness.

Unique Wine Country Experiences

Wine regions must stress authentic cultural and lifestyle experiences in which wine is an important ingredient. That is what sets them apart from other destinations. Marketing efforts have to be directed towards establishing the desired image of uniqueness that will yield competitive advantages. This involves destination branding, so that each wine region is clearly recognizable for its wines and attractive tourist experiences.

Attractions and Services: Critical Mass

Wineries are the core attraction in wine tourism. Where there exists a critical mass in terms of numbers, visitor orientation, and quality service, wine tourism will flourish. Most wineries are located in viticultural areas, but wine tourism can clearly be successful by taking the product to the people. Other attractions and services are necessary to support a successful wine tourism industry. Interpretive visitor centers, wine villages, winery and wine country tours, wine-themed festivals and events, wine routes, fine dining, and a range of complementary recreation activities are key components on the supply side. Specialty accommodations, such as country inns, spas, and bed and breakfast, are highly complementary to wine tourism.

Resource Protection

Wine requires special places with attractive scenery and favorable climates. The industry depends on having the right soils and it often needs substantial water resources, in order to flourish. It might come into conflict with other resource users, with local regulations, or even with an unsupportive community.

Therefore, protection of the physical resource base through sustainable development and operational practices is essential, as is good community relations.

Accessibility

European wine regions have a major advantage in being close to very large populations of consumers and international tourists. But some wine regions, especially in the New World, are remote from cities and extra effort is required to lure wine tourists. Wine routes and sign posting are necessary investments. Overcoming the barriers of "perceived distance" becomes a primary marketing goal.

Focus on Quality, High-Yield Segments

Wine tourism cannot be mass tourism. Wineries and destination must pursue the niche markets that will provide high yield (defined as longer stays in the area and higher spending) and high quality (they come specifically for the area's attractions and will respect the environment and community). At some point in their development, the DMO—as in Napa Valley—must focus more on destination management than on promotions.

Leadership and Cooperation

Who will take the lead role in wine tourism, and how will the necessary partnerships be formed? This might be the critical factor separating successful destinations from "also-rans." A key wine company or local winery owner might provide leadership, but it should be expected that tourism and wine industry organizations get together for planning and marketing initiatives. In Australia, which leads the world in elevating wine tourism to prominence, national and state strategies have been formulated, with individual wine regions preparing their own positioning and branding efforts.

Branding

Competitive advantages will flow from successful branding efforts. This is in part "positioning" to certain target market segments, but it is much more. Wines, wine companies, wineries, and wine countries can be branded to attract loyal consumers. Consistent themes used of imagery, names, designs, and promotions are required. Consumer research is required. Quality must be guaranteed.

Specialty Programming and Events

Event marketing brings wineries and wine regions alive, all year round. It facilitates packaging and sponsorship, leads to increased industry partnerships, and can make the difference between "interesting" and "highly attractive." Wineries are great places for functions and special events, while wine festivals help make "wine villages" and "wine countries" especially inviting during off-peak tourist seasons. Events provide unlimited image-enhancement opportunities, free publicity, and can foster community support for wine tourism in general. Every wine region should have at least one "hallmark" wine-themed event that gives it high value in terms of visitor numbers, spending, and exposure.

Packaging

For wine country experiences, as in all forms of cultural tourism, the package often is the product. Free, independent wine tourists will remain the core market segment in many areas, especially those near big cities, but even they can be sold event-related and all-inclusive getaway packages. For group tours and international or interstate visitors, some degree of packaging is highly desirable and frequently necessary to make the sale.

Synergy of Wine and Lifestyle (Food, Heritage, Leisure)

Ultimately, wine tourism is cultural tourism. It is the synergy of wine country experiences, a creative and sensual blending of wine, food, and lifestyle that will continue to attract and satisfy the discriminating wine tourist.

RESEARCH PRIORITIES

This book illuminates what we know and do not know about wine tourism, especially regarding the wine consumers and wine tourists themselves. As more conferences on wine tourism are held, books written, and destinations developed, we will get better at filling the knowledge gaps and improving our collective ability to plan, market, and manage this exciting field. Here are a number of research priorities that can become an agenda for academics, industry groups, and destinations, hopefully working together.

The Wine Consumer

We know that wine consumption is highly correlated with income and age, so that "baby boomers" are the predominant group of wine consumers. We do not know how wine consumers become wine tourists. What are the exact benefits sought? What marketing or destination-specific factors influence the decision to travel? What does the ideal wine tourism experience include, for distinct market segments? Most importantly, how can the next generation of wine consumers be cultivated?

The Wine Tourist

Limited research has been conducted on wine tourists, usually through surveys at wineries. More comprehensive surveys in wine countries have to be commissioned, and compared, in order to examine the entire bundle of wine tourism experiences, including: How can tourists not motivated by wine be convinced to try a wine tourism product? What is the role of friends and relatives in getting visitors to local wineries, and how can that process be heightened? Other key questions are: Who makes the best wine tourist in terms of yield? How can new markets, say in Asia, be cultivated for international wine tourism?

Marketing Effectiveness

Little if any research has been conducted on the effectiveness of wine tourism marketing actions. The main questions should be:

• What imagery and messages work best?

• What are the most effective communications media?

• What types of events and packages have the greatest appeal?

• How sensitive to price changes are wine tourists?

All these questions must be addressed in the context of different target market segments, as each segment might behave differently. Winery and destination marketing efforts must both be examined, especially with regard to the results of partnerships.

Impacts of Wine Tourism

More data are required on the positive and negative impacts of the wine industry and wine tourism on the economy, environment, and community. Like any other form of special-interest tourism, wine tourism has its own unique impacts. These include land use changes, water consumption, use of chemicals versus organic viniculture, impact on traffic patterns, and use of related services and other area attractions. Monitoring changes over time is desirable, especially to determine the long-term impacts of wine tourism development. Comparison of emerging and well-established regions is desirable.

Success Factors for Wineries

Many critical success factors have been identified in this book, including those arising from a survey of industry experts. But how valid are they, and under what circumstances do they work best? This can only be answered through case studies and comparisons at successful wineries, and through examination of failures. There are many possible strategies for success, so examination of many types is desirable.

Success Factors for Destinations

Similarly, the key success factors identified in this book for destinations must be tested in the real world. Cross-cultural comparisons will be useful, as well as comparisons among planned wine tourism destinations and those struggling without concerted efforts. Will the Australian model prevail? What lessons can be applied globally?

Note: Some of these sources proved useful in researching Wine Tourism Management but are not directly cited in the text.

Adelaide Hills Grapegrowers and Wine Makers Association. (n.d.). Untitled brochure.

Adelaide Hills Regional Tourist Association. (n.d.). Untitled brochure.

Allegra, A., & Gillette, R. (1997). *Napa Valley: The ultimate winery guide.* San Francisco: Chronicle Books.

Australia, Department of Industry, Science and Tourism (1996). *Developing tourism: Projects in profile.* Canberra: Author.

Australian Wine Foundation. (1996). *Strategy 2025.* Adelaide: Winemakers' Federation of Australia.

Australian Bureau of Tourism Research. (1996). *International visitor survey.* Canberra: Author.

Barossa Tourist Association and Tourism South Australia. (n.d.). *Barossa Valley scenic heritage drive* [Brochure].

Barossa Vintage Committee. (n.d.). *Barossa Vintage Festival 1997 program* [Brochure]. Tanunda: Author.

Barossa Wine and Tourism Association. (1996). *Barossa Australia* [Brochure]. Tanunda: Author.

Barossa Wine and Tourism Association. (1997). *Barossa South Australia 1997 visitors guide.* Tanunda: Author.

Baum, M. (1998). Measuring and enhancing sustainability in California Vineyards and wineries. *vineyard and winery management* [On-line]. http://wines.com/vwm-online/archive/25-1/sustain.html

Bentley, D. (1998, October). Stand by your brand. *United Airlines Hemispheres, 34.*

Bitner, M. (1993). Managing the evidence of service. In E. Scheuing & W. Christopher (Eds.), *The service quality handbook* (pp. 358–370). Amacom.

Boddy, T. (1998, October 21). Where grapes of hope are stored. *The Globe and Mail,* p. A-17.

Bramwell, B. (1993). *Tourism strategies and rural development.* Paris: OECD.

Budd, J. (1996). *Appreciating fine wines.* London: Chartwell Books/Quintet Publishing.

Cambourne, B. (1999). Creating tourism vintages: A practitioner's guide to wine tourism. In R. Dowling & J. Carlsen (Eds.), *Wine tourism: Perfect partners. Proceedings of the first Australian wine tourism conference, Margaret River, May, 1998* (pp. 51–71). Canberra: Bureau of Tourism Research.

Campbell, B. (n.d.). *New Zealand wine annual 1998.* Auckland: Cuisine Publications Ltd.

Canadian Tourism Commission. (1998). *The American tourist market evaluation to 2010.* Ottawa: Author.

Cartiere, R. (1997, July). After aging baby boomers, who is the next generation? *Wine Business Monthly, 4*(7).

Chateau des Charmes. (1998). *Heritage of fine wines* [Newspaper advertising supplement]. Niagara-on-the-Lake.

Chidley, J. (1998a, August 24). Haute Canuck. *Macleans: Canada's Weekly Newsmagazine,* 36–40.

Chidley, J. (1998b, August 24). Grape white north: Canada is now a producer of exquisite, prize-winning wines. *Macleans: Canada's Weekly Newsmagazine,* 42–43.

Choisy, C. (1996). Le poids du tourisme viti-vinicole. *Espaces, 140,* 30–33.

Commonwealth Department of Tourism, Australia. (1994). *National rural tourism strategy.* Canberra: Author.

Conaway, J. (1990). *Napa.* New York: Avon Books.

Cox, G. (1998, October/November). Sonoma County's tasting room treasures. *The Wine News,* 38–42

Crockett, S. (1999). The Western Australian perspective: A tale of two regions. In R. Dowling & J. Carlsen (Eds.), W*ine tourism: Perfect partners. Proceedings of the first Australian wine tourism conference, Margaret River, May, 1998* (pp. 185–190). Canberra: Bureau of Tourism Research.

Cusick, H., & Gillette, R. (1995). *Sonoma: The ultimate winery guide.* San Francisco: Chronicle Books.

Davidson, C. (1998). The Montalchino syndrome. *WineX Magazine, 3*(2), 42–46.

Dawes, G. (1998, October/November). The Basque country: A wine and food pilgrimage through northern Spain. *The Wine News,* 50–55.

Delroy, N. (1998). *Viticulture 2000.* Paper presented to a seminar on Agribusiness Research and Management, Margaret River, Western Australia.

Desplats, B. (1996). Un tourisme valorise ou valorisant? Examples compares de L'Armagnac et du Cognac. *Espaces, 140,* 34–42.

Deves, M. (Ed.) (1995). T*he Australian and New Zealand wine industry directory* (13th annual edition). Marleston: Winetitles.

Deves, M. (1997a). Regional report: Sea and vines, McClaren Vale. *Wine Industry Journal, 12*(1), 15–28.

Deves, M. (1997b). Art features in state-of-the-art winery. *Wine Industry Journal, 12*(4), 375–376.

Deutsche Weinakademie. (1997). *Wine drinking and health.* Mainz: Author.

Deutsche Weinakademie. (1996). *A short guide to German wines.* Mainz: Author.

Deutsche Weininstitut. (1993-1994). *The wines of Germany.* Mainz: Author.

Dodd, T. (1995). Opportunities and pitfalls of tourism in a developing wine industry. *International Journal of Wine Marketing, 7*(1), 5–16.

Dodd, T., & Bigotte, V. (1997). Perceptual differences among visitor groups to wineries. *Journal of Travel Research, 35*(3), 46–51.

Doerper, J. (1996). *Wine country: California's Napa and Sonoma Counties.* Oakland, CA: Compass American Guides.

Dowling, R., & Carlsen, J. (Eds.) (1999). *Wine tourism: Perfect partners. Proceedings of the first Australian wine tourism conference, Margaret River, Western Australia, May 1998.* Canberra: Bureau of Tourism Research.

Dunstan, D. (1990). Victoria's historic wineries: A resource for tourism? *Historic Environment, 7*(3/4), 47–54.

Edmondson, B. (1998, March). The line between beer and wine. *American Demographics,* 18–19.

Eilender, E. (1998, June 15). Food for thought. *Wine Spectator* [On-line, article archives]. www.winespectator.com

Elkjer, T. (1998, June 15). Blast from the past. *Wine Spectator* [On-line, article archives]. www.winespectator.com

Euromonitor (1998, November 21). Report on global wine industry. *Calgary Herald,* p. E9.

Farrell, E. (1997, March). Wining and dining on the Rhine. *Europe, 364,* 33–35.

Fattorini, J. (1997). *Managing wine and wine sales.* London: Thomson International Business Press.

Folwell, R., & Grasell, M. (1989). *Characteristics of tasting rooms in Washington wineries* (Research Bulletin XB1013). Pullman: College of Agriculture and Home Economics Research Center, Washington State University.

Foot, D. (1996). *Boom bust and echo: How to profit from the coming demographic shift.* Toronto: Macfarlane Walter and Ross.

Fuller, P. (1997). Value adding the regional wine experience. *Wine Industry Journal, 12*(1), 35–39.

Fuller, P. (1997). The Barossa: An old, new world region comes of age. *Wine Industry Journal, 12*(4), 328–339.

Getz, D. (1993). Tourist shopping villages: Development and planning strategies. *Tourism Management,* 14(1), 15–26.

Getz, D. (1997). *Event management & event tourism.* New York: Cognizant Communication.

Getz, D. (1999). Wine tourism: Global overview and perspective on its development. In R. Dowling & J. Carlsen (Eds.), *Wine tourism: Perfect partners. Proceedings of the first Australian wine tourism conference, Margaret River, May, 1998* (pp. 13–33). Canberra: Bureau of Tourism Research.

Gilbert, D. (1990). Touristic development of a viticultural region of Spain. *International Journal of Wine Marketing, 4*(2), 25–32.

Global Tourism and Leisure. (1998). *National wine tourism strategy green paper* (Draft). Winemakers' Federation of Australia Inc.

Great Southern Touring Route Committee. (n.d.). *Great southern food and wine guide.* Victoria: Author.

Hackett, N. (1997). *Surprise success: Wine, tourists, and the woes of free trade.* Paper presented to the TTRA annual conference, Virginia.

Hackett, N. (1998). *Vines, wines, and visitors: A case study of agricultural diversification into winery tourism.* Unpublished thesis, Master of Natural Resource Management, Simon Fraser University.

Hall, M., & Johnson, G. (1999). Wine and tourism: An imbalanced partnership? In R. Dowling & J. Carlsen (Eds.), *Wine tourism: Perfect partners. Proceedings of the first Australian wine tourism conference, Margaret River, May, 1998* (pp. 51–71). Canberra: Bureau of Tourism Research.

Hall, M., & Macionis, N. (1998). Wine tourism in Australia and New Zealand. In R. Butler, M. Hall, & J. Jenkins (Eds.), *Tourism and recreation in rural areas* (pp. 197–224). Chichester: Wiley.

Hardesty, K. (1997, February 28.). Where the wines are. *Wine Spectator* [On-line, article archives]. www.wine-spectator.com

Hardy, T., & Roden, M. (1995). *Australian wine: A pictorial guide.* Unley South Australia: Winestate Publications.

Howley, M., & van Westering, J. (1999). Wine tourism in the United Kingdom. In R. Dowling & J. Carlsen (Eds.), *Wine tourism: Perfect partners. Proceedings of the first Australian wine tourism conference, Margaret River, May, 1998* (pp. 73–80). Canberra: Bureau of Tourism Research.

Iland, P., & Gago, P. (1997). *Australian wine: From the vine to the glass.* Adelaide: Patrick Iland Wine Promotions.

Iles-Hunt, E. (1998). *Marketing and promotional techniques used by English vineyards.* Unpublished Honors thesis, Thames Valley University.

Ioannou, N. (1997). *Barossa journeys: Into a valley of tradition.* Kent Town, South Australia: Paringa Press.

Johnson, G., 1997. Surveying wine tourism in New Zealand. In *Quality tourism: Beyond the masses. Proceedings of the first national tourism students' conference* (pp. 61–66). Dunedin: The Tourism Club, University of Otago.

Kaplan, S., Smith, B., & Weiss, M. (1996). *Exploring wine.* New York: Van Nostrand Reinhold and the Culinary Institute of America.

Kenihan, K. (1991, March). Sparkling times in Barossa. *The Australian Way,* 27–31.

King, C., & Morris, R. (1997). To taste or not to taste: To charge or not to charge. *Wine Industry Journal, 12*(4), 381–384.

Lane, B. (1994). What is rural tourism? *Journal of Sustainable Tourism, 2,* 7–21.

Laws, E. (1995). *Tourist destination management.* London: Routledge.

Lawson, R., Thyne, M., & Young, T. (1997). *New Zealand holidays: A travel lifestyles study.* Dunedin: Department of Marketing, University of Otago.

Leiper, N., & Carlsen, J. (1998). Strategies for winery managers contemplating tourist markets: A case history— what happened to a winery positioned to remain on the fringe. In R. Dowling & J. Carlsen (Eds.), *Wine tourism: Perfect partners. Proceedings of the first Australian wine tourism conference, Margaret River, May, 1998* (pp. 197–208). Canberra: Bureau of Tourism Research.

Lockshin, L. (1997). Branding and brand management in the wine industry. *Wine Industry Journal, 12*(4), 386–387.

Lucas, M. (1997, August 6). Do beer and wine mix? *Los Angeles Times.*

Lynch, R. (1997). *The Sonoma Valley story: Pages through the ages.* Sonoma: The Sonoma Index Tribune, Inc.

Macintosh, G., Lockshin, L., & Spawton, T. (1998). The effects of salesperson/consumer relationships in wine retailing. In *International wine marketing study guide.* Adelaide: School of Marketing, University of South Australia.

Macionis, N. (1996). Wine tourism in Australia. In G. Kearsley (Ed.), *Tourism down under 2, conference proceedings* (pp. 264–286). Dunedin: University of Otago.

Macionis, N. (1997). *Wine tourism in Australia: Emergence, development and critical issues.* Unpublished Masters thesis, University of Canberra.

Macionis, N. (1999). Wineries and tourism: Perfect partners or dangerous liaisons? In R. Dowling & J. Carlsen (Eds.), *Wine tourism: Perfect partners. Proceedings of the first Australian wine tourism conference, Margaret River, May, 1998* (pp. 35–50). Canberra: Bureau of Tourism Research.

Mallon, P. (1996). Vin et tourisme: Un developpement dans la diversite. *Espaces, 140,* 29–48.

Margaret River Wine Industry Association. (1997). *A vision of fine wine.* Author.

McArthur, S. (1997, July/August). Port appeal. *Europe, 368,* 38.

McBoyle, G. (1996). Culture and heritage: Keys to success of Scottish malt whisky distilleries as tourist attractions. In M. Robinson, N. Evans, P. Callaghan et al. (Eds.), *Culture as the tourist product* (pp. 279–295). Newcastle: University of Northumbria.

McIntosh, C. (1997, June). Promoting tasting room sales out in the vineyard. *Wine Business Monthly* [On line]. http://smartwine.com/wbm/1997/9706/bmf9718.htm

Miller, A. (1994). The whisky experience: Interpretation and brand identity. In J. Fladmark (Ed.), *Cultural tourism, papers presented at the Robert Gordon University heritage convention* (pp. 283–290). London.

Melbourne Food and Wine Festival. (n.d.). A *guide to Melbourne's food streets and markets* [Brochure].

Mondavi, R., with Chutkow, P. (1998). *Harvests of joy: My passion for excellence.* Orlando: Harcourt Brace and Co.

Morgan, J. (1995, September 15). Touring the finger lakes. *Wine Spectator* [On-line, article archives]. www.winespectator.com.

Morgan, J. (1996, May 15.). California's 'other' coast. *Wine Spectator* [On-line, article archives]. www.winespectator.com

Morris, R., & King, C. (1997). *The cellar door report: Margaret River region winery/tourism research.* For the Margaret River Wine Industry Association and the Margaret River Tourism Association [unpublished]. Bunbury: Edith Cowan University.

Morrison, A. (1996). *Hospitality and travel marketing* (2d ed.). Albany, NY: Delmar.

Morse, J. (1999). Australia's international image. In R. Dowling & J. Carlsen (Eds.), *Wine tourism: Perfect partners. Proceedings of the first Australian wine tourism conference, Margaret River, May, 1998* (pp. 113–117). Canberra: Bureau of Tourism Research.

Munsters, W. (1996). Cultural tourism in Belgium. In G. Richards (Ed.), *Cultural tourism in Europe* (pp. 109–126). Wallingford, Oxon: CAB International.

Murphy, R. (1998, October/November). The state of Texas wine. *The Wine News,* 45–48.

New Zealand Tourism Board. (1996). *New Zealand international visitors survey 1995/96.* Wellington: Author.

NFO Research Inc. (1997). *SIP STUDY 1997* [provided directly by the Wine Institute].

O'Brien, A. (1997). Strategic plan to take WA wine into the next century. *Wine Industry Journal, 29*(4), 368–369.

Page, S., & Getz, D. (1997). *The business of rural tourism: International perspectives.* London: International Thomson Business Press.

Parsons, C. (1999). Corker projects. In R. Dowling & J. Carlsen (Eds.), *Wine tourism: Perfect partners. Proceedings of the first Australian wine tourism conference, Margaret River, May, 1998* (pp. 131–138). Canberra: Bureau of Tourism Research.

Pavan, D. (1994). L'Enoturismo tra fantasia e metodo. *Vignevini, 21*(1/2), 6–7.

Peters, G. (1997). *American winescapes—the cultural landscapes of America's wine country.* Boulder: Westview Press/Harpers Collins.

Philips, C. (1998, July 11). Bicycle tours offer taste of Niagara Peninsula's best: Fine food, great wine and lush scenery all part of weekend tours. *Calgary Herald,* p. G9.

Pollard, A. (1998, October). Bordeaux birdies. *United Airlines Hemispheres,* 49–50.

Ready, Set, Go. (1997, August 31). *Wine Spectator.*

Rees, C., & Delforce, J. (1998). Outlook for wine grapes. *ABARE Outlook Conference.*

Rees, C., & Grivas, X. (1997). Winegrapes—projection of winegrape production and winery intake to 1999–2000. *ABARE Research Report* 97.10.

Reilly, A. (1996). *A marketing approach for small winemakers in regional areas.* Unpublished thesis, Masters of Business Administration, University of Adelaide.

Richards, G. (1996). European cultural tourism: Trends and future prospects. In G. Richards (Ed.), *Cultural tourism in Europe* (pp. 311–333). Wallingford, Oxon: CAB International.

Robins, R. (1999). Potential research into wine tourism. In R. Dowling & J. Carlsen (Eds.), *Wine tourism: Perfect partners. Proceedings of the first Australian wine tourism conference, Margaret River, May, 1998* (pp. 81–96). Canberra: Bureau of Tourism Research.

Robinson, J. (Ed.) (1994, reprinted 1997). *The Oxford companion to wine.* Oxford: Oxford University Press.

Roby, N. (1998, October/November). Selling wine at the source. *The Wine News,* 12.

Salvatore, S. (1999). Study: Moderate alcohol consumption may protect against stroke. *CNN Interactive* [On-line]. www.cnn.com/health/9901/05/stroke

Sambidge-Mitchell, G. (1999). Tourism and wine Australia. In R. Dowling & J. Carlsen (Eds.), *Wine tourism: Perfect partners. Proceedings of the first Australian wine tourism conference, Margaret River, May, 1998* (pp. 125–129). Canberra: Bureau of Tourism Research.

Saunders, D. (1996, August 16). Niagara wine country uncorks a feud. *The Globe and Mail,* p. A-1.

Schaefer, D. (1997). *Touring the California wine country.* Houston: Gulf Publishing Co.

Shapiro, L. (1998, October 5). A glass half empty. *Newsweek,* pp. 74–76.

Silbergh, D., Fladmark, M., Henry, G., & Young, M. (1994). A strategy for theme trails. In J. Fladmark (Ed), *Cultural tourism, papers presented at the Robert Gordon University heritage convention 1994* (pp. 123–146). London.

Simmons Market Research. (1996). *Wine Business Monthly.*

South Australian Tourism Commission. (1995). *South Australia wine and food touring guide.* Adelaide: Author.

South Australian Tourism Commission.(1997). *Wine and tourism: A background research report.* Adelaide: Author.

South Australian Tourism Commission. (n.d.). *South Australian Tourism Commission Corporate Plan, 1998–2003.* Adelaide: Author.

Spahni, P. (1995). *The international wine trade.* Cambridge, MA: Woodhead.

Spawton, T. (1998). *International wine marketing study guide.* University of South Australia, School of Marketing.

Stuller, J. (1998, October). California Cheese Trail. *United Airlines Hemispheres,* 117–121.

Sullivan, C. (1994). *Napa wine: A history from mission days to present.* San Francisco: The Wine Appreciation Guild.

Texas Wine Marketing Research Institute. (1996). *A profile of the Texas wine and wine grape industry.* Lubbock: Texas Tech University.

Thevenin, C. (1996). Quands les vignerons font du tourisme. *Espaces, 140,* 43–48.

Tourism New South Wales. (1996). *Food and wine in tourism: A plan.* Sydney: Author.

Tourism South Australia. (1991). *Barossa Valley Vintage Festival visitor survey, research report.* Adelaide: Author.

Victoria Wineries Tourism Council. (1997). *Victoria's wine and food: Strategic business plan 1997–2000.* Melbourne: Author.

Victoria Wineries Tourism Council and Victoria Tourism Commission. (n.d.). *Victoria's wine and foodlovers short breaks 1998–99.* Melbourne: Author.

Vine, R. (1997). *Wine appreciation* (2nd ed.). New York: Wiley.

Vintners Quality Alliance of British Columbia. (n.d.). *BC's wine country* [Brochure].

Wine Council of Ontario. (n.d.). *Wine regions of Ontario winery tours map.* St. Catherines: Author.

Wine Council of Ontario. (1998). *The six unforgettable weekends of summer: 1998 calendar of events, the wine regions of Ontario.* St. Catherines: Author.

Wine Institute of New Zealand. (1997). *Annual report.* Auckland: Author.

Wine Institute and Gomberg, Fredrikson and Associates. (1997). Data on U.S. consumption, provided directly by the Wine Institute.

Winegrape Growers' Council of Australia Inc. and Winemakers' Federation of Australia Inc. (1994). *Sustaining success: National industry submission to the winegrape and wine industry inquiry.*

Winegrape Growers' Council of Australia Inc. and Winemakers' Federation of Australia Inc. (1995). *National industry response to the winegrape and wine industry inquiry draft report.*

Winters, M. (1997, July). Airports, tourist towns spout wineries. *Wine Business Monthly, 4*(7).

Woehler, B. (1998). Vintage of the decade. *Wine Press, 1*(2), 15–18.

Ziraldo, D. (1995). *Anatomy of a winery: The art of wine at Inniskillin.* Toronto: Key Porter Books.

247

Publishers Note:
For travel to sites listed and other wine destinations, I have used with great satisfaction Tallyho Travel:
tallyho475@aol.com.